AF662573

2019 WILL MODI WIN ?

2019 WILL MODI WIN?

Pankaj Sharma
Saurav Sanyal

KNOWLEDGE WORLD
KW Publishers Pvt Ltd
New Delhi

Copyright © 2018
Pankaj Sharma and Saurav Sanyal

All rights reserved. No part of this publication may be reproduced, stored in a retrieval system, or transmitted in any form or by any means, electronic, mechanical, photocopying, recording or otherwise, without the prior written permission of the copyright owner. The views expressed in this book are of authors and do not represent the viewpoint of the publisher.

ISBN 978-93-87324-17-6 Paperback
ISBN 978-93-87324-18-3 ebook

Published in India by Kalpana Shukla

KNOWLEDGE WORLD

KW Publishers Pvt Ltd
4676/21, First Floor, Ansari Road
Daryaganj, New Delhi 110002
Phone: +91 11 23263498/43528107
Marketing: kw@kwpub.com
Editorial: jose@kwpub.com
Website: www.kwpub.com

Printed and Bound in India.

Contents

Acknowledgements ix

The Story behind this Book – From Pankaj xiii

Introduction xix

1. The Opposition will be Better Prepared for Modi 1
2. 2014 Mandate: UPA - The Story of Self Goals 39
3. The Role of Economy in Elections 59
4. 2014 Mandate: BJP's Statistical Peak? 91
5. Modi's Pinnacle: Was it 2014 or Will it be 2019? 105
6. Anti-Incumbency Against State Governments 123
7. The Implications for 2019 151
8. The Key Takeaways for BJP for 2019 169
9. The Key Takeaways for Opposition for 2019 183

Epilogue 201

Notes and References 211

About the Authors 233

Index 235

*For the unknown and unnamed soldier,
without whom there is no freedom and
no democracy!*

ACKNOWLEDGEMENTS

> Feeling gratitude and not expressing it is like wrapping a present and not giving it.
>
> — William Arthur Ward[1]

John F. Kennedy[2] has said "As we express our gratitude, we must never forget that the highest appreciation is not to utter words, but to live by them". This applies to everyone. Even if we are partially successful in our attempt to do the same in whatever we do, it is a huge achievement.

We dedicate this book to the unknown soldiers who are nameless, faceless and most often don't get enough recognition from the countrymen. This is strange. The last 1000 years of our history has provided us with enough examples which prove that weak rulers and countries can't talk of peace, it is only the powerful that can defend themselves. Only the militarily strong countries can successfully protect their land and population from aggressors and can negotiate peace with respect and dignity intact.

Without the soldier who is committed to give up his (or her) comforts and willing to make even the supreme sacrifice when required during wartime or peace, there is no nation that can survive. Without the soldier, neither freedom nor democracy can flourish in a country. This book is about elections and democracy, and in a very small and insignificant way, this is our tribute to the Indian soldier. We are forever indebted to his/her selfless service.

We are immensely grateful to all the teachers, colleagues, professional associates, friends and family members who have not only influenced our thought process knowingly or unknowingly, but also helped in molding who we are, as a person and as a professional. There are so many that it would be virtually impossible to remember each and every one but still, none of them would have a contribution which is not significant. We owe a deep sense of gratitude towards each and every one of them.

The consent to go ahead and cooperation from immediate family is never a sufficient condition for an endeavour like this but is almost an absolute necessity. Pankaj is thankful to his wife, Shikha and son, Pulin for their patience and accommodation keeping in view the enormous demand on Pankaj's time this book had warranted during the background research and writing phase. It would not have been possible without the support from them. Pankaj would be keen to acknowledge the contribution and encouragement received from many people that the list below is really long but still, incomplete. The first inspiration which comes to his mind was from his maternal grandfather, Late Shri Janardan Shastri to whom he would attribute his love for reading and writing. His friends (Sandip Bansal, Saswat Sarangi, Sunil Teluja, Niraj Khare, Rupal Mehrotra, Rohan Arora, Pavitra Kumar, Ramesh Mantri, Sanjeev Soni and Unmesh Sharma), his teachers at Morar, Kharagpur and Delhi (Late Shri Kulwant Singh Sachdeva, Mahavir Sir, Sharma Madam, Bhupendra Sir, Rakesh Sir, Maheshwari Sir, Dr Gokarn, Dr Raheja, Dr Sha, Dr Ghosh, Dr Satsangi, Dr

Narag, Dr Mitra, Dr Singla, Dr Pandit and Dr Kaur to name a few of them), his workplace superiors at different points of time (Suhas Hari, Suresh Mahadevan, Venkatesh Balasubramaniam, Srikant Bharti, Ashish Gupta, Ajay Garg, Gordon Gray and Kishore Gandhi), his brothers who provided solid support in this journey (Ranjan Sharma, Neeraj Sharma and Pushkar Shukla). So were his parents (Mr. Kamlesh Kumar Sharma/Mrs. Veena Sharma and Dr Ram Gopal Shukla/Mrs. Mithlesh Shukla).

Saurav wishes to acknowledge the support extended by his father, Sanjib Kumar Sanyal and mother Ruma Sanyal for giving him freedom to continue to exercise the choices of career as researcher and business professional. He wishes to acknowledge the consistent support of his wife Ms. Sujata Sanyal who has been a pillar of strength and son Shubhraneel Sanyal who is a bundle of energy, ideas and keeps bringing new perspective to life. He also wishes to acknowledge all family members especially Ms. Shruti Chatterjee, Commodore A. Chatterjee, Dr. S.S. Chakravarti, Smt. Sumita Chakravarti, Col. S. Chakravarti, Ms. Rashi Chakravarti, Mr. Gaurav Sanyal, Ms. Suranjana Lahiri, Shri A.K. Sanyal, Mr. Supriyo Sanyal and Dr. Purandar Chakraborty and Ms. Shikha Chakraborty who kept the DNA of free thinking alive. He remains indebted to the indelible inspirations from Prof. B. Viswanathan (Emeritus Professor, IIT Madras), Prof. J.K. Mitra (Former Dean, Faculty of Management Studies, Delhi University) and Prof. V. S. Srinivasan (Ram Krishna Mission Vivekananda College, University of Madras) along with inspiring faculty at Department of Chemistry, IIT Madras (1996-1998). My special friend and FMS batch mate Pankaj Sharma (my co-author) deserves a special word of thanks for taking our common inspiration to a different level and providing an excellent motivation to move beyond the obvious and create the knowledge that we have assimilated through experience and joint expertise of 40 years. My special note of thanks and acknowledgement to friend Mr. Anish Andheria (President and CEO, Wildlife Conservation Trust), who provided sustainable ideas and long lasting virtues in promoting wild life conservation. I also wish to thank my seniors in the RELX Group specifically Mr. Sander Verboom; Mr. Saurabh Sharma, Mr. Kok Keng Lim, Dr. Lalit Singh for their support and understanding to ideas and suggestions provided for Elsevier South Asia Office Business.

We wish to acknowledge our sincere gratitude for Ms. Kalpana Shukla of KW Publishers Pvt Ltd, whose continuous support and encouragement made this book possible. We were never very good in making a realistic and fair assessment of what were the key areas of development for this book since the time we had submitted the first version of our manuscript but it was Kalpana and her team, who helped us at each step. We are also grateful to Jose Mathew at KW for his unwavering patience all the time during which this book took shape.

THE STORY BEHIND THIS BOOK — FROM PANKAJ

> But there's a story behind everything. How a picture got on a wall. How a scar got on your face. Sometimes the stories are simple, and sometimes they are hard and heartbreaking.
>
> — Mitch Albom, For One More Day[1]

Every book has a story and this too has one. Mr. Rakesh Jhunjhunwala[2] was an investor in one of the firms I earlier worked with. The owner of that firm and he was my manager as well, naturally was on very good terms with Mr. Jhunjhunwala. For those who don't know Rakesh Jhunjhunwala, he is one of the most well-known and successful stock market investors Indian Stock Market has ever seen. And for those who are interested in numbers, Jhunjhunwala would be worth a few billion dollars easily. So, coming back to the point, it was in one of the evenings of the hot and humid summer of 2016 in Mumbai that we were invited as a team by Rakesh for dinner and drinks.

During the course of the evening, the topics of discussion varied from his beginnings in the Indian stock market, his family, his investment philosophy and his views on philanthropy. He also shared his views on how much money is needed for a good and purposeful life as well as what percentage of an individual's net worth should be the risk tolerance for a single bet i.e. how much money you can afford to lose if things don't go your way.

Since he is so good at investing, people also asked Rakesh about his view and outlook for markets, his stock selections and how to choose winners among thousands of stocks available. Rakesh is a very good host and may be not to make his guests feel bad, he also asked almost each one of us what do we think about the markets and which are our favorite stocks. When it was my turn and I had to tell about how I think about markets, my reply was that I foresee an entirely local, political risk for the markets in 2019. It was because I saw a threat to Modi getting reelected in 2019.

My rationale was that since the local and foreign investors in Indian markets are in favour of Prime Minister, Narendra Modi[3] and his pro-reforms and business friendly approach, market correction is inevitable if Modi fails to return to New Delhi after the next General Elections in 2019. Honestly, I have no qualms in admitting now that it was a completely wrong answer. Most of the times, these outcomes are only event risks and are not that relevant for the broader direction of the equity markets over medium to long run. More often, they do not really change the fundamentals for the economy. This is not to discount the political factors and importance of decision making at the very top, but markets are fairly efficient in incorporating the new information and events and the event risks only (in most cases if not all) have a transient impact.

Nevertheless, this answer had already triggered a "what if" process in my mind. This possibility and the implications of various political scenarios on what could happen in 2019

General Elections certainly needed a more thoughtful and careful analysis of the available data. Moreover, I was fully aware that a primary research or a "dip test" at this point may not be very sensible as that would just give us a false sense of confidence in our findings. So, we started to run with whatever data we had and though history may not be a good student, it is almost always a very good teacher. And we had enough of history spread over last 65+ years of General Elections in independent India, the process which is one of the most important pillars in our parliamentary democracy.

In this book, we have made a conscious attempt to keep our personal ideologies, biases, prejudices linked with our political preferences separate. To ensure this, we are not trying very hard to judge the performance of the Central Government on subjective parameters and how that would affect the choices people would make in 2019. We have also tried to resist the temptation of making assumptions about how people could vote in 2019 and view only what the available data tells us and what we learnt from the history of elections in independent India. We are under no illusions that our attempt will throw up a definitive answer to such questions because that is likely to compromise the integrity of our analysis in the first place. We are not driven by the ambition to reach a definite answer on how 2019 verdict would look like.

Many a times we try to find explanations post the occurrence of an event and indeed, a few available theories fit very nicely in providing a reason for what has happened and why. However, the real life is messy and unpredictable. Things change very quickly at times without any warning. This is even more relevant in the context of elections globally. For example, whether it was a surprising victory of Donald Trump[4] in US presidential elections in November 2016 or much less than expected popular mandate for Theresa May[5] in UK during parliamentary elections in June 2017, the scenarios changed very fast and glorious uncertainties of popular mood were very difficult to assess. No matter how certain or uncertain a Modi victory in 2019 looks today, one cannot be absolutely sure of the result till the process is actually over.

The National Democratic Alliance or NDA[6] Government has already completed its first three and a half years in this term and it looks that the popularity of BJP is on the rise. With a massive mandate in Uttar Pradesh in March 2017[7] and an expanding footprint across the country, it looks impossible to stop the Modi juggernaut in 2019. Also, the opposition is in complete disarray with no possible challenger to Modi on the horizon. Among the opposition leaders, there is no one at this stage who can effectively counter Modi and match him in his political acumen and popularity. Even on the issue of presidential elections in July 2017, there was no effective consensus among opposition parties. In this kind of a situation, how can we even think that there could be a credible threat for Modi in 2019 and why he would not get reelected in the next General Elections? But, is the reality that simple and straight forward?

For example, BJP was able to win a simple majority of 282 seats in 2014 with the least number of percentage vote-share in the history of independent India because opposition vote was fragmented. Opposition is unlikely to repeat similar mistake in 2019. Also, there was a massive anti-incumbency wave against UPA in 2014 and this tail wind will not be available for BJP in 2019. There are many states which have only a nominal presence of BJP and during General Elections, the party is able to fight only in about 350-360 seats practically.

In this book, we look at the factors which would determine if Modi would get second term. Will Modi return or will it be a coalition Government in Delhi in 2019? Or BJP's dependence on allies would be so high in the next term that the "compulsions of coalition politics" will influence policies? Read on to get an impartial and non-ideological take on what the future holds for the country from the perspective of 2019 General Elections.

How successful we have been in our endeavour to keep this work unbiased and useful..........*that is for you to decide.*

INTRODUCTION

> Popularity should be no scale for the election of politicians. If it would depend on popularity, Donald Duck and The Muppets would take seats in senate.
>
> — Orson Welles[1]

There are enough instances in the history when mere numbers in favour alone did not make a decision right or wrong. For example, according to one very interesting part of the 'Mahabharata'[2] (a popular Hindu legend), the size of Pandavas' army in the war at Kurukshetra was 7 Akshauhinis, and that of Kauravas' was 11 Akshauhinis. An Akshauhini consists of 21870 chariots, 21870 elephants, 65610 cavalry and 109350 infantry. Had there been an election to decide the winner, Kauravas would have won the Mahabharata comfortably. But, that was not to be. Eventually, Pandavas emerged victorious though there was a massive and widespread destruction on both the sides.

To whom, the saying *"War Does Not Determine Who Is Right — Only Who Is Left"* should be attributed, is always disputed, but the deep philosophical meaning of it makes a lot of sense. We are not pointing out who was right or who was wrong, because history is always written by the winners and still there are several glitches in the Pandavas' side of the story (the elevation of Pandu over Dhritrashtra to the throne, Yudhisthir's habitual gambling, Draupadi's derogatory comments about Duryodhan, Krishna's questionable role in the entire episode, use of deceit against Bheeshma, Karna and Dronacharya during the war). To be clear, we are only drawing attention to the result as to who was the eventual winner (Pandavas) and who could have been (Kauravas) if the issues between the warring parties were sorted out through democratic elections.

Mathematics and elections[3] are poles apart. But, anything which is about numbers (and elections of course are about numbers), has a relationship with Mathematics. Moreover, with the advent of social media and election analytics[4], the role of Mathematics in elections and how it can influence the outcome is out in the open. It would not be an exaggeration that the wave of targeted and data backed election campaign which began with Barack Obama's election in 2008[5], is unlikely to be reversed in the near future and on the contrary, it will get stronger and stronger.

Even in India, the prominent role of election strategists such as Prashant Kishor[6] in the 2012 Gujarat Assembly Elections (or *Vidhan Sabha* Elections) followed by the 2014 General Elections and then again in the 2015 Bihar Elections is proof that election campaigns are getting more and more scientific and less and less intuitive. Similarly, the Prime Minister, Narendra Modi and BJP[7] President, Amit Shah[8] have also accorded special importance to new-age campaign mediums and role of analysis in devising a better election campaign. All other politicians have to learn about these aspects quickly and there is simply no other choice for them.

While the role of complex modeling and analytical techniques may not be rare anymore and they do influence the end results, this book is not about them.

Yes, we will be talking about numbers but only the ones which are far more basic and which don't require an advanced educational background in Mathematics. It is important to point out that the basic principles which are being followed in the context of elections in India, have not really undergone much change since the time we as a country started voting more than 65 years ago. A lot may have changed on how the elections are conducted but at the same time, many of the things have remained totally the same as to how people would choose their political representatives.

But before we get into this in more detail, there are three things which we want to highlight and clarify:

- This book is not about making a forecast for 2019 on the basis of popular sentiment today and that is for an important reason. We think it is a little premature to do that on the basis of either opinion polls or speaking informally to the voters. We have seen time and again and more recently in the elections in United Kingdom that voter preferences can change very quickly. Even in India, the NDA Government had advanced the poll dates in 2004 as the surveys were indicating that it had a very good chance of winning the elections.
- We are also not making an assumption on how the voters' preferences will change (or will remain same, for that matter) to claim what we would be elaborating over the course of this book. This effectively means that at no point, we are implying that BJP is going to lose because there is a large scale shift of voters away from it, or BJP will win because the voters would continue to remain loyal to the party in 2019.

- We are assuming that there is no massive wave either against Narendra Modi or in favour of him, as happened in 1977 (the Janata wave after Emergency), in 1984 (the sympathy wave after Indira Gandhi's assassination) and in 2014 (the Modi wave combined with anti-UPA wave). This doesn't mean that Modi will be unpopular in 2019 but only suggests that the quantum of difference that was noticed because of "Modi factor" between 2009 and 2014 is unlikely to be repeated in 2019.

In this book, we are primarily analysing factors which we believe could influence the 2019 outcome:

- How a realignment of political forces against Narendra Modi and BJP could influence the 2019 General Elections outcome even when we assume that there is no widespread shift of voters away from the party? If the vote share BJP had won in 2014 remains the same or even increases marginally, would BJP be able to retain the same number of seats if Opposition vote is not fragmented?
- What role the state of Indian economy at the time of General Elections in 2019 would be playing? Several factors such as GDP growth, inflation, industrial production, job creation are important and these worked heavily against UPA in 2014, have things changed on the ground or would this provide a strong head wind for BJP in 2019? Would people be disillusioned with Modi because they had expected much more from him in spite of the fact that those expectations were unrealistic in the first place?

- How the final tally of seats in *Lok Sabha* could undergo a drastic change even when the support towards Modi is intact but anti-incumbency against elected local representatives and the state Governments become important in the political outlook of the people.
- Is it possible that there could be a very different result in 2019 elections than what we are expecting today on state wise basis? Is there enough scope for BJP to increase its seats tally or would it be a daunting endeavour to even maintain the number it has today?
- Finally, what could be the important lessons both BJP and Opposition parties can draw to do better in 2019?

It is difficult to predict the result of elections specifically in the Indian context. The political opinion across the country is extremely varied because of the country's diversity and vastness. The fact that in many cases, the regional aspirations can be handled better by state level parties is an important influence in determining the final results in General Elections. In many cases, the electoral contest involves three or four serious candidates.

In a first-past-the-post system, even a small change in percentage of votes won by a party can make a big difference in the number of seats. This implies that even a very small shift either in favour or against a party can drastically change the number of seats the party would eventually win. For example, the shift in vote share from one party to another in most bi-polar contests is very small but that is enough to change the final outcome completely.

Even in 2014 elections when there was a strong Modi wave in North and West, there were only 206 (out of total

543) candidates who had got more than 50 percent of total valid votes to win the elections. In most cases, the margin of victory is really small and the number of seats won by a party is not just dependent on the percentage of votes the party will get, there are several other factors involved. For any party, three important things are:

- Is the support base of the party concentrated in certain geographical areas so that the party candidates can win those seats or the party is receiving a lot of votes but these votes are scattered over many constituencies.
- How many votes the principal Opposition party is getting and if a political party can make the main Opposition weaker, this will automatically enhance the chances of getting a higher number of seats for the party.
- Is the Opposition fragmented because if the votes are getting distributed over many competitors, that is good for a party's prospects.

In other words, it can be explained this way, a) if the vote percentage remains unchanged for a party, it would be better for it if the support is concentrated in lesser number of constituencies e.g. despite being the No. 3 party in total votes in 2014 *Lok Sabha* elections, the BSP didn't win a single *Lok Sabha* seat, b) unless you win more than 50 percent votes in a constituency, the win or loss is dependent on how many votes your nearest competitor is getting, and, c) the party's chances of winning is adversely affected if the Opposition is united because of political realignment and pre-election seat sharing agreements.

At the end of the day, the vibrancy of democracy is more important than fortunes of a particular party or a particular leader. The bigger worry for Indian political system today is that there is a vacuum at the national level in the Opposition space and if BJP falters, the probability of a rag-tag coalition assuming power at the Centre is very high. As history has proven time and again (1977-79, 1989-91, 1996-98), the coalition Governments[9] lead to political instability and that is bad for policy making and implementation. Even the former Prime Minister, Dr. Manmohan Singh[10] infamously remarked *'compulsion of coalition politics'* when quizzed about the unruly allies and why he as the Prime Minister or Congress as the most senior party in UPA I[11] and UPA II[12] could not really rein in the wayward partners and Ministers from allies' quota.

Hence, we think there is a much larger question on the horizon in this regard. Even in a "Not really bad" scenario for BJP in 2019, the possibility of a weaker NDA coalition Government is extremely realistic and that will be bad for India on a longer term basis. The economy and the Government machinery does not work in isolation and politics is always an overriding factor. Hence, we believe that it is important to look at these possibilities. As Donald Trump is showing in USA and that is a lesson to the entire world, a country can never be fully prepared for political disruptions. Still, it is important to be aware of political and governance related risks.

Before we move on, we would also spend some time about the possibilities where we could go wrong. There could be many reasons. First of all, we need to admit (and of course have no hesitation in doing that) the limitation in our work that despite all the advanced models and huge amount of effort put in by experts, the fact remains that predicting the outcome of elections is extremely tough.

Secondly, our assessment is based on historical data and extrapolation of past trends. Our analysis is subject to a scenario that resembles some kind of a steady state and we are excluding the exceptional events between now and next elections and to name a couple of these examples, the 1977 election verdict was influenced by Emergency[13] and in 1984, by then Prime Minister, Mrs. Indira Gandhi's assassination[14].

1

THE OPPOSITION WILL BE BETTER PREPARED FOR MODI

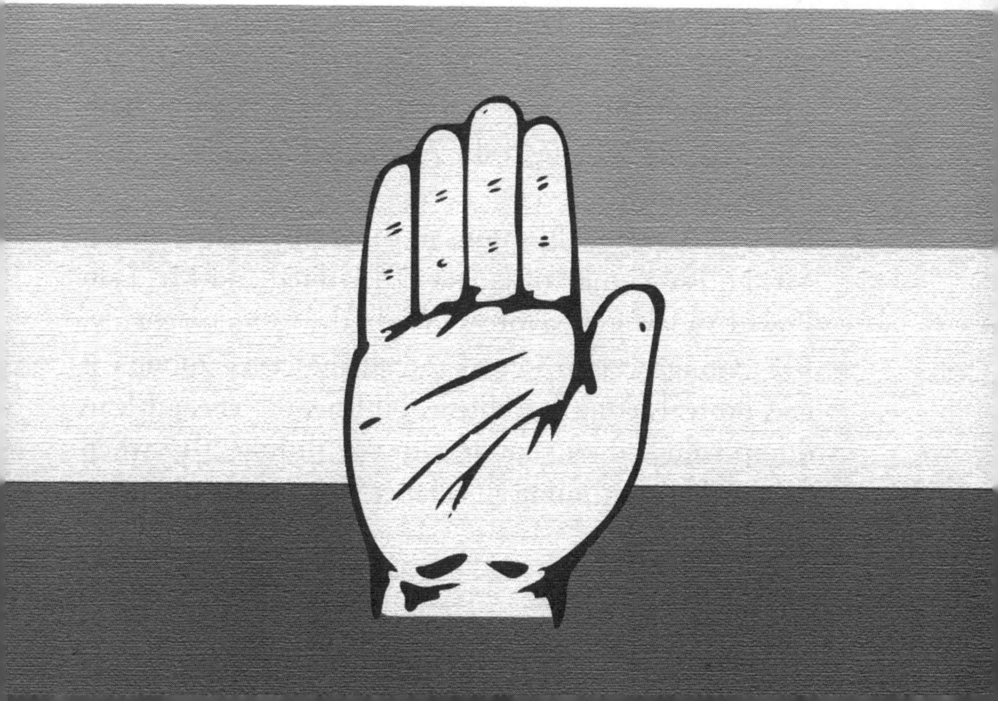

> If you know your enemies and know yourself, you will not be imperiled in a hundred battles...if you do not know your enemies nor yourself, you will be imperiled in every single battle.
>
> — Sun Tzu[1] (c. 6th century BCE), Chinese General, Military Strategist, and Author of 'The Art of War'

Otto Eduard Leopold von Bismarck[2] (Bismarck) was a German statesman who is widely credited as one of the key architects behind unification of Germany in the 19th century. Bismarck had remarked "Politics is the art of the possible, the attainable - the art of the next best". However, many subsequent events have time and again indicated that politics in reality is an art of "the impossible" and to prove this, there are no better examples available than from a country like India.

Even if we don't go beyond the very recent political events in India, there are enough such instances available which will prove that the word "impossible" doesn't really exist in the dictionary of Indian politicians. For example,

- Dr. Ram Manohar Lohia[4], who is proclaimed as the chief ideologist and inspiration for Samajwadi Party[5] (SP) was a prominent anti-Congress force and very recently, both Congress and SP fought the Assembly Elections in Uttar Pradesh jointly.
- In 2015 Assembly Elections in Bihar, the arch-enemies, Mr. Nitish Kumar[6] of Janata Dal United and Mr. Lalu Prasad Yadav[7] joined forces to fight the common enemy, BJP. Congress also joined the alliance even though it had no real liking for Nitish. Nitish was very quick to dump Lalu and join hands with BJP in July 2017 when he saw that continuing an alliance with Lalu could harm his clean image.

- Communist Party of India (Marxist)[8] or CPI (M) was fighting an extremely bitter battle with Congress during previous Assembly Elections in Kerala, but at the same time, both these parties had no hesitation to form an alliance against Trinamool Congress[9] in West Bengal.
- In the state of Jammu and Kashmir (J&K), Jammu and Kashmir Peoples Democratic Party (JKPDP or PDP[10]) and BJP formed a coalition to run the State Government. PDP and BJP had been staunch opposition to each other in the past on several key issues and even today, it is an uneasy coalition between them in the state.

To be fair, this trend runs across party lines and it is not really new,

- Rashtriya Swayamsevak Sangh[11] (RSS) and Shiromani Akali Dal[12] were always treated as communal by other political parties but that didn't deter anyone from joining forces with them in 1977 to fight Congress and Mrs. Indira Gandhi.
- Both BJP and Communist Parties can't see each other eye to eye, but both of them provided outside support to a Janata Dal Government led by Vishwanath Pratap Singh[13] (V P Singh) after 1989 General Elections.
- Chaudhary Charan Singh[14] of Bharatiya Lok Dal and Chandra Shekhar[15] of Janata Dal (he started his political career with Congress and after he left Janata Dal, formed Samajwadi Janata Party), Congress was a bitter enemy for both of them. But, they accepted the support from Congress Party to become Prime Ministers in 1979 and 1990 respectively.

- BJP was untouchable for many parties, but in 1998 and 1999, it became perfectly acceptable for many of these parties which shunned BJP because of their belief that BJP is a communal force.
- The origin and evolution of the Leftist movement was based on anti-Congress ideology but CPI and CPI-M supported Congress in 2004.

When there are several examples of continuous flip-flop from political parties, it would be futile to even attempt how an individual's loyalties change in Indian Politics.

But, there are still some extraordinary individual cases. For example, let us take a look at the interesting political careers of Shri Chimanbhai Patel[16] in Gujarat and Shri Bhajan Lal[17] in Haryana. Chimanbhai Patel was a Minister in the Congress Government led by Ghanshyam Oza[18]. But, he toppled the Ghanshyam Oza government in 1973 and became the Chief Minister of the state. After he was forced out of office in 1974 by the Nav Nirman movement[19] and was expelled from the Congress party, he helped in the formation of Janata Morcha government in 1975. During Emergency (1975-77), he helped Congress in toppling the Janata Morcha government. He again became the Chief Minister in 1990 heading the Janata Dal-BJP coalition government. After the breakup of the coalition, he managed to retain his post with the help of legislators of Congress. Later, he joined Congress and continued as the Chief Minister of Gujarat till his death in 1994.

The case of Mr. Bhajan Lal is even more bizarre. He became the Chief Minister (CM) of Haryana in 1979. After Mrs. Indira Gandhi came to power in January 1980, Bhajan Lal who was heading a Janata Party Government as a Chief Minister defected with some Janata Party's MLAs to Congress and continued as CM of the state. This act of open and immediate switchover in party loyalties is still unparalleled in the history of Indian politics in many ways. Effectively, his first term continued from 1979 to 1985. He served a second term from 1991 to 1996. In 2005, after the victory of Congress in Haryana, the party opted for Bhupinder Singh Hooda[20] as the Chief Minister instead of Bhajan Lal. Bhajan Lal was not happy with the choice of Congress High Command and in 2007, he announced the launch of a new party, Haryana Janhit Congress[21], after his son, Kuldeep Bishnoi[22] was expelled from the Congress party.

It is a norm accepted and understood in India that the decision to have a tie-up or not with other parties is made purely based on possible electoral gains and that is the only consideration in most cases. For a political party, sometimes the objectives behind political alliances are strategic and at other times, alliances happen for short term gains but ideology is rarely the driving force. It is also not uncommon that to keep an opposition party away, two smaller parties form an alliance. This is very similar to the concept of *"Dushman ka dushman, dost hota hai"* (An enemy's enemy is a friend) which usually happens in movies e.g. in several Bollywood films, an important sub-plot is two villains uniting against the Lead Actor or the Hero. By the way, we are not saying who is a villain or who is a hero here. That is for the reader to figure out.

On a serious note, it is to be noted that we are not taking this opportunity to express regret as to how the only loyalty in Indian politics is towards power and how ideology has long been dead. We are discussing this because we think that this characteristic has important implications for the possible political alignments in the 2019 General Elections. The flexibility, with which political parties can forge pre-poll and post-poll alliances and how coalitions can be formed to arrive at seat sharing agreements, will play a crucial role in what we are going to see in next elections. But, that comes later in this chapter. In the first instance let us look at the 2014 popular mandate and how that learning can help us to understand the possible decision making process of non-BJP opposition parties in 2019.

2014 Election was unique in several different ways

We strongly believe that to make sense of the complete range of possibilities in 2019, it is immensely helpful to study the 2014 Elections well. In this section, we will start with the most important changes that occurred in 2014 as compared to the previous elections and then we will talk about how the result was different in terms of vote percentage and number of seats won for BJP.

- **2014 General Elections in India were like presidential elections in USA** – There have been powerful leaders earlier e.g. Pandit Jawaharlal Nehru[23] who was able to influence the fortune of the Congress party in post-Independence era and the name of Indira Gandhi was good enough for many Congress leaders even without any mass base, to get elected. However, this trend was less visible afterwards, until 2014 Elections. In 2014, the primary appeal of BJP to the voters was to elect Narendra Modi as their Prime Minister. As reflected in many such slogans like "*Abki Baar, Modi Sarkaar*" (This time, it is going to be a Modi Government), *Har-Har*

Modi, Ghar-Ghar Modi (there is Modi at every home, this slogan was modeled after the popular chant "*Har Har Mahadev*", dedicated to Hindu God, Lord Shiva). Quite literally, the appeal made was that it will not be a BJP Government but a Narendra Modi Government, people and voters were promised. The interesting fact is that while BJP pushed forward Modi as the leader of the party and the Prime Ministerial candidate, the other parties were extremely confused. For example, while it was likely that even if UPA comes back to power, Dr. Manmohan Singh will not be leading the Government but whether Rahul Gandhi[24] will be taking over or someone else will be pushed forward just like Dr. Singh in UPA victory of 2004, was not made very clear to the voters. So, this was a case where only one side was making an attempt to build a personality cult around a Prime Ministerial candidate. And, it ultimately proved to be a very successful strategy for BJP.

- **Congress won less than 100 seats for the first time in history** – Even in 1977, the Congress had won more than 150 seats despite being the prime target of voters' anger because of *"Emergency"* linked resentment. This pathetic performance of Congress was despite the fact that in 1977, the Congress was completely wiped out in North India and the party's win percentage was less than 1 percent in more than 200 seats across the eight states of Punjab, Himachal Pradesh, Haryana, Delhi, Rajasthan, Uttar Pradesh (Uttarakhand was not a separate state then), Madhya Pradesh (Chhattisgarh was a part of Madhya Pradesh) and Bihar (Jharkhand was a part of Bihar then). Before 2014, the previous low for Congress was in 1999 when the party was able to win only 114 seats. In 2014 Elections, Congress could only win just 44 seats. Even in terms of vote share, 2014 was the first time when the Congress party's vote share plunged to below 20 percent. In these elections, Congress could only win 19.3 percent vote share as against the previous low of 25.8 percent in 1998. In fact, Congress didn't even have the required number of seats to qualify as the official opposition party (the requirement is to have minimum 1/10th of the total *Lok Sabha* strength).

- **In thirty years, it was the first clear mandate** – After 1984, the popular mandate was not fractured for the first time in 2014. For as many as seven elections since 1984 (in 1989 - Congress won 197 seats, 1991 - Congress won 244 seats, 1996 - BJP won 161 seats, 1998 - BJP won 182 seats, 1999 - BJP won 182 seats, 2004 - Congress won 145 seats, 2009 - Congress won 206 seats), no single party could reach the half way mark. In 2014, the BJP won 282 seats and became the first party that could reach 272+ after 1984. It was also the first time when BJP won a simple majority on its own as a party and this performance was really special as BJP has improved its position by 100 seats or by 55 percent compared to its previous best of 182 seats. Not only this was an incredibly good performance from BJP, it was also extremely important to reduce the need for support required from its associates and smaller parties under the NDA fold. In the past, the excessive dependence on smaller parties has led to fall of Governments in the worst case (for example, the one vote loss of BJP in floor test at *Lok Sabha* in 1999) and significantly reduced maneuvering capability in the best of the cases. So, it was a positive change and a clear mandate for the BJP and Narendra Modi, who was expected to provide a strong and stable Government at the Centre. After a long period of time, the Government at the Centre was free from the shackles of whimsical coalition politics and unjust blatant extortion of regional satraps for ministerial berths. We will take a look at this aspect again as to whether the verdict was really as clear as it was made out to be or the multi-cornered contest simply made the fractured mandate hidden. Did the people indicate their preference so clearly in favour of Modi and BJP in 2014 or because the Opposition was fragmented, the BJP won a massive number of seats despite garnering a relatively (as compared to the previous elections when a party had won an absolute majority in *Lok Sabha*) small vote share?

- **Third largest party in terms of votes polled didn't win a single seat** – There were several new, unprecedented and interesting things that happened in 2014 Elections that not everything important and path breaking did get enough attention. However, we think that one of the *Top Five* take away from this election was Bahujan Samaj Party[25] or BSP's performance. Behind the BJP and Congress, Bahujan Samaj Party (BSP) was the third largest party in popularity as its vote share was 4.14 percent. While BSP was the choice of as many as 23 million people in India, it failed to win even a single seat in the 16th *Lok Sabha*. Many other parties were far more successful even with a significantly lower vote share. For example, All India Trinamool Congress (Trinamool Congress) won 34 seats with a 3.84 percent vote share and All India Anna Dravida Munnetra Kazhagam[26] (AIADMK) won 37 seats with only 3.27 percent vote share. There were a few others, Telugu Desam Party[27]or TDP (16 seats with 2.55 percent vote share), Shiv Sena[28] (18 seats with 1.85 percent vote share) and Biju Janata Dal[29] or BJD which was successful in winning 20 seats with just 1.71 percent vote share. This was also the first time when BSP contested a *Lok Sabha* election and failed to win even a single seat. In a first-past-the-post system, unless a party crosses a certain threshold, the vote percentage may not always be converted into seats. This is an important point and we will continue to discuss the implications of this.

- **Influence of technology and social media** – 2014 was the first General Elections in India where social media combined with use of technology and advanced analytics played an important role. The campaign of BJP and Narendra Modi was not just based on extensive travel by the Prime Minister candidate. Mr. Modi addressed as many rallies and meetings as he could, but it was also based on a coordinated and concerted effort by BJPs' powerful machinery. Both BJP as a party and Narendra Modi as a leader made a special effort to target the young first time voters by using these new tools. Also, the usage of three dimensional holograms and new age audio-visual mediums gave BJP an edge in election campaigning. Other parties were far behind and though it is difficult to assess how much contribution this would have made in the end-result, it would be impossible to argue that this didn't play an important role.

Majority in Lok Sabha with only 31 percent votes–An Unprecedented Result

In 2014 General Elections, BJP won 282 seats (out of total 543) in *Lok Sabha* with only 31 percent vote share. We think that defining characteristic of 2014 General Elections was that the single largest party that crossed the simple majority mark by winning 272+ seats was able to do so with such an unprecedentedly low vote percentage.

Even when we exclude the General Elections till early 1970s when Congress (1951 – 364 seats with 44.99 percent vote share, 1957 – 371 seats with 47.78 percent vote share, 1962 – 361 seats with 44.72 percent vote share, 1967 – 283 seats with 40.78 percent vote share, 1971 – 352 seats with 43.68 percent vote share) was the dominant political party, this is an extremely important result that BJP was able to win so many seats with only 31 percent vote share.

This had never happened earlier and it was unique in the history of electoral politics of independent India. In contrast to this, when Congress made a grand comeback in 1980 after the failure of "Janata Party Experiment[30]" in Indian Politics, the party won 351 seats but it needed a 42.69 percent vote share to do so. December 1984 was an outlier because of a massive sympathy wave in favour of Congress after Mrs. Indira Gandhi's assassination, Congress had its best ever vote share with winning 49.01 percent of votes and the party under the leadership of Rajiv Gandhi[31] won 415 seats.

Table 1.1: 2014 Election Results
(Number of Seats and Vote Percentage)

Party Name	Seats	Votes percentage
Bharatiya Janata Party (BJP)	282	31.00
Indian National Congress (Congress)	44	19.31
Bahujan Samaj Party (BSP)	0	4.14
All India Trinamool Congress (Trinamool Congress)	34	3.84
Samajwadi Party (SP)	5	3.37
All India Anna Dravida Munnetra Kazhagam (AIADMK)	37	3.27
Communist Party of India (Marxist) or CPI (M)	9	3.25
Telugu Desam Party (TDP)	16	2.55
Yuvajana Sramika Rythu Congress Party (YSR Congress)	9	2.53
Aam Aadmi Party (AAP)	4	2.05
Shiv Sena (SS)	18	1.85
Dravida Munnetra Kazhagam (DMK)	0	1.74
Biju Janata Dal (BJD)	20	1.71
Nationalist Congress Party (NCP)	6	1.56
Rashtriya Janata Dal (RJD)	4	1.34
Telangana Rashtra Samithi (TRS)	11	1.22
Janata Dal (United) or JD (U) or JDU	2	1.08

Note: Parties with more than one percent vote share are included in the table.
Source: Election Commission of India[32]

Before May 2014, it had never happened in General Elections in India that a party had needed less than 40 percent vote share to win more than half the seats in *Lok Sabha*. Most non-BJP parties would admit (though not that openly, for obvious reasons) that they could not really gauge the extent of "Modi wave" in 2014. Perhaps his rivals in other parties knew that Modi would prove to be a formidable competitor, but he would prove to be so strong that the entire Opposition would be swept away, not many in BJP's Opposition parties may have imagined for sure.

However, the opposition parties at present have a clear idea as to how strong the Modi phenomenon is and in 2019, they are likely to bury their differences and fight the common enemy (BJP and Narendra Modi), united despite the fact that many of these Opposition leaders would have to swallow their ego and pride to arrive at a pre-poll alliance. But in all probability, the opposition parties would probably still forge this anti-BJP alliance in 2019 because for them, that is the most pragmatic thing to do. And who can deny that politicians are among the most pragmatic people. The moot point is that by forging pre-poll seat sharing arrangements, the Opposition leaders would be willing to concede some ground before 2019 polls in the hope that they would gain a lot more in the post-poll 17th *Lok Sabha*.

In several ways, the 2019 Elections could turn out to be quite similar to what had happened in 1977 and 1989. It was Indira Gandhi vs. everybody else in 1977 and Rajiv Gandhi vs. everyone else in 1989. In 1977, when Congress had lost massively and could only win 153 seats, the party's vote share was 34.5 percent (more than BJP's 31 percent in 2014). Similarly, in 1989 General Elections, Congress could only win 197 seats despite winning 39.5 percent vote share (significantly more than BJP's 31 percent in 2014). The Congress had lost despite winning 34.5 percent vote share in 1977 and once again, with a 39.5 percent vote share in 1989. The vote share of Congress in 1977 and 1989 was much more than what BJP managed to garner in 2014, still it was Congress that ended up on the wrong side of the poll results in 1977 and 1989 and had to sit on the Left to the Speaker in *Lok Sabha*.

The verdict of 1977 and 1989 was hailed as a clear rejection of Indira Gandhi and Rajiv Gandhi respectively. On the contrary, with only 31 percent people voting for BJP in 2014 was projected as a clear and popular mandate for Narendra Modi to govern India. Of course, no one can deny that it is the number of seats which matters more than vote share in absolute terms. However, the credit for Modi's victory in 2014 should also go to a fragmented Opposition. A multi-cornered contest and an Opposition which was fighting Modi each one individually were also responsible for BJP's spectacular victory in 2014.

2014 elections: BJP's big win hides the reality of a very fragmented verdict

2014 is often seen as an election where people voted for political stability and in favour of a single party rule. The media has promptly and repeatedly highlighted that after several years and a number of successive coalition Governments (some of them stable yet non-performing and some of them not so stable) at New Delhi, the popular mandate was not fragmented in 2014 and this was lauded as a sign of maturity of the electorate. Many experts also pointed out that the main highlight of this verdict was that people are tired of unstable and indecisive coalition governments and they are making a decisive choice by voting for BJP and choosing Narendra Modi as their Prime Minister.

However, the reality is a little more complicated and the fact that BJP has been able to win more than 50 percent of seats in 16th *Lok Sabha* does not mean that the vote was not fragmented in 2014 General Elections. Only 31 out of

100 voters chose BJP in 2014 and still, the party won 52 percent of seats and this indeed is as fractured a verdict as it could be. Also, the two largest parties (BJP and Congress combined) won only about 50 percent votes and the next competitor was at 4 percent vote share indicates that voters in 2014 were as indecisive and confused as ever. As we have discussed earlier, an individual voter had no control over the outcome in 2014 general elections (just like other previous elections) on how the final tally of seats would look like and not many would have thought that they are voting for Modi because they wanted to hand over a clear mandate to Modi or wanted to give 282 seats for BJP.

In elections, people vote for particular parties and candidates. They don't really bother with the final outcome in terms of how many seats they want the various parties to win because they don't have any control over the final tally. The 2014 verdict was fractured and only because BJP crossed 272+ seats, the verdict does not become clear and unambiguous. This is important because, a) though BJP was able to increase its vote share by almost 50 percent over the course of five years between 2009 and 2014, the change in voter's preferences was not big enough in absolute terms to not call it fragmented, b) as we have seen that final tally of seats is much less dependent on vote share and much more determined by political alignment at the time of elections.

In 2019, are we going to see a repeat of 1977 and 1989?

The key feature of 1977 and 1989 *Lok Sabha* Elections was that the Opposition was united against Congress. The Opposition parties at that time understood the ground reality that if they don't come together and form a coalition to fight, they would not be able to defeat Congress led by Indira Gandhi and Rajiv Gandhi respectively. In 1977, the Opposition had realised it very well that no matter how unpopular Indira Gandhi is, it is impossible to defeat her without unity and forging a common front against her.

In 1989, the Opposition leaders understood very well that despite anti-corruption popular sentiment against Rajiv Gandhi, they can put up a spirited fight only when they are united and not allow splitting of votes against Congress. This could be repeated in 2019 and there is a strong possibility that the Opposition parties will be united against BJP and Narendra Modi.

In 1977, the common enemy was Indira Gandhi. In 1989, it was Rajiv Gandhi. And in 2019, the common enemy for the entire opposition could be Narendra Modi.

The template for Opposition - Bihar verdict in 2014 General Elections vs. 2015 Assembly Elections

In Bihar, BJP and NDA had an impressive performance in 2014 General Elections. There are 40 *Lok Sabha* seats in Bihar and in 2014, BJP had won 22 seats and BJP's allies, Lok Janshakti Party won 6 seats and Rashtriya Lok Samata Party was successful in 3 seats. In all, NDA won 31 seats, more than 75 percent success rate. The Opposition to BJP, Janata Dal United led by Nitish Kumar and Sharad Yadav, Rashtriya Janata Dal led by Lalu Pradad Yadav and Congress led by Sonia Gandhi and Rahul Gandhi along with local leadership was nowhere close.

The Opposition read the message loud and clear for Bihar Assembly Elections which were held about eighteen months later. Nitish Kumar and Lalu Pradad Yadav decided to ignore their differences and forged a coalition called *Mahagathbandhan*[33] or Grand Alliance. Congress also joined this coalition. On the other hand, the strength of NDA was more or less the same as it was in 2014 except for the fact that a break-away faction from JDU (Hindustani Awam Morcha led by former Chief Minister Jitan Ram Manjhi) had also joined NDA at the time of 2015 Assembly Elections.

So, what was the major difference in 2015 vs. 2014 in terms of pre-poll scenario? While in 2014 General Elections, Nitish Kumar and Lalu Prasad Yadav were separately fighting against BJP; both of them joined hands in 2015 Assembly Elections. The result of 2015 Assembly Elections in Bihar was in complete contrast to 2014 General Election results. Of 243 seats in Bihar assembly, JDU won 71 seats, RJD 80 and Congress won 27 seats. The best performance was that of RJD which was successful in 80 percent of the seats it contested. On the other hand, BJP won 53 seats, Lok Janshakti Party won 2, Rashtriya Lok Samata Party 2 seats and Hindustani Awam Morcha could win only 1 seat.

The *Mahagathbandhan* coalition (JDU-RJD-Congress) won 178 seats (almost $3/4^{th}$ in a 243 member Bihar legislative assembly) and NDA only 58 (less than $1/4^{th}$ of total seats). The interesting thing is that in terms of vote share, BJP came first with 24.4 percent, followed by RJD with 18.4 percent and JDU with 16.8 percent. But, the fortunes of NDA were completely reversed in a matter of only eighteen months as a result of seat sharing agreement between JDU, RJD and Congress.

Lalu Prasad Yadav in an election fight with BJP was not a surprise. He had been a bitter critic of Modi and BJP for several years. Lalu was the one who arrested BJP leader L K Advani in 1990 at the time of Advani's Rath Yatra from Somnath to Ayodhya, prior to demolition of the disputed structure at Ayodhya during Ram Janma Bhoomi Movement[34]. But, Nitish Kumar had snapped ties with BJP only recently when Modi was selected as the PM candidate for the party. But, both Lalu and Nitish could not fight BJP separately and they had to unite to make the *Mahgathbandhan* coalition work.

Lalu Yadav and Nitish Kumar coming together is an interesting story in itself. Both Lalu and Nitish had started their political careers in Bihar around the same time in 1970s and they had been close associates for many years. But immediately before forging this RJD-JDU-Congress alliance, they had been sworn enemies for decades. Not many people would have imagined this to be possible that Lalu and Nitish can form a coalition. But, this was exactly what happened because there was a bigger enemy in BJP and both of them had to help each other if they had to defeat Modi.

Uttar Pradesh verdict: 2014 General Elections vs. 2017 Assembly Elections

In Uttar Pradesh (UP), BJP and NDA had an even more impressive (compared to Bihar) performance in the 2014 General Elections, something that surpassed all expectations and pre-poll/exit-poll forecasts. There are 80 *Lok Sabha* seats in Uttar Pradesh and in 2014, BJP won 71 seats and its ally, Apna Dal won 2 seats. NDA was successful in 73 seats with a success rate of more than 90 percent. The Opposition

(Samajwadi Party or SP led by Mulayam Singh Yadav[35] and his son Akhilesh Yadav[36], Bahujan Samaj Party led by Ms. Mayawati[37] and Congress led by Sonia Gandhi and Rahul Gandhi) was completely decimated.

Unlike Bihar, the Opposition in UP was overconfident and failed to read the ground reality when Uttar Pradesh Assembly Elections were held about two and a half years later in February-March 2017. Both Akhilesh Yadav and Mayawati decided to fight the 2017 Assembly Elections on their own perhaps thinking that Elections for *Lok Sabha* and Assembly are completely different ball game altogether. Though Congress had joined Samajwadi Party in a pre-poll alliance, SP itself was struggling as a result of serious infighting between the old guard led by Mulayam's younger brother, Shivpal Singh Yadav and the new generation led by Akhilesh Yadav and supported by Mulayam's cousin Ram Gopal Yadav. Even a smaller group led by Ajit Singh (Rashtriya Lok Dal) was not accommodated in the SP-Congress alliance because of differences over seat sharing. So, Opposition to BJP remained fragmented in UP.

BJP, SP and BSP were three most powerful political parties in UP at the time of 2017 Assembly Elections and there was no major difference in terms of pre-poll scenario vs. 2014. While in 2014 General Elections, Mulayam/Akhilesh Yadav and Mayawati were separately fighting against BJP and NDA; both of them had still chosen to remain separate against the BJP/NDA. Hence, the result in 2017 Assembly Elections in UP was exactly similar to the 2014 General Election results. There are total 403 seats in UP legislative assembly, BJP and its allies won 325 seats while SP was successful in 47 seats, BSP in 19 and Congress won 7 seats.

In terms of vote share, BJP combined with its allies was the first with 41.4 percent, followed by BSP with 22.2 percent, SP with 21.8 percent and Congress with 6.2 percent. The combined vote share of SP, BSP and Congress was more than 50 percent and had there been a pre-poll alliance among these three parties, the result could have been completely different. The basic difference in the situation existing in Bihar in 2015 and UP in 2017 was that while in Bihar, the sworn enemies (Lalu and Nitish) forgot the personal enmity and formed an alliance to fight BJP, this was not the case with Akhilesh Yadav and Ms. Mayawati in Uttar Pradesh.

After the election results were announced, if we go by the statements of both Akhilesh Yadav and Ms. Mayawati, there is a clear sense of regret on this issue and they realised (though much later in the day) that they could have defeated BJP had BSP and SP forged a pre poll alliance. Will both Akhilesh Yadav and Ms. Mayawati learn from this experience and fight as a unified force against BJP in 2019? It is too early to get a final confirmation on that but this possibility is extremely realistic.

It is easier to see common enemy in a ruling party

Another important point to be noted here is that it is much more likely and a lot easier to identify a common political threat in an incumbent Government than someone who is a challenger. In 2014, Mr. Modi was a challenger and it would have been very difficult for Congress to accept that the party requires a coalition to counter the Modi challenge, irrespective of the fact that whether this threat was real or only perceived.

It is possible that some non-BJP and non-Congress parties were able to see the writing-on-the-wall in 2014 but could not really find an alternative other than the one already existing, UPA. Apart from this, there were some leaders in 2014 who themselves were contenders for the post of PM and it was difficult for them to align with UPA which would not have conceded the pole position easily. For example, Mulayam Singh Yadav from Samajwadi Party was a PM contender himself.

Even for Congress, it would have been a bitter pill to swallow if they had talked about an anti-Modi coalition in 2014 because at that time, a) it was leading the Government in New Delhi, b) the party had more than 200 MPs in *Lok Sabha*, c) the party was comfortably ahead of BJP in terms of vote share and number of seats as per the results in 2009. For the common people and for the party itself, any such step by Congress would have been a clear sign of admission of defeat and sheer desperation of Congress leadership.

Hence, it is very likely that though several Congress leaders internally may have been wary of Modi's appeal among voters, it was not practically possible for them to talk about a coalition openly. In addition, even if Congress had tried, the other parties would not have been willing to become a part of this front, or they would have been more demanding and Congress had to concede a lot more in terms of seat sharing. Hence, practically speaking, an anti-Modi coalition was much more difficult to achieve before 2014 elections.

The situation now is completely different and it is very likely to remain the same in 2019 except for some unforeseeable and drastic political developments. Narendra

Modi and BJP have been extremely successful in successive elections across the length and breadth of the country with the only exceptions of Bihar and Delhi. As for the Punjab Assembly Elections in first half of 2017, the lion's share of blame for SAD-BJP loss went to anti-incumbency against SAD.

Keeping in view the prevailing circumstances, Congress should have no problems in accepting the fact that the party and its allies need to fight BJP by sticking together and forging a formidable pre-poll alliance. Being in opposition, Congress is already occupying the space of the challenger and aligning with other parties and agreeing to a seat sharing arrangement which is more acceptable to other parties should not pose any serious conflict. If we have to go by the examples of important recent elections, Congress now it seems is ready to accept that.

In Bihar Assembly Elections, the party readily agreed to play second fiddle to both RJD and JDU and similarly, Congress accepted the fact that it is a junior partner to Samajwadi Party in UP Assembly Elections. Not just the Congress, other parties are also more willing to share space with each other in their attempt to fight BJP. For example, the RJD-JDU combine was more generous than expected in seat sharing with Congress in Bihar and Samajwadi Party too offered more number of seats to Congress than what many thought was the fair share of Congress in UP.

Uttar Pradesh and Bihar: the passage to New Delhi

We think it makes sense to see what could happen in 2019 in two of the most important states i.e. Uttar Pradesh and Bihar. These two states contribute 120 seats in *Lok Sabha*

(80 in UP and 40 in Bihar, which is 22 percent of the total strength of *Lok Sabha*). UP and Bihar are also very important from NDA's perspective as these two states had sent more than 100 MPs to *Lok Sabha* for NDA in 2014 (which is almost one-third of NDA's strength in *Lok Sabha* today). For BJP as a standalone entity, this number was 93 (71 MPs from UP and 22 from Bihar) and for BJP too, these two states constitute 33 percent of total MPs the party currently has in *Lok Sabha*. Essentially, there is no doubt that these two states when combined, holds the key as to how BJP and NDA could perform in 2019. For BJP, if it can win UP and Bihar again in 2019 the way it did in 2014, half portion of the task can be considered as done.

We will first have a look at Bihar. Why? Bihar Assembly Elections took place in the second half of 2015 and the opposition to BJP witnessed a fresh realignment and new pre-poll alliances which was very different from 2014 General Elections. In one of the previous sections in this Chapter *(The template for Opposition - Bihar verdict in 2014 General Elections vs. 2015 Assembly Elections)*, we have seen that between 2014 and 2015, the results were completely opposite. The number of seats won by BJP/NDA to Opposition was in the ratio of 75 and 25 in 2014 and it got reversed to 75:25 against BJP/NDA in 2015 because of the alliance worked out between Nitish Kumar and Lalu Prasad Yadav.

However, the situation has changed again in Bihar. Nitish Kumar resigned on the evening of 26th July 2017 after RJD refused to budge on the issue of resignation of Deputy Chief Minister Tejashwi Yadav, son of Lalu Prasad Yadav. Tejashwi Yadav is facing serious corruption charges and Nitish wanted him to resign in order to protect the *"zero tolerance for corruption image"* of Nitish and his government. Immediately after his resignation, BJP announced its support for Mr. Kumar, and with this, he again achieved the majority to remain the CM in the state. Nitish took oath as the CM on the morning of 27th July and BJP joined him in the Govt. Up to this point; he had Rashtriya Janata Dal (RJD) and Congress as partners. Now, he has BJP as his partner in the state government.

Bihar in 2019 General Elections

From the time RJD-JDU alliance was announced in 2015 and till the time Assembly Elections were held, there were concerns as to how this is the most unnatural partnership, why it would not work and why people would reject this. Even after the victory of *Mahagathbandhan* (JDU, RJD and Congress) in Assembly Elections, there were doubts about the fate of this Government.

For more than one and a half years, the JDU-RJD-Congress government led by Nitish Kumar survived. Despite having more MLAs, Lalu Yadav was surprisingly restrained and Nitish was pragmatic enough to respect the coalition *dharma*. In a coalition government, things are never smooth but if the partners are pragmatic enough to appreciate that the alternative in the form of each one going their own way is much worse, they will be willing to go extra length. His family had been Lalu's weakness for long and Nitish could not continue with Tejashwi Yadav in his cabinet as his clean image is the only political capital Nitish had. That led to a complete 180 degree shift in the political scenario. RJD-JDU alliance had to break down and JDU-BJP are the new friends.

But, could the crumbling of opposition unity in Bihar be a big help for BJP in 2019? For the Opposition parties, Bihar was touted as an example to prove that why Narendra Modi and BJP are not invincible. With Bihar gone BJP's way, the task of Opposition parties to launch a joint common front against BJP in 2019 General Elections looks more difficult. Nitish Kumar had a clean image and he could have been PM candidate of the joint opposition. At least for now, it seems that Nitish has kissed his national ambitions good-bye. He was at least one of the three-four leaders who could have become challengers to Modi in 2019. With the departure of Nitish from opposition camp, the task of Congress (the main opposition party) becomes more difficult in finding reliable partners who can be aligned with, to fight BJP in 2019.

Now when Nitish Kumar and JDU switched sides and came back to BJP and are part of NDA, how this change will reflect in 2019? In this case, JDU and BJP are likely to have a seat sharing arrangement and will become the most potent political force in the state. The trouble with this coalition is that unless Nitish Kumar is desperate to remain a part of this arrangement, the number of seats BJP could win on its own will be much lesser than the acceptable level for the party. JDU ideally will ask for equal number of seats to contest in 2019 *Lok Sabha* elections and accommodating JDU, LJP and a few other smaller parties will be a challenge for BJP. This will not be conducive for BJP to win 22 or more seats in 2019 in Bihar.

There are two other points, a) the image of Nitish Kumar as a secular leader will be dented after his tie-up with BJP and he will lose some of his Muslim vote as leaders like Sharad Yadav are already unhappy with Nitish which means that Nitish may not be as helpful for BJP in 2019, b) Nitish has been proven to be an unreliable partner and no matter how much he praises Modi and BJP today, the chances are never hundred percent that he will remain with BJP for 2019 elections. This is also linked to the fact that what has happened between Modi and Nitish in last eight to ten years, none of them would give each other an inch in terms of political space in Bihar.

The whole idea behind this discussion on Bihar is to realistically assess the chances if BJP can win 22 or NDA can win 31 seats out of 40 in 2019. The repeat of 2014 performance for NDA could certainly be possible now when Nitish has rejoined NDA but BJP winning 22 out of 40 seats doesn't look easy.

Uttar Pradesh in 2019 General Elections

BJP had the biggest of its success in Uttar Pradesh in 2014 elections and that was the primary reason for the party to have a comfortable majority in the 16th *Lok Sabha*.

Table 1.2: Uttar Pradesh - 2014 *Lok Sabha* Elections Results

	Vote share percentage	Seats won	percentage Seats
Bharatiya Janata Party	42.6	71	88.8
Samajwadi Party	22.4	5	6.3
Bahujan Samaj Party	19.8	0	0.0
Congress	7.5	2	2.5

Source: Election Commission of India[38]

Though there were many states where BJP swept the *Lok Sabha* Elections in 2014 (Rajasthan – 25 out of 25 seats, Gujarat – 26 out of 26 seats, Madhya Pradesh – 27 out of 29 seats, Chhattisgarh – 10 out of 11 seats, Delhi – 7 out of 7 seats, Uttarakhand – 5 out of 5 seats), but there was nothing as spectacular as UP. From 80 seats in UP, BJP bagged 71 and BJP's ally, Apna Dal won 2 seats.

The extent of BJP's sweep was so enormous that in 2014, no one else other than Gandhi family (Two seats - Sonia Gandhi at Rae Bareli and Rahul Gandhi at Amethi, for Congress) and Mulayam Singh Yadav's family (Five seats for Samajwadi Party) won in UP among candidates contesting from non-NDA parties, Congress, Samajwadi Party or Bahujan Samaj Party.

In the March 2017 Assembly Elections in Uttar Pradesh, BJP repeated the extraordinary feat. This was despite the fact that there was already a seat sharing arrangement between Samajwadi Party and Congress. We also think that the SP-Congress alliance for whatever it is worth may continue, notwithstanding the poor Assembly Election results for both the parties.

Table 1.3: Uttar Pradesh - 2017 Assembly Elections Results

	Vote share percentage	Seats won	Percentage of Seats
Bharatiya Janata Party	39.7	312	77.4
Samajwadi Party	21.8	47	11.7
Bahujan Samaj Party	22.2	19	4.7
Congress	6.2	7	1.7

Source: Election Commission of India[39]

Another addition to SP-Congress alliance we could see is that of Rashtriya Lok Dal (RLD) which is led by Ajit Singh, son of former Prime Minister and UP Chief

Minister, Chaudhary Charan Singh. So, if nothing much is changing in the situation during the intervening period, we are likely to witness a three-cornered fight between BJP, SP-Congress-RLD and BSP. That is not going to be a huge challenge for BJP as long as the party is able to hold on to its vote share. Of course, winning 71 seats once again in 2019 is not going to be easy for BJP but it may certainly be possible if BSP and SP do not forge an alliance.

Can things get worse for BJP? That depends on with whom BSP would ally itself. It is almost impossible to forecast how BSP would decide on the issue of alliance for 2019 General Elections, a) if it will go alone, b) if it will ally itself with SP-Congress, or, c) BSP will become an ally of BJP. For an outsider, all three possibilities exist and only Ms. Mayawati would know which one is more likely.

However, we think that after the disastrous *Lok Sabha* and Assembly Election results for the party in UP, the possibility of BSP allying itself with either SP or a SP-Congress combine is extremely realistic. Moreover, from a strategic perspective for both SP and BSP, an alliance is much more probable in *Lok Sabha* Elections in 2019. Except for 2017, the UP Assembly Elections were a direct fight between SP and BSP for many years now and hence, they have been arch enemies for decades. They couldn't simply afford to have an alliance for Assembly Elections. Both of them were candidates to form a Government in the state and are contenders to be the "King" and because of what were at stake in Assembly Elections, none of them would have been content to be a "King Maker".

The situation in 2019 *Lok Sabha* elections will be different. At best, these parties can be the "King Maker" at the Centre and for them, having more MPs in *Lok Sabha* would always be desirable even when it comes at the cost of allying with each other. Ideally, both BSP and SP can afford to experiment in *Lok Sabha* elections. Another important factor is that as the command of SP was passed on (or rather it was snatched depending on which narrative you would like to believe more) to Akhilesh Yadav, the relationship between SP and BSP may improve. Mulayam Singh Yadav and his brother, Shivpal Singh Yadav, have always been very hostile towards Ms. Mayawati and she reciprocated accordingly. The animosity may not remain as intense and as personal as it was earlier, now when Akhilesh Yadav is coming to the fore and will be the key decision maker for Samajwadi Party on decisions about forming the alliance and with whom.

Despite their pathetic performance in 2014 and 2017, both SP and BSP still command a very solid, stable and significant vote bank in UP and if the party has to fight the combined SP-BSP-Congress coalition, it would be nothing short of a disaster for the BJP. It can be debated how likely this alliance could be but there is no doubt that the result of SP-BSP alliance would be extremely bad for BJP and NDA. For the people who believe that BSP and SP can never come together, a) many strange things have happened in Indian politics, b) the fear of a common and much more powerful enemy is incentive enough for sworn enemies to come together, and, c) before the Lalu-Nitish alliance became a reality, there were enough skeptics to the idea that this can ever be possible.

The third scenario of BSP allying with BJP would depend upon how BSP would perceive the advantages or disadvantages of being a part of the Central Government. From BJP's perspective, whether BJP is interested in forming such a coalition to defeat SP and Congress is dependent on how BJP would see the long term, strategic advantages of such a move. But, even if a coalition between BSP and BJP happens and if there is a seat sharing agreement between BSP and BJP, the BSP is unlikely to settle for less than a respectable number and that may not be acceptable for BJP. And even if seat sharing between BJP and BSP goes through, it would certainly bring down the number below 71 (the number of seats it won in 2014) for BJP.

The conclusion is that in all the three scenarios, the worst outcome for BJP is a SP-BSP-Congress combine in opposition in UP in the 2019 General Elections. For BJP's tally, a three cornered fight among BJP, Congress-SP and BSP will be better than BSP alliance with BJP. However, irrespective of the pre-poll alliance situation in 2019, it is very likely that a repeat of 2014 for BJP is not going to be easy.

Another unexpected scenario which could emerge in UP is linked to the entry of Priyanka Gandhi[40] into the electoral battle. So far, she has been resisting the demands from party cadre and the Congress leaders alike to join and lead them. It seems that her mother and Congress President, Mrs. Sonia Gandhi is also not keen on Priyanka joining politics in near term. Of course, there is no method to forecast the timing of her entry into the arena or if at all this will happen. But, if it happens before 2019 General Elections, this will certainly invigorate the Congress workers at least in UP. For many voters who are otherwise loyal to

Congress but don't see much of a future for the party under the leadership of Rahul Gandhi, this change would act as reason to give Congress one more chance.

Like Bihar and UP, a similar scenario may play out in a few other states

From the perspective of BJP and how the number of MPs could change in 2019 because of realignment of opposition parties, there are a few other critical states which will matter for the party. Let us take examples of Maharashtra, Andhra Pradesh and Punjab.

The coalition politics is likely to play an important role in Maharashtra (48 *Lok Sabha* seats in the state with four key parties – BJP, Shiv Sena, Congress and NCP), Andhra Pradesh (25 *Lok Sabha* seats with four key parties –TDP, YSR Congress, BJP and Congress) and Punjab (13 *Lok Sabha* seats with four key parties – BJP, SAD, Congress and AAP). In many states, the Opposition Parties against BJP are likely to be more united in 2019 than they were in 2014.

There are states where BJP had won a significant number of *Lok Sabha* seats despite getting less than 40 percent votes. Haryana is an interesting example, BJP's vote share in the state was only a little more than $1/3^{rd}$ but the party still won 70 percent of the seats in the state. In such scenarios, a united opposition could damage the BJP significantly.

The following table shows that there are at least 20 percent seats (of total strength in *Lok Sabha*) in the four states (Assam, Bihar, Haryana and Maharashtra) where the gap between BJP's vote share and seat share was significant. It is important to point out that Maharashtra is a unique case because BJP was not fighting all the seats in 2014 and the party's vote share does not truly capture the support for BJP in the electorate. To some extent, this is true with Bihar as well.

Table 1.4: 2014– States where BJP performed well despite winning less than 40 percent vote

	BJP's seats	Vote percentage for BJP	Total Seats in State	Percentage of seats for BJP
Assam	7	36.86	14	50.0
Bihar	22	29.86	40	55.0
Haryana	7	34.84	10	70.0
Maharashtra	23	27.56	48	47.9

Source: Election Commission of India[41]

BJP will be vulnerable in many states if the Opposition is united

There is a strong possibility that notwithstanding Nitish joing NDA and a JDU-BJP tie up in Bihar, the experiment of 2015 Assembly Elections in Bihar could play out at the national level in 2019 *Lok Sabha* Elections. In each and every state where BJP benefitted because of a split in the Opposition vote, the possibility of a united opposition can make BJP vulnerable.

It is important to note here that if we look at the vote share of BJP in subsequent Assembly Elections, it has declined in most states in comparison to 2014 General Elections. This means that despite the impression being created by multiple victories of BJP in Assembly Elections which were held after 2014 General Elections, the support for Narendra Modi and BJP has not really expanded after 2014 General Elections.

However, to draw a best case scenario for BJP, we ignore that point because it can be argued that *Lok Sabha* elections are different from Assembly Elections and the *Lok Sabha* Election is a much better yardstick to judge the support for Modi. Hence, in the next section, we only refer to the vote shares of BJP and its opponents in 2014 *Lok Sabha* Elections. From this exercise, some important messages are emerging. Please note that in this section, we are not really commenting on how realistic these possibilities of realignment are, but we are only trying to assess the impact these new alignments could potentially have on the success of BJP in 2019. In some ways, this could only be a theoretical exercise at this point. But as Mark Twain had said: "Truth is stranger than fiction, but it is because Fiction is obliged to stick to possibilities; Truth isn't.", even completely theoretical possibilities can become real very quickly in politics.

In bracket against the state, we show the total number of seats and the seats BJP had won in 2014.

Uttar Pradesh (Total seats: 80, BJP: 71)
In 2014, BJP had 42.6 percent vote share followed by SP (22.4 percent), BSP (19.8 percent) and Congress (7.5 percent). From BJP's perspective, SP and BSP if combined will be a formidable competitor and all three SP, BSP and Congress if united will certainly spell disaster. The possible scenarios in UP because of new political realignment in 2019 as compared to 2014 and 2017, we have already discussed in detail in this chapter earlier.

Maharashtra (Total seats: 48, BJP: 23)
BJP had 27.6 percent vote share followed by Shiv Sena (20.8 percent), Congress (18.3 percent) and Nationalist Congress Party or NCP (16.1 percent). From BJP's perspective, Shiv Sena aligning with either NCP or Congress could adversely impact BJP's tally and all the three parties, Shiv Sena, Congress and NCP, forming an alliance against BJP will be even more damaging.

Bihar (Total seats: 40, BJP: 22)
BJP had 29.9 percent vote share followed by RJD (20.5 percent), Janata Dal United (16.0 percent) and Congress (8.6 percent). NDA had won 31 seats (BJP won 22) in Bihar in 2014 and the number of seats may come down for BJP after its tie up with JDU though NDA's tally may increase. This is under the assumption that JDU and BJP will have a pre-poll alliance in 2019 *Lok Sabha* elections and JDU will not agree for anything less than 16-18 seats out of 40 in seat sharing.

Karnataka (Total seats: 28, BJP: 17)
BJP had 43.4 percent vote share followed by Congress (41.2 percent) and Janata Dal (S) (11.1 percent). From BJP's perspective, Congress and Janata Dal (S) if united could negatively impact the party in a big way.

Jharkhand (Total seats: 14, BJP: 12)
BJP had 40.7 percent vote share followed by Congress (13.5 percent), Jharkhand Vikas Morcha – Prajatantrik (12.3 percent) and Jharkhand Mukti Morcha (9.4 percent). Even if all three opposition parties Congress, Jharkhand Vikas

Morcha (Prajatantrik) and Jharkhand Mukti Morcha are united, BJP would still have numerical advantage. However, the possibility of a loss of a few MPs in the next *Lok Sabha* exists.

Assam (Total seats: 14, BJP: 7)
BJP had 36.7 percent vote share followed by Congress (29.9 percent) and All India United Democratic Front (15.0 percent). From BJP's perspective, Congress and All India United Democratic Front if united in fighting against BJP could negatively impact the party in a big way.

Haryana (Total seats: 10, BJP: 7)
BJP had 34.8 percent vote share followed by Indian National Lok Dal (24.4 percent) and Congress (23.0 percent). For BJP, Indian National Lok Dal and Congress if united for fighting against BJP in next elections would spell a huge disaster for BJP.

Delhi (Total seats: 7, BJP: 7)
BJP had 46.6 percent vote share followed by Aam Aadmi Party or AAP (33.1 percent) and Congress (15.2 percent). It may sound extremely improbable today, but AAP and Congress if united for fighting against BJP will be very bad for the party.

Conclusion and the implications for 2019
We think that a spilt in non-BJP vote in 2014 helped BJP in achieving 272+ seats with only 31 percent vote share. Even if BJP maintains the vote share or increases it slightly, a united Opposition could mean a significant decline in the number

of seats BJP can win in 2019 General Elections. Opposition parties have realised that in 2014 elections, fighting BJP separately was a disastrous mistake in judgment; they are unlikely to repeat this mistake in 2019. The Opposition parties (both individually and collectively) have heavily suffered for that indiscretion and it is very likely that they won't make the same mistake again.

There is a high probability that anti-BJP parties would form an alliance and fight the 2019 elections united against BJP. If the other parties at the national level and the regional parties in their respective states identify BJP as the common threat, are willing to accommodate each other and able to set aside their differences at least temporarily by forging pre-poll alliances, the outcome could be disastrous for BJP in 2019. BJP may keep its vote share intact but may still lose several seats in 2019 because the Opposition might not allow the anti-BJP vote to get fragmented. If there is no split in anti-BJP vote, the number of seats BJP would be able to win in 2019 is going to be much less. The transfer of votes between coalition partners may not be fully efficient but it would be good enough in 2019 to stop the BJP juggernaut that was on a roll in 2014.

In the next Chapter

We have seen in this chapter that more than the absolute vote share of BJP in 2014, its tally of seats was driven by huge split in the anti-BJP vote. And, this could change in 2019. In the next chapter, we will look at how the strength of opposition is important in determining the victory margin. Even for the strongest of teams, playing with a weaker opposition increases the probability of a bigger difference in final score. We would also look at how the sentiment against incumbent Government influences election result. The anti-incumbency against UPA in 2014 helped BJP in steamrolling the opposition and why that critical support would be missing in 2019 for BJP.

2

2014 MANDATE: UPA — THE STORY OF SELF GOALS

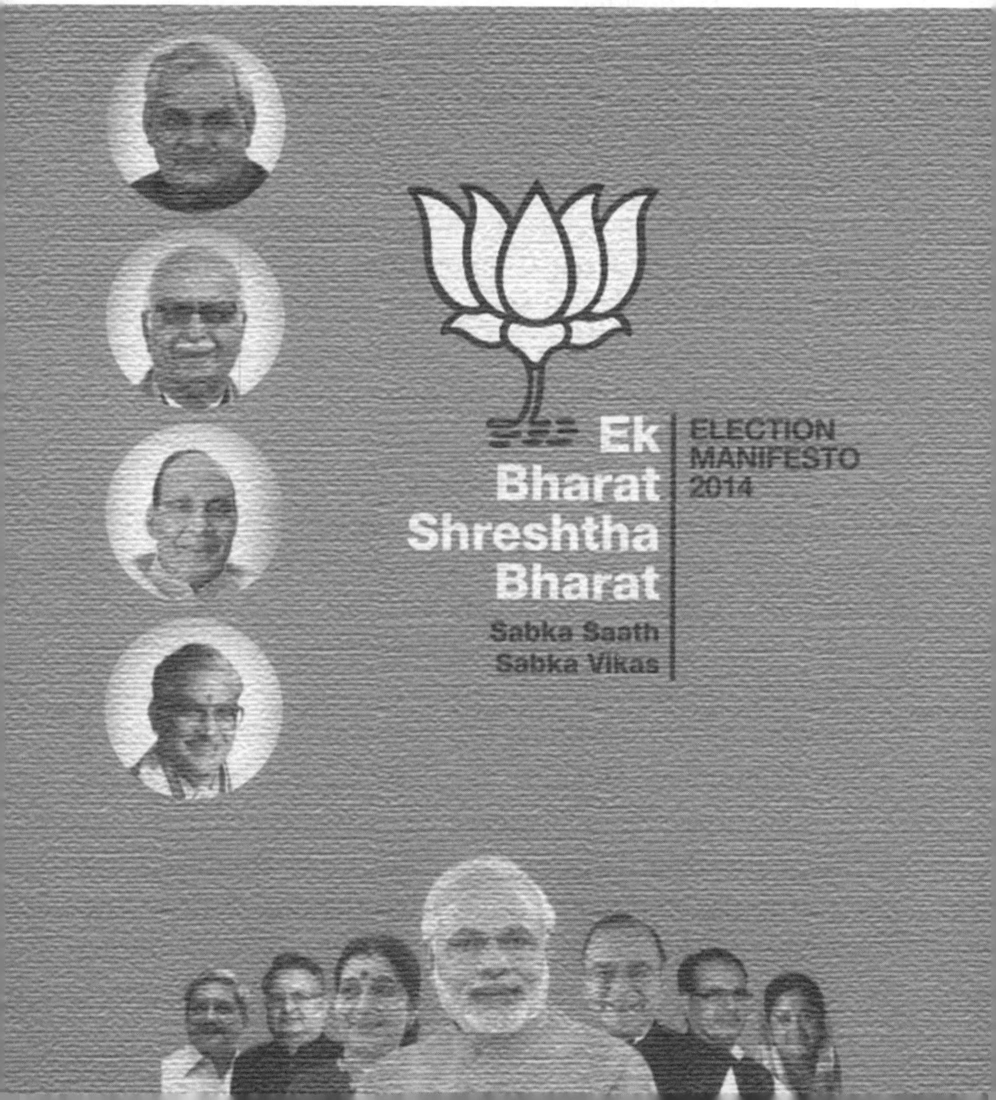

> Anti-incumbency, not PM Narendra Modi's charisma is behind poll results. If he (Modi) is invincible, what happened to his charisma in Punjab where the BJP lost so badly... (also) in Manipur and Goa?
>
> —CPI General Secretary S Sudhakar Reddy, post assembly election results March 2017[1]

UPA: Surprise winner in 2004 with a legitimate claim of being popular in 2009

After the unexpected defeat of NDA under the leadership of Atal Bihari Vajpayee[2] in 2004, the UPA Government took charge under the leadership of Dr. Manmohan Singh. It is interesting to note that though BJP had lost to Congress and its performance was significantly below expectations, the difference between Congress and BJP was not huge. Compared to BJP's 138 seats, Congress had won 145 seats in 2004. If there was not much difference between BJP and Congress, why did not the BJP make an attempt to form a coalition Government?

Congress was much more acceptable to many other non-BJP and non-Congress parties such as Left (CPI-M had 43 seats, CPI had 10 seats), RJD (Lalu Prasad Yadav's RJD had 24 seats), DMK (16 seats) and NCP (9 seats). As a result, UPA with Congress as the leading partner in the coalition was able to form the Government. After Sonia Gandhi declined to become Prime Minister and instead appointed Dr. Manmohan Singh as the PM, she was hailed as the epitome of sacrifice and selflessness. This was one of the key factors that helped in creating a positive vibe around UPA.

It is also important to note that the first three to four years of UPA's first term (from 2004 to 2007/08 during

2004-09 term of UPA I) was a great time for global economy as well. We will discuss the economic factors in much more detail in the next Chapter but at this point, it would be sufficient to note that the world back then was flush with liquidity and global trade was booming. In this kind of environment, it was not a surprise that Emerging Markets such as India were doing well as investors were discovering new investment destinations and opportunities. It also helped UPA that the previous NDA Government had done well on the fiscal discipline front and had put great emphasis on the development of infrastructure, economic reforms and disinvestment.

As a result, UPA I (2004-09) had an excellent environment to govern. UPA I also had a solid platform available to launch many populist schemes such as MNREGA[3]. On the other hand, the BJP cadre and leaders could not really recover from the jolt of 2004 defeat. In addition, there were question marks on NDA's leadership as Lal Krishna Advani's attempts to portray himself as a more acceptable leader by praising Muhammad Ali Jinnah (founder of Pakistan) as secular leader, while he was on a visit to Pakistan created big confusion and resentment in BJP cadre and the party's core voter base[4]. It can be speculated with a fair degree of conviction that even the ordinary *Swayamsevak* (volunteer) of *Rashtriya Swayamsevak Sangh* and BJP worker was also not solidly behind the party in 2009 Elections.

In 2009 *Lok Sabha* Elections, Congress did spectacularly well and crossed the 200 seats mark first time in eighteen years, after 1991. Its allies such as Trinamool Congress (19 seats), DMK (18 seats) and NCP (9 seats) also did well.

Compared to 2004, the NDA and BJP slid further with the party being reduced to 116 seats in *Lok Sabha*. Sensing that Congress is on a very solid footing now, some other parties such as Ms. Mayawati's BSP (21 seats) also extended support to UPA.

If Congress in UPA I (2004-09) at all had any constraints in providing a stable and effective Government, almost all of it was removed after a significantly better show in the 2009 General Elections. The Congress not only had a comfortable majority along with allies, some of the fence sitters and so-called neutral (non-NDA and non-UPA) parties also didn't see any logic in fighting with Congress unnecessarily.

After 2009 General Elections, the setting was perfect for UPA to deliver and build a solid base for 2014 Elections. Alas! This is not how it was meant to be.

UPA II – The story of self-goals

The results of 2009 elections provided a very good platform for UPA to prepare for a return in 2014 with an even bigger mandate. But, the reality in politics is never that simple and straight forward. Though we will have a detailed observation on the prominent developments which were responsible for such extreme unpopularity of UPA during 2009-14, it is important at this stage to highlight a crucial difference between the earlier defeats of Congress and the one it was handed over in 2014.

After being in power, Congress had lost in 1977, 1989 and 1996 as well. But, in any of those years, it would not be very easy to point out that the party had even lost the will to fight. In all the previous elections when Congress had lost after being in power (1977, 1989 and 1996), it had given a good fight and tried to give a good account of itself. In short, elections were not a one sided affair in 1977, 1989 and 1996. But in 2014, the party had completely given up and virtually conceded defeat even before the commencement of election process. Congress cadre was completely demoralised and the party leadership could not really do much to motivate them.

The charges of Corruption against senior Ministers and Officials in UPA

This issue of corruption was the biggest and naturally, much exploited by Opposition. This was perhaps the most important reason behind UPA's debacle in the 2014 General Elections as there was an all-round impression that UPA was leading a corrupt government. Since corruption was perceived to be flowing from the top, people saw the Government as totally inept in handling and controlling the situation. The number of incidents and the amounts involved in the allegations would be huge if we starting discussing all the corruption scandals during UPA rule. But we would highlight only three major cases, a) Coal Blocks Allocation Scam[5] (Rs 1.86 trillion), b) 2G Spectrum Scam[6] (Rs 1.76 trillion), and, c) Commonwealth Games Scam[7].

The general perception was that either some Congress leaders are themselves beneficiaries of large scale corruption in the Government (at the worst) or the Congress is responsible for shielding the corrupt (at the best). All of these stories were easy fodder for the media. The incessant coverage by print and electronic media also helped in creating an anti-UPA sentiment to a great extent. The net result was that people were extremely disappointed with Congress and UPA on the corruption issue.

In 2011, anti-corruption activist and renowned social worker Anna Hazare[8] began a hunger strike at the Jantar Mantar in New Delhi. The main objective of the movement was to target corruption at senior political posts through introduction of the *Jan Lokpal* Bill[9]. Arvind Kejriwal[10] who was an activist and had worked with Anna Hazare earlier also joined the movement led by Anna. Kejriwal later on formed a new political party called Aam Admi Party (AAP)[11]. Arvind Kejriwal and AAP seized the initiative and started attacking the Congress Government and were able to do very well in Delhi Assembly Elections.

However, the biggest beneficiary of anti-UPA sentiment created on the issue of corruption was Narendra Modi. Modi was able to maintain a very clean image despite being at the helm in Gujarat as a Chief Minister for more than 12 years. No wonder, he coined the slogan "*Na Khaoonga, Na Khaane Doonga*" (I will not take bribe nor I would allow anyone else in the Government to take). The public anger against UPA on the issue of corruption became one of the key factors in building a favourable sentiment for Modi and led to BJP's spectacular performance in 2014.

Policy Paralysis and crumbling Economy – Mix of controllable and uncontrollable

As the global economy went into a recession from 2008 onwards[12], this downturn also impacted countries like India. Under such an environment, there were a lot of sectors where the positive intervention of the Central Government became necessary. Even otherwise, in the areas of core infrastructure development (power, roads, ports, airports etc.), there are a lot of approvals and clearances which are required. In these sectors, land acquisition is also an integral component of project development.

This requires consistent, coherent and efficient policy formulation along with swift decision making from the Government. Similarly, many other industries such as Mining and Mineral Exploration, Manufacturing, Process, Oil and Gas and Telecom need clearly laid out rules and guidelines. Hence, they are dependent on Government for providing an enabling environment that works smoothly. However, efficient decision making and coordination among various Government departments and Ministries was lacking under UPA II.

There were also many new rules and guidelines (sometimes arbitrary and whimsical as well) which were introduced and this entire situation was collectively referred to as *"Policy Paralysis"*. For example, in case of MoEF (Ministry of Environment and Forests), there was an accusation that the introduction of *"Go"* and *"No Go"* areas created unnecessary difficulties for coal mining and that led to severe shortage of domestic coal despite India having one of the largest coal reserves in the world. The end user industries like power plants had to resort to more expensive coal imports which was logistically difficult as well or had to cut down on the plant utilisation i.e. had to stop power generation on the account of insufficient coal availability.

It has been more than three years since UPA lost power. With the benefit of hindsight and to be a little bit more sympathetic to the previous Government now, we can say that some of things which went wrong for UPA were clearly beyond Government's control. For example, the significantly lower than expected gas production from Reliance Industries Ltd's Natural Gas field KG-D6 led to massive issues for gas based power generation capacity and for Banks in the form of NPAs (Non performing assets or Bad loans). Also, Oil prices went up and since India is a large net importer, this created increased difficulties for the Government and the people.

On the other hand, Narendra Modi's Gujarat was marching ahead on vital parameters like Foreign Direct Investment (for example, *Vibrant Gujarat*[13] was a very successful event) and GDP growth rate in the state[14]. Sensing which way the wind was blowing, many industrialists and people who were considered influential and important voice of expertise openly started criticising the UPA Government and started advocating a regime change in general and in favour of Narendra Modi in particular. Though UPA Government made an attempt to address these concerns from time to time, most of these efforts didn't look adequate before the people.

Dual Power Centers in Party and Government – Confusion and dilution of authority

What worked like a precise division of responsibilities in UPA I where Dr. Manmohan Singh was leading the Government and Mrs. Sonia Gandhi was handling Congress party affairs, became the Achilles' heel for the administration in UPA II. There was a basic difference in people's perception towards the abdication of Prime Minister's post by Mrs. Sonia Gandhi. What people saw in

2004 was an act of detachment with power and an act of great sacrifice and morality, the same thing done in 2009-14 phase was seen as an attempt by Mrs. Sonia Gandhi to have "Hundred percent power and Zero percent accountability". This became really difficult to defend for the Government and Congress party.

To be fair, there were reasons behind that perception. The seemingly questionable and in many instances, the State Government facilitated land deals by Mrs. Sonia Gandhi's son-in-law, Mr. Robert Vadra in Rajasthan and Haryana hardened the impression in public that Mrs. Gandhi was enjoying all the perks and privileges associated with power without being bothered with day-to-day responsibilities on how to run the administration. As per media reports and grapevine from corridors of power, some of her close associates were also not beyond suspicion in many business deals. That certainly impacted Mrs. Sonia Gandhi's image negatively.

In many ways, it was such a situation though not as bad but still quite similar to 1975 to 1977 phase when Sanjay Gandhi[15] was seen as an extra-constitutional authority. During that phase though Mrs. India Gandhi remained the Prime Minister officially, if we believe the grapevine it was her son, Sanjay Gandhi who was calling the shots. It was Sanjay who was enjoying all the perks and privileges which come with power but had absolutely zero accountability for his actions. Many people saw Mrs. Sonia Gandhi the same way in UPA government.

Most of the Ministers from Congress in the UPA Government knew that they owe their jobs to the equation they had with Mrs. Sonia Gandhi and this became a big hindrance in governance. Dr. Manmohan Singh virtually had very little authority over some of these Ministers. This created several parallel power centers and a source of huge confusion for bureaucracy.

Similarly, many of the Congress party's allies never really bothered even to at least create an impression of harmony and coordination in the Cabinet and the Ministers filled from the allies' quota continued to work as they pleased. The Cabinet of Dr. Manmohan Singh was also filled with people who were more politically experienced than the PM himself and also, there were many who were themselves contenders for the post of PM (Mr. Pranab Mukherjee[16], Mr. P Chidambaram[17], Mr. Sharad Pawar[18] to name a few).

Public opinion would be subjective more often than not, but Dr. Singh also never had any single Indo-US nuclear deal type of moment in his second term. He came across as someone who had his heart at the right place but was simply not equal to the task. A lot of people from general public held the opinion that Dr. Singh was using the shield of his honesty and personal integrity and was hiding behind it, but he was ignoring the inefficiency and rampant corruption in his Government.

People believed that Dr. Singh was directly responsible for why there was so much corruption in the UPA Government or why Dr. Singh was not wielding his authority over his colleagues and bureaucracy. It is only a conjecture but had Dr. Singh resigned mid-way, history would have been more sympathetic towards him and would have judged him more favourably.

As the perception grew stronger that the authority of Prime Minister's Office (PMO) has been severely diluted under Dr. Manmohan Singh as the Prime Minister, people started to witness that even his own party had lost confidence in him. The open acts of defiance for example, Rahul Gandhi tore the ordinance on convicted politicians in front of a press briefing attended by full complement of journalists, were absolutely disastrous for the image of PM.

We don't know who the political advisers to Rahul Gandhi were at that point, but there is no way you can act like an activist against your own government. In a major embarrassment to the UPA government led by Dr. Singh and also for the Prime Minister personally, Rahul Gandhi in September 2013 publicly denounced the controversial ordinance to negate the Supreme Court verdict on convicted lawmakers. Rahul Gandhi claimed that this ordinance was "complete nonsense" and openly said that what the government had done was wrong. Similarly, towards the end of UPA II tenure, Mrs. Gandhi seldom openly tried to restore the credibility of PMO and expressed her full and absolute confidence under the leadership of Dr. Singh. Even if Dr. Singh and Mrs. Gandhi had no difference of opinion at all, this never became apparent to the outsiders and general public.

No wonder that the campaign of BJP capitalised very well on this opportunity. In his 2014 election campaign, Modi projected the image of himself as a strong and decisive leader who will not shy away from taking difficult and bold decisions. There were hopes that he will end the policy paralysis and he will be firm in dealing with China and Pakistan. It was also hoped that Modi will do everything possible to meet the aspirations of youth and a burgeoning Indian Middle Class by offering a development focused agenda and a clean, transparent Government.

The Unruly Allies damaged the Government and Congress

This was something really very strange and difficult to understand. While the number of seats Congress had won increased substantially in 2009 (206 seats in 2009 General Elections vs. 145 in 2004), the bargaining power it had with its allies either didn't change much or had even considerably diminished. At least this was the general impression. Either Congress was too timid in dealing with its allies or simply, the party did not have intent to deal with unruly allies in a stern manner. This made Congress guilty in the eyes of people.

Despite being critically dependent on the Left Parties in the UPA's first term, Dr. Manmohan Singh overruled their objections on Indo-US nuclear deal and went ahead. Congress and Mrs. Gandhi also supported Dr. Singh's decision. It was a completely different picture during the second term of UPA II as allies went berserk and Congress didn't make any effort to salvage this situation. The Government may not be "in control" always but there is nothing worse for its public image than the impression that a Government doesn't look to be "in control". For example, the "2G scam" as a whole was being seen as a brazen act of misappropriation by Ministers from DMK and in which, Congress had very little role. But, since Congress didn't do anything in the matter, the party had to suffer the consequences.

In UPA II, the general public noted that some of the alliance partners were guilty but Congress and Dr. Singh overlooked those serious lapses and acts of financial irregularities and misappropriation. This was seen as a much bigger crime. It may only be a subject of post-facto analysis but Dr. Singh blaming the "compulsions of coalition politics" for the troubles in administration made the situation even worse. His attempt was seen by people as a feeble effort to justify corruption and poor standards of governance. Though every coalition Government has to face these challenges, the difference was that the Congress was not even seen as making an attempt to correct the situation.

Excessive dependence on Populist Measures

The unexpected loss of NDA in 2004 was primarily attributed to the fact that the Atal Bihari Vajpayee led Government ignored the rural areas and agriculture. This angered these voters and as a result, BJP suffered in 2004. Perhaps learning from this experience, UPA launched several welfare measures in its first term and this worked very well as Congress along with its allies came back to power in 2009. Unfortunately, this led to disastrous consequences in future.

This political model which was based on Government largesse was hailed as the template for future elections by campaign managers of Congress. The inherent assumption was that as long as you take care of the bottom of the pyramid[20] by offering them generous benefits, they will continue to vote for you. The evidence which was used to support this assertion was that people had ousted NDA in 2004 and brought back UPA in 2009.

Unfortunately, this model had a few flaws, a) the benefits are welcome at the bottom of the pyramid but it should not seem like that the governance is suffering and corruption at the top has increased, b) the Government needs to find resources before they can be distributed and if there are external and internal shocks that limits the Government's financial maneuverability, it would be difficult to sustain this expenditure, c) it is a vicious cycle and the Government needs to offer more and more benefits to get the same results and there would be times when the system would collapse under its own weight. These measures are not sustainable in the long run.

The welfare measures based political model is also responsible for alienation of those people who don't really benefit from this excessive populism of the Government. The people especially from middle class felt that the Government is taking undue advantage of them and not offering any commensurate improvement in the governance standards and public services. The middle class and upper middle class would be more interested in development work and creation of infrastructure and they won't appreciate an excess of populist measures by the Government.

Contrary to this, the image of Narendra Modi's governance model in Gujarat was development based. In public perception, better governance was achieved in this model by attracting foreign and domestic investment, improving infrastructure, achieving higher industrial growth and providing better amenities to public. Modi offered the hope of a better tomorrow and stoppage of wasteful expenditure on populist measures to people and they responded by voting for him in 2014.

Reasons were many, but result was same: A huge anti-incumbency against UPA

India is a cricket crazy nation and sometimes, we understand the language of cricket better than anything else. So, while any similarity to any living or dead cricketer would be purely coincidental, UPA towards the end of its second term in 2014 resembled more and more like a batsman who was poor in technique on a Sabina Park pitch at Kingston, Jamaica in the 1970s and 1980s against the pace battery[21] of West Indies. The agony had to end; sooner the better it would be.

Jokes apart but as we have seen, the reasons were many why people started to feel disgruntled with Congress and UPA and why they wanted a change; a) the charges of Corruption against UPA, b) Policy Paralysis and a crumbling Economy, c) Dual Power Centers in the Party and the Government, d) the Unruly Allies, and, e) Excessive dependence on Populist Measures. With all these factors, the result was: **A massive ANTI-INCUMBENCY against Congress in 2014 elections.**

Combined with this anti-incumbency mood against UPA, the people also had a credible alternative available in Narendra Modi. Modi was a choice people were willing to bet on, a) he was seen as strong and decisive, b) he had delivered in Gujarat, c) he had the vision of progress and development, d) his image was clean, and, e) he was perceived as someone who is above the push and pull of intra-party politics and was not under the influence of powerful and rich people despite being business friendly.

People thought that Narendra Modi was an outsider who deserved a chance. And, the choice was made simple for people by perceived non-performance of UPA and it worked in favour of Modi in 2014. Just like sports, a stronger opposition may not be able to change the final result but it can certainly make a huge difference to the score line.

Similarly, it is highly possible that BJP would have scored a victory in 2014 because they were the stronger team than UPA but had UPA not been struggling with massive anti-incumbency, BJP's victory margin would not have been as big as it was in 2014 General Elections.

BJP's win in 2014 was big because of Modi wave plus Anti UPA wave

The victory margins of BJP's winning candidates also suggests that there was a strong wave in party's favour (we can surely argue over if it was a Modi wave or an Anti-UPA wave or a combination of both). In 2014, more than 40 percent of BJP's candidates had won with a victory margin of more than 200,000 votes and only about 10 percent had victory margin of less than 50,000.

Table 2.1: BJP's winning candidates and their victory margin in number of votes

	< 10,000	10,000-50,000	50,000-100,000	100,000-200,000	200,000-300,000	>300,000	Total
No. of candidates	9	23	44	90	74	42	282
Percentage of Total Candidates	3	8	16	32	26	15	

Source: Election Commission of India

On the other hand, almost 50 percent of Congress candidates were successful with a margin of less than 50,000 votes. The candidates with a victory margin of more than 200,000 were very rare. Only three of total 44 Congress MPs in 16th *Lok Sabha* had victory margin of more than 200,000 votes. This figure is a meager 7 percent compared to 40 percent plus of BJP MPs winning with a margin of 200,000 votes or more.

Table 2.2: The winning candidates of Congress and their victory margin in number of votes

	< 10,000	10,000-50,000	50,000-100,000	100,000-200,000	200,000-300,000	>300,000	Total
No. of candidates	7	14	10	10	1	2	44
Percentage of Total Candidates	16	32	23	23	2	5	

Source: Election Commission of India

However, UPA will be a distant memory by the time it is 2019

There is an old trick very commonly used by many real estate agents. They would have a ready inventory of houses which are bad and still quoting a high rate. Before they actually show the prospective clients the real inventory they have, they will make it a point to show this poor and expensive sample inventory to their prospective clients. These agents know it very well that this bad inventory won't fly with the clients. Still, they show it every time.

The purpose of showing this inventory to clients is to make the other, real inventory look good in comparison. And, it works very well most of the times. Playing with the psychology of a customer is not just limited to the sales people; it is also common during the elections. The political parties and candidates would use similar techniques by highlighting, a) how they are good and, b) how others are bad. This is done with an almost equal emphasis on both these comparisons.

In comparison of the time candidates spend on telling the prospective voters that how good they are, they spend a lot more time in telling voters how the other candidates are bad. Another phenomenon which is observed in the campaigns is that the political parties spend most of their time in running down the principal opposition which they think is their main competitor.

The candidate's objective is twofold, a) the best case scenario is when the voter vote for him or her, and, b) the next best choice is that when the voters don't vote for him/her but they should not at least vote for the candidate who is their strongest competitor. As we have seen in detail in **Chapter 1, *The Opposition Will be better prepared for Modi*** that the winning candidate doesn't need to win the majority vote; the purpose is served equally well if no one else wins more votes irrespective of the absolute number of votes the winning candidate has received.

In the previous 2014 election, people wanted to throw UPA out and in comparison, Modi certainly looked very good. There were many voters who were keen to send UPA packing and they ensured that they visited the polling booths on the Election Day. They may have opted for Modi but the primary objective was not to elect Modi, it was to change the Government and vote against UPA for them.

But that won't be the case in next elections

In 2019, people would evaluate Modi on how well he has performed in the preceding five years. And, no Government or administrator can make everyone happy. Not just that, Narendra Modi is also carrying a massive burden of expectations and there would certainly be a few disappointments for his support base and there is a chance that some of these people may shift their loyalties elsewhere. For some it could be not enough new jobs and for some others, the worsening internal security situation in Jammu and Kashmir. Some may get unhappy with demonetisation[22] or Goods and Services Tax (GST[23]) and some may believe that law and order situation has not really improved under Modi's rule. It is very likely that in 2019, BJP will not be benefitting from the negative UPA vote which was coming to them in 2014.

Let us consider a different argument. In 2019, it is possible that people may still decide to vote for Narendra Modi because they don't find any of the alternatives available appealing. But, they would certainly not be as angry with today's Opposition as they were in 2014. The electorate would not really blame the Congress for whatever happened and/or didn't happen during 2014 to 2019.

Hence, no matter how good the performance of NDA Government is or how popular Narendra Modi remains as a Prime Minister, the comparison effect which massively helped BJP in 2014 will be missing in 2019.

In the next Chapter

We have seen in this chapter that a powerful anti-incumbency sentiment against UPA significantly helped BJP in 2014. This strong tailwind would not be available in 2019. In the next Chapter, we will take a look at the role economy plays in elections. Congress would not have performed this badly or BJP this well in 2014 elections had the Indian economy not been in a very bad shape during last two years of UPA II. Poor growth rates, inadequate investment in infrastructure, higher inflation and many other things which are associated with a poor economy actually do hurt the electoral prospects of ruling party. Unfortunately for BJP, things have not really improved much which may prove to be a very difficult challenge for Modi to handle in 2019.

3

THE ROLE OF ECONOMY IN ELECTIONS

It's the economy, stupid!

— A popular phrase used by Bill Clinton's team during his successful 1992 presidential campaign against sitting US President George H. W. Bush.[1]

The economy was struggling especially in the second half of UPA II rule

It is a fact that poor state of economy and dissatisfaction because of economic factors hurt the electoral prospects of any ruling party. For example, price rise is a very sensitive subject for people and this alone can seal the fate of incumbent Governments. For an interesting case, please refer to the section ***Onions and BJP's loss in Delhi Assembly Elections in 1998*** in ***Chapter 5, Modi's Pinnacle: Was it 2014 or Will it be 2019?***

More importantly, it is entirely immaterial if the poor state of economy is a result of controllable factors or uncontrollable reasons. The controllable reasons can be classified as things which are of Government's own making such as delayed policy decisions, bad planning, unnecessary bureaucratic delays, massive top level corruption and poor coordination among various Government departments.

The uncontrollable factors are the factors where the Government is completely helpless such as oil shocks for a crude importing nation, volatile world economy, artificial barriers for the flow of trade and services, adverse geo political developments and poor foreign direct investment flows. These are the things which can turn favourable or unfavourable purely on the basis of chance events and how lucky or unlucky an administration is.

If we take a look at several important economic indicators which we are going to explain in more detail next, there was a particularly bad patch the country was going through during the second half of UPA II tenure (2009-14). And this played an important role in making the UPA's loss in 2014 much bigger than it would have been otherwise. UPA had to suffer for the poor performance of economy and this helped in making BJP's victory much bigger.

GDP growth rate[2]–There was a serious decline in India's GDP growth rate in last three years of UPA's second term. It may only be a conjecture but had the order been reverse (poor growth in initial years followed by good years in 2012-13 and 2013-14), we don't think election outcome would have been this bad for Congress or UPA in 2014.

Table 3.1: GDP Growth Rate for India during UPA II rule

Year	India's GDP Growth rate
2008-09	6.7 percent
2009-10	8.6 percent
2010-11	8.9 percent
2011-12	6.7 percent
2012-13	5.5 percent
2013-14	6.4 percent

Source: Government of India Estimates as per Central Statistical Organization, http://mospi.nic.in/

Inflation[3] –The rate of inflation, based on annual average Wholesale Price Index (WPI), was 7.8 percent in 2012-13 and 8.8 percent in 2011-12. During 1999-2013, the maximum WPI inflation (9.6 percent) was observed in 2010-11. Over the nine-years span (from 1999-2000 to 2007-08), WPI inflation remained below 7 percent except one breach in 2000-01 (7.2 percent) and in five-years span, 2008-09 to 2012-13, WPI inflation remained well above 7 percent except in 2009-10 when it went down to 4.1 percent . The rate of inflation, based on annual average Consumer Price Index (CPI), was 8.0 percent in 2012-13 and 9.0 percent in 2011-12. During 1999-2013, maximum CPI inflation (13 percent) was observed in 2009-10. Throughout the nine year span, 1999-2000 to 2007-08, CPI inflation remained below 7 percent and in five year span, 2008-09 to 2012-13; CPI inflation remained above 7 percent every year. There is hardly any doubt that a high inflation or Government's inability to control prices makes the voters angry.

Table 3.2: Consumer Price Inflation in India

Year	India's Inflation Rate
2009-10	13.0 percent
2010-11	9.5 percent
2011-12	9.0 percent
2012-13	8.0 percent
2013-14	9.5 percent

Source: http://pib.nic.in/newsite/PrintRelease.aspx?relid=106245, www.data.gov.in

Table 3.3: Average inflation India (measured in Consumer Price Inflation)

Year	India's Inflation Rate
2009	10.8 percent
2010	12.1 percent
2011	8.9 percent
2012	9.3 percent
2013	10.9 percent
2014	6.4 percent

Source: http://www.inflation.eu/inflation-rates/india/historic-inflation/cpi-inflation-india.aspx

Industrial Growth[4] –There was a decline in India's Industrial growth rate in UPA's second term. Poor industrial growth impacts job creation and also indicates a sluggish economy. Neither this is good for the country nor is it helpful for the government in getting reelected.

Table 3.4: Industrial Growth Rate in India on Year-on-Year Basis (Base Year 2004-05)

Year	Industrial Growth rate
2009-10	5.3 percent
2010-11	8.2 percent
2011-12	2.9 percent
2012-13	1.1 percent
2013-14	-0.1 percent

Source: https://rbidocs.rbi.org.in/rdocs/Publications/PDFs/0HANDB_F0651BA902A5244DFB75DA46261B53726.PDF (RBI Handbook on Indian Economy)

Currency Exchange rate[5] –The UPA Government was in power till mid-May in 2014 and in 2012 and 2013, the Rupee lost almost 25 percent of its value against dollar. A depreciating currency does not reflect too well on the health of an economy and though currency exchange rate as such may not be a factor when people make their voting decisions, exchange rate is an important parameter to assess the stability of an economy.

Table 3.5: USD: INR exchange rate

Year	bid	ask	Average	Percentage change
2009	48.42	48.85	48.64	
2010	45.72	45.94	45.83	5.8
2011	46.85	47.24	47.04	-2.7
2012	53.46	53.76	53.61	-14.0
2013	58.44	58.59	58.52	-9.1
2014	60.89	61.03	60.96	-4.2

Note: In the table, a positive number in percentage change column denotes Rupee's appreciation vs. US dollar.
Source: www.oanda.com

Table 3.6: INR against major currencies

Year	SDR	US Dollar	Pound Sterling	Japanese Yen	Euro
2009	74.59	48.41	75.73	51.81	67.39
2010	69.75	45.73	70.69	52.17	60.67
2011	73.64	46.67	74.77	58.62	64.88
2012	81.79	53.44	84.70	67.03	68.67
2013	89.06	58.60	91.77	60.08	77.90
2014	92.73	61.03	100.54	57.79	81.12

Notes: 1. The exchange rate for Japanese Yen is in per 100 Yen. 2. Data are based on FEDAI (Foreign Exchange Dealers' Association of India) indicative rates till April 2012.RBI reference rates are used w.e. f. May 2012. 3. The currency value of the SDR is determined by summing the values in U.S. dollars, based on market exchange rates, of a basket of major currencies (the U.S. dollar, Euro, Japanese yen, pound sterling and the Chinese renminbi). SDR is an international reserve asset, created by the IMF in 1969 to supplement its member countries' official reserves. As of March 2016, 204.1 billion SDRs (equivalent to about $285 billion) had been created and allocated to members. SDRs can be exchanged for freely usable currencies.

Source:https://rbidocs.rbi.org.in/rdocs/Publications/PDFs/0HANDB_F0651BA902A5244DFB75DA46261B53726.PDF (RBI Handbook on Indian Economy), http://www.imf.org/en/About/Factsheets/Sheets/2016/08/01/14/51/Special-Drawing-Right-SDR, http://www.imf.org/external/np/fin/data/rms_sdrv.aspx

Core Industries Growth[7] – The core industries include Coal, Crude Oil, Natural Gas, Refinery Products, Fertilizers, Steel, Cement and Electricity. The eight core industries contribute approximately 40 percent in the IIP and this is an important benchmark for assessing the health of core sector. There was a decline in core industries' growth rate in UPA's second term. However, it was not as pronounced as the slow-down in broader industrial growth which we had discussed a little earlier.

Table 3.7: Core Industries Growth Rate in India (Base Year 2004-05)

Year	Core Industries Growth rate
2009-10	6.6 percent
2010-11	6.6 percent
2011-12	5.0 percent
2012-13	6.5 percent
2013-14	4.2 percent
2014-15	4.5 percent

Note: Refinery Products' yearly growth rate of 2012-13 is not comparable with other years on account of inclusion of RIL (SEZ) production data since April, 2012 and this impacted 2012-13 figure. Refinery products reported 29 percent growth rate in 2012-13.

Source: https://rbidocs.rbi.org.in/rdocs/Publications/PDFs/0HANDB_F06 51BA902A5244DFB75DA46261B53726.PDF, RBI Handbook on Indian Economy and http://pib.nic.in/newsite/erelease.aspx?relid=0

On important parameters, we find that Indian economy was in a difficult phase in UPA II, especially during second half of the Government's tenure. Things such as an unusually high inflation hurt the common people and leads to anger against ruling dispensation and that is exactly what had happened in 2014 General Elections.

In the next section, we will analyze whether things have changed in Indian economy under NDA.

How the economy is doing under Modi Government?
The Modi Government took charge in May 2014 and to make a comparison, we take a look at the key parameters to assess if the Indian economy has done better in last three years.

GDP Growth
Under NDA Government, GDP growth has been better than the worst years of UPA II tenure. However at the same time, it has been worse than the best years of UPA II tenure. There are two ways to look at it. The supporters of Modi will claim that the economy was in such bad shape that it will take time to recover while his critics will claim that some recovery was expected because of cyclical nature of an economy and due to base effect. Nevertheless, it is difficult to claim that NDA government has been able to perform better than UPA on GDP growth.

Table 3.8: GDP Growth Rate for India during UPA II rule

Year	India's GDP Growth rate
2014-15	7.5 percent
2015-16	8.0 percent
2016-17	7.1 percent
2017-18 (E)	7.2 percent
2018-19 (E)	7.5 percent
2019-20 (E)	7.7 percent

Note: The estimates for FY18, 19 and 20 are as per World Bank.
Source:http://www.livemint.com/Politics/Ig7hWnKkVbhVGXxovJOYGO/GDP-grows-at-61-in-fourth-quarter-below-estimate-of-71.html,http://www.thehindubusinessline.com/economy/world-bank-pegs-indias-gdp-growth-at-72-in-fy18/article9715141.ece, http://www.moneycontrol.com/news/business/economy/world-bank-pegs-indias-fy18-growth-at-7-2-2291905.html

It is relevant here to discuss the impact of demonetisation on GDP. As per official estimates, India's GDP growth rate was only 6.1 percent in the fourth quarter of 2016-17 from 7.9 percent in the April-June quarter primarily because of the negative impact of demonetisation on economy. In 1Q Financial Year 2018 (FY 18), the GDP growth declined further to 5.7 percent. The following table shows a worrisome trend as the GDP growth date indicates that the economy is in a downward spiral over last 12-18 months.

Table 3.9: GDP Growth Rate in Financial year 2017 (FY 2017) and Financial Year 2018 (FY 18) (Quarterly data)

Year	India's GDP Growth rate
1Q FY17	7.9 percent
2Q FY17	7.5 percent
3Q FY17	7.0 percent
4Q FY17	6.1 percent
1Q FY18	5.7 percent

Source: http://www.livemint.com/Politics/Ig7hWnKkVbhVGXxovJOYGO/GDP-grows-at-61-in-fourth-quarter-below-estimate-of-71.html, http://www.livemint.com/Industry/acEAx2TJIDMMzZbuhOBpLN/India-GDP-growth-slumps-to-57-in-Q1-hit-by-GST-implementa.html

Another way to look at it is the slowdown in second half of FY17 vs. the first half (1H). There is 115bps (bps is basis points and 1 percentage point is equal to 100 bps) decline from 1H to 2H in FY17 and this means that the nascent recovery in economy was derailed because of demonetisation. In 1Q FY18, there has been another decline in GDP growth rate by 85bps vs. 2H FY17. Effectively, the GDP growth rate has declined by full 200bps from 1H FY17 to 1Q FY18 and demonetisation has been the main reason for this negative impact.

Table 3.10: GDP Growth Rate in 1Q FY18, 2H FY17 and 1H FY17

Year	India's GDP Growth rate
1 H FY17 (Average of 1Q and 2Q)	7.70 percent
2 H FY17 (Average of 3Q and 4Q)	6.55 percent
1 Q FY18	5.70 percent

Source: http://www.livemint.com/Politics/Ig7hWnKkVbhVGXxovJOYGO/GDP-grows-at-61-in-fourth-quarter-below-estimate-of-71.html, http://www.livemint.com/Industry/acEAx2TJIDMMzZbuhOBpLN/India-GDP-growth-slumps-to-57-in-Q1-hit-by-GST-implementa.html

The sub-sector data reflects another interesting feature. Because of good monsoon in CY16, a) the growth in agriculture has been significantly better in 3Q and 4Q than 1Q and 2Q. b) the slowdown in Industry and Services is much more pronounced in 3Q and 4Q vs. 1Q and 2Q. Had this not been the case, the headline GDP numbers for 3Q and 4Q could have been even worse.

Table 3.11: GDP Growth Rate in FY17
(Year on Year change in percentage)

	Q1	Q2	Q3	Q4
GVA at basic prices	7.6	6.8	6.7	5.6
Private consumption	8.4	7.9	11.0	7.3
Investment demand	7.4	3.0	1.7	-2.1
Agriculture	2.5	4.1	6.9	5.2
Industry	7.4	5.9	6.2	3.1
Services	9.0	7.8	6.9	7.2

Note: GVA is Gross Value Added.
Source:http://www.livemint.com/Politics/Ig7hWnKkVbhVGXxovJOYGO/GDP-grows-at-61-in-fourth-quarter-below-estimate-of-71.html

Demonetisation was a big event and since its impact is much more severe on informal sector, the people from lower strata among general population are much more affected than what the official numbers are reflecting. It is also possible that the impact of demonetisation may continue to affect GDP numbers in 2Q and 3Q of FY18 as well. Another important factor for GDP growth is potential impact of Modi government's other big move, the Goods and Services Tax (GST).

The economic activity has also been affected with the GST roll out in July. While it will require more data points to be available, the initial signs from GDP numbers and IIP data are that GST is likely to impact growth rates negatively. For example, the Index of Industrial Production (IIP) numbers for June were shockingly disappointing and launch of GST had a negative impact on industrial production. Similarly, 1Q FY18 GDP growth rate was only 5.7 percent and GST has been highlighted as the main reason for this decline.

In this context, it is important to highlight the Government of India's mid-year economic survey which was presented in the second week of August 2017. This was the first time that the government presented a mid-year economic survey for the year 2017-18 and it is not very optimistic at least about the current financial year. The survey says that the high end of the 6.75-7.5 percent range for growth rate in GDP for the year 2017-18 projected previously will be difficult to achieve due to several challenges including the appreciation of rupee, farm loan waivers and disruption from implementing GST. The Economic Survey also said that important indicators of the health of an economy - GDP, IIP, credit, investment and capacity utilisation are indicating a slowdown and unfortunately, it seems to have got worse over last two or three quarters.

After the 1Q GDP growth rate of 5.7 percent, it is very likely that for full year FY18, the growth rate may not even touch 7 percent. For economy which has been severely hit from GST and demonetisation, the recovery will take time because the primary reason for such a poor GDP growth figure was dip in manufacturing sector growth which has declined to 1.2 percent. This is significantly worse than 10.7 percent growth rate in the manufacturing sector in Q1 FY17. Another important characteristic is that the Q1 FY18 GDP growth rate is lowest in more than three years.

Inflation –Over last three years under NDA government, the price rise has largely been in control. The average CPI inflation declined from 9.5 percent in 2013-14 to 5.9 percent in 2014-15 and 4.9 percent in 2015-16. It declined further to 4.6 percent in FY17, up to February 2017. Food inflation based on consumer food price index (CFPI) which was in double digits during 2012-2014 declined to 6.4 percent in 2014-15 and 4.9 percent in 2015-16. It declined further to 4.4 percent in FY17, up to February 2017. The Government, in consultation with RBI has also fixed the inflation target of 4 percent with tolerance level of +/- 2 percent for the period beginning from 5th August, 2016 to 31st March, 2021.

Table 3.12: Consumer Price Inflation in India

Year	India's Inflation Rate
2013-14	9.5 percent
2014-15	5.9 percent
2015-16	4.9 percent
2016-17	4.6 percent
2017-18	2.1 percent

Note: For 2017-18, data is up to May 2017.
Source:http://pib.nic.in/newsite/PrintRelease.aspx?relid=162005, www.data.gov.inmhttp://pib.nic.in/newsite/printrelease.aspx?relid=165557

Table 3.13: Average inflation India
(measured in Consumer Price Inflation)

Year	India's Inflation Rate
2014	6.4 percent
2015	5.9 percent
2016	5.0 percent
2017	2.3 percent

Source: http://www.inflation.eu/inflation-rates/india/historic-inflation/cpi-inflation-india.aspx

Inflation has fallen sharply in India. If we refer to the latest available data, inflation in India is trending at low levels and depressed food prices is primarily the reason behind this trend. The inflation numbers reported for last many months indicate a benign inflation and in the short term, this is also prompting the Government to ask for rate cuts by Reserve Bank of India (RBI).

Table 3.14: All India Inflation Rates (percent) based on CPI (General) and CFPI (Food)

	July 2017 (Prov)			June 2017 (Final)			July 2016 (Final)		
Indices	Rural	Urban	Combined	Rural	Urban	Combined	Rural	Urban	Combined
CPI (General)	2.41	2.17	2.36	1.52	1.41	1.46	6.66	5.39	6.07
CFPI	0.07	-0.99	-0.29	-1.62	-3.16	-2.12	8.18	8.80	8.35

Note: Inflation for July 2017 (as reported on 14th August 2017).
Source: http://www.mospi.gov.in/sites/default/files/press_release/CPI_PR_14aug17m.pdf (MoSPI, Government of India)

Vegetables and Pulses are driving food inflation lower. High inflation creates a lot of difficulties for the general public and the Government tries to tame it very religiously. However, the detailed, component wise analysis presents a slightly different picture. The low inflation is being reported because of a sharp decline in some of the agricultural commodities. For example, let us observe the inflation data for May 2017. Food inflation has remained in negative and this implies that the food prices have actually come down compared to last year.

Table 3.15: Component wise Inflation for May 2017 (as reported on 12th June 2017)

	Inflation (percent)
Food and beverages	-0.22
Cereals and products	4.81
Meat and fish	1.87
Egg	0.72
Milk and products	4.56
Oils and fats	2.7
Fruits	1.4
Vegetables	-13.44
Pulses and products	-19.45
Sugar and Confectionery	9.84
Spices	0.52
Non-alcoholic beverages	2.66
Prepared meals, snacks, sweets etc.	5.17
Pan, tobacco and intoxicants	6.17
Clothing and footwear	4.41
Housing	4.84
Fuel and light	5.46
Miscellaneous	3.81
General Index (All Groups)	2.18
Consumer Food Price Index	-1.05

Source: http://mospi.nic.in/sites/default/files/press_release/CPI_PR_12jun17m.pdf (MoSPI, Government of India)

Is low food inflation linked with farm distress and demands for farm loan waivers?

The low inflation and especially very low or even negative food inflation is creating huge distress in the agriculture sector. The low prices of end produce are also leading to the demand for loan waivers from farmers. Since *"farmers in distress"* is a huge political issue in the country, it becomes very difficult for the state Governments to resist this temptation as seen recently in the case of Maharashtra and Uttar Pradesh. In both these states put together, the state governments have announced farm loan waivers of more than US$ 10 billion.

We think that very low food inflation may be bad for the economy.

- For farmers, the input prices don't change that quickly and if the farm produce is fetching significantly lower prices, it creates genuine difficulty for farmers.
- Despite only contributing approximately 15 percent in Gross Domestic Product, agriculture is important for almost half of India's population for their livelihood.
- Since farm distress becomes a huge political issue, the demands for sops for farmers such as farm loan waivers and increase in MSP (Minimum Support Price, the price at which farmers can sell their produce to the Government) increase.
- The populist measures such as farm loan waivers don't really help in addressing the structural issues in Indian agriculture and they are very bad for financial discipline in states.
- Technically, the banks don't get hit from farm loan waivers. However, these loan waivers are bad for credit culture in the country and create larger structural issues in the system.

Industrial Growth –It is observed that IIP has not picked up under NDA rule.

Table 3.16: Industrial Growth Rate in India on Year-on-Year Basis

Year	Industrial Growth rate
2013-14	-0.1 percent
2014-15	2.8 percent
2015-16	2.4 percent
2016-17	2.7 percent

Note: For the base year 2004-05.
Source: https://rbidocs.rbi.org.in/rdocs/Publications/PDFs/0HANDB_F0651BA902A5244DFB75DA46261B53726.PDF, RBI Handbook on Indian Economy and http://mospi.nic.in/sites/default/files/press_release/iip_PR_12may17.pdf (MoSPI, Government of India)

The Central Statistics Office (CSO), Ministry of Statistics and Programme Implementation (MoSPI), revises the base year of the macroeconomic indicators, as a regular exercise, to capture structural changes in the economy. This also improves the quality and representativeness of the indices. Accordingly, in May 2017, the base year of the all-India Index of Industrial Production (IIP) was revised from 2004-05 to 2011-12 to reflect the changes in the industrial sector and to align it with the base year of other macroeconomic indicators like the Gross Domestic Product (GDP), Wholesale Price Index (WPI).

The comparable figures for 2004-05 vs. the new base year are as follows.

Table 3.17: Annual Growth Rates of IIP for Base 2011-12 vis-à-vis 2004-05

Base Year	2012-13	2013-14	2014-15	2015-16	2016-17
2011-12	3.3	3.4	4.0	3.4	5.0
2004-05	1.1	-0.1	2.8	2.4	2.7

Source: http://mospi.nic.in/sites/default/files/press_release/iip_PR_12may17.pdf (MoSPI, Government of India)

The IIP numbers for June 2017 were extremely disappointing. Negative IIP is not very common and June's monthly IIP data was in the negative zone for the first time in many years. This means that despite a revision in the series a few months back; the reported industrial production has been stagnant. The IIP growth for June 2017 was -0.1 percent on year to year basis. For April-June 2017 or in first quarter of FY18, IIP was up only 2.0 percent yoy which is an abysmally poor performance. The 1Q FY18 IIP growth is worse than previous five years' record; please refer to the first row data in the table above, which shows annual Growth Rates of IIP for Base 2011-12 for five years, from 2012-13 to 2016-17.

The cumulative y-o-y growth in these three sectors (Mining, Manufacturing and Electricity) during April-June 2017 was 1.2 percent, 1.8 percent and 5.3 percent respectively. Manufacturing which is the dominant and most important segment has been a huge disappointment. 15 out of the 23 industry groups in the manufacturing sector have shown negative growth during the month of June 2017. This indicates that the slowdown in Manufacturing is widespread. As such, the IIP picture does not give any comfort on industrial recovery hopes and we think the IIP is showing a worsening trend year-on-year even when FY17 was not a great year for Industrial Production in India. We also think that the poor growth in manufacturing sector reported in 1Q FY18 GDP data is consistent with IIP data.

The IIP data suggests, a) Industrial activity has not picked up under NDA rule if we look at the data under the older series, b) if we go by the new series of data, it can be implied that the economy was not doing that badly under UPA rule either.

Exchange rate of Indian Rupee against major currencies There has been more stability in exchange rates under NDA rule and the Rupee depreciation has been much smaller in last three years.

Table 3.18: USD: INR exchange rate

Year	bid	ask	Average	percent change
2014	60.89	61.03	60.96	-4.2
2015	64.03	64.20	64.12	-5.2
2016	67.08	67.27	67.18	-4.8
2017	65.69	65.87	65.78	2.1

Source: https://www.oanda.com/currency/average

Table 3.19: INR against major currencies (Average Rates)

Year	SDR	US Dollar	Pound Sterling	Japanese Yen	Euro
2014	92.73	61.03	100.54	57.79	81.12
2015	89.75	64.15	98.13	53.02	71.24

Notes: 1. The exchange rate for Japanese Yen is in per 100 Yen.2. Data are based on FEDAI (Foreign Exchange Dealers' Association of India) indicative rates till April 2012.RBI reference rates are used w.e. f. May 2012. 3. The currency value of the SDR is determined by summing the values in U.S. dollars, based on market exchange rates, of a basket of major currencies (the U.S. dollar, Euro, Japanese yen, pound sterling and the Chinese renminbi).SDR is an international reserve asset, created by the IMF in 1969 to supplement its member countries' official reserves. As of March 2016, 204.1 billion SDRs (equivalent to about $285 billion) had been created and allocated to members. SDRs can be exchanged for freely usable currencies.

Source: https://rbidocs.rbi.org.in/rdocs/Publications/PDFs/0HANDB_F0651BA902A5244DFB75DA46261B53726.PDF (RBI Handbook on Indian Economy), http://www.imf.org/en/About/Factsheets/Sheets/2016/08/01/14/51/Special-Drawing-Right-SDR, http://www.imf.org/external/np/fin/data/rms_sdrv.aspx

Table 3.20: INR against major currencies (Average Rates)

Year	SDR	US Dollar	Pound Sterling	Japanese Yen	Euro
2013-14	92.26	60.50	96.31	60.40	81.17
2014-15	90.8	61.14	98.57	55.83	77.52
2015-16	91.35	65.47	98.73	54.59	72.29

Notes: 1. The exchange rate for Japanese Yen is in per 100 Yen.2. Data are based on FEDAI (Foreign Exchange Dealers' Association of India) indicative rates till April 2012.RBI reference rates are used w.e. f. May 2012. 3. The currency value of the SDR is determined by summing the values in U.S. dollars, based on market exchange rates, of a basket of major currencies (the U.S. dollar, Euro, Japanese yen, pound sterling and the Chinese renminbi).SDR is an international reserve asset, created by the IMF in 1969 to supplement its member countries' official reserves. As of March 2016, 204.1 billion SDRs (equivalent to about $285 billion) had been created and allocated to members. SDRs can be exchanged for freely usable currencies.

Source: https://rbidocs.rbi.org.in/rdocs/Publications/PDFs/0HANDB_F0651BA902A5244DFB75DA46261B53726.PDF (RBI Handbook on Indian Economy), http://www.imf.org/en/About/Factsheets/Sheets/2016/08/01/14/51/Special-Drawing-Right-SDR, http://www.imf.org/external/np/fin/data/rms_sdrv.aspx

Core Industries Growth –The pickup has not been visible under NDA government in growth of core industries which include Coal, Crude Oil, Natural Gas, Refinery Products, Fertilizers, Steel, Cement and Electricity. These eight core industries contribute 40 percent in the IIP and this is an important benchmark for assessing the health of core sector.

Table 3.21: Core Industries Growth Rate in India (Base Year 2004-05)

Year	Core Industries Growth rate
2014-15	4.5 percent
2015-16	4.0 percent
2016-17	4.5 percent

Source: https://rbidocs.rbi.org.in/rdocs/Publications/PDFs/0HANDB_F0651BA902A5244DFB75DA46261B53726.PDF, RBI Handbook on Indian Economy and http://pib.nic.in/newsite/erelease.aspx?relid=0
The base year for core industries growth data was revised from 2004-05 to 2011-12 along with the base year revision for IIP.

Table 3.22: Core Industries Growth Rate in India (Base Year 2011-12)

Year	Core Industries Growth rate
2012-13	3.8 percent
2013-14	2.6 percent
2014-15	4.9 percent
2015-16	3.0 percent
2016-17	4.8 percent
2017-18 (Apr – Jul)	2.5 percent

Source: http://pib.nic.in/newsite/erelease.aspx?relid=0

We find that the performance of Modi Government has been largely mixed. There are positives, a) Notwithstanding a recent slowdown, the GDP growth rate has been better though not as good as the best years in UPA, b) inflation is largely under control and, c) INR is more stable against major international currencies. However, the track record of NDA Government on industrial growth is poor and core industries continue to struggle.

When we compare NDA Government vs. UPA, we can conclude that:

- *In the last more than three years after Modi Government took charge, Indian economy has done better than how it has been doing in last 2-3 years of UPA II tenure.*
- *However, the performance of the Indian economy has been lower as compared to the best years of UPA administration.*
- *It is difficult to prove whether there was a cyclical downturn in 2012-14 which happens in every economy or was it a bad performance of the economy for which UPA was solely responsible.*
- *It is difficult to substantiate the claim that NDA Government after May 2014 has been able to resolve the issues in the economy.*

The other important things in an economy and how NDA Government is performing

Apart from analysing the headline numbers on GDP growth, Inflation and Industrial growth, we also need to look at a few other important parameters. These indices track the changes on the ground to realistically assess how things have been after the Modi Government has taken charge. These may include:

- Capacity Utilisation in the Industry,
- The pace of new orders for the companies,
- Project execution,
- Investment cycle,
- Job creation.

Capacity utilisation is low and new orders are not coming fast enough

Reserve Bank of India (RBI) releases a survey every quarter on indicators of manufacturing activity in the country (though with a three month lag). It is called Order Books, Inventories and Capacity Utilisation Survey (OBICUS) and covers almost 700-800 companies which make this data extremely useful. Though this set of data is a little bit dated, we think there are important messages in it because the time series runs across cycles and across political administration.

For example, Capacity utilisation is an important parameter to determine if there would be more capex and if the facilities are fully employed. Overall, if we look at last several quarters of data, we don't see a meaningful improvement in the capacity utilisation trend and it remains below 75 percent level which could broadly be seen as a threshold where the companies need to think about new capacity addition.

Another data point is the pace of new orders. The flow of new orders has not shown any significant improvement either on a quarter-on-quarter basis or on a year-on-year basis. There is not much improvement in order inflow after NDA Government has taken over.

Table 3.23: Capacity Utilisation and Growth in New Orders

	Capacity Utilisation (percent)	QoQ Growth in New orders (percent)	YoY Growth in New orders (percent)
Q4 FY12	78.4	6.7	7.3
Q1 FY13	73.2	-0.1	23.7
Q2 FY13	75.2	-10.7	0.7
Q3 FY13	74.4	4.9	-0.2
Q4 FY13	75.7	1.3	-5.3
Q1 FY14	71.6	3.8	-3.8
Q2 FY14	73.7	6.4	9.0
Q3 FY14	74.1	6.7	12.6
Q4 FY14	74.4	-0.7	8.5
Q1 FY15	70.2	-1.6	11.0
Q2 FY15	73.6	6.5	12.6
Q3 FY15	71.3	-8.5	-8.4
Q4 FY15	73.6	5.2	-1.5
Q1 FY16	71.3	0.9	3.4
Q2 FY16	70.6	3.1	0.1
Q3 FY16	72.2	-1.3	5.6
Q4 FY16	74.6	3.9	0.0
Q1 FY17	73.6	-3.7	-2.3
Q2 FY17	73.1	-3.1	-4.3
Q3 FY17	72.7	1.9	-1.3
Q4 FY17	74.1	26.5	12.3

Note: 1) NDA Government had taken over in Q1 FY15. 2) Note: The Quarterly Order Books, Inventories and Capacity Utilisation Survey (OBICUS) of Reserve Bank of India (RBI) tracks the capacity utilisation and order inflow for a large set of companies.

Source: https://www.rbi.org.in/Scripts/QuarterlyPublications.aspx?head =Quarterly Order Books, Inventories and Capacity Utilisation Survey

In OBICUS of 4Q FY17, the order inflow increased on a q-o-q basis and on a y-o-y basis. For last four quarters, this was the first time order inflow on a y-o-y basis has reported an increase. This is a positive sign however, it is largely because of a base effect. If we see the order backlog, the q-o-q growth was only 2.5 percent and on a y-o-y basis, there has been a decline of 9.5 percent.

Project execution is still struggling[8]

After the Modi Government took charge, the hope was that the Government would move quickly and decisively to expedite the resolution of key bottlenecks and would remove the bureaucratic hurdles. It was also expected that the new administration would focus on an enhanced public spending to revive growth and push for increased activity in the economy.

It has been more than three years and the data on this front is not very encouraging. It is possible that some of the issues are much deeper, for example the bad loans problem with banks which is a structural challenge. There are other headwinds as well including real exchange rate appreciation which is impacting the competitiveness of Indian exports, farm loan waivers which could impact the money available with states for putting into productive use and stress in balance sheets of companies that could impact the pace of execution. So, it may not be possible for Government to sort them out so quickly and, hence the administration is not directly responsible for them.

However, the fact remains that implementation of projects is not moving as quickly as it was expected. There are two clearly identifiable basic issues we think, a) there are a lot of projects which continue to remain stalled and we have not really seen a huge positive change on this front, and, b) the private sector is still much ahead in terms of announcing investments in new projects which means that the Public spending has not picked up to the extent it was expected, both in terms of the intent and the execution.

An analysis by Centre for Monitoring Indian Economy (CMIE) suggests that apart from the first six months immediately after NDA Government assuming power, the picture on public spending has not been that good. The public capex announcements have fallen since then though private sector project announcements have increased. However, there have been challenges on lack of available funding, continuous land acquisition challenges and delays in receiving project clearances. As a result, stalling of project is a common occurrence.

It is not really difficult to conclude that the Government has been not very successful in eliminating the bottlenecks and the picture on the ground has not changed much. Also, there is no big change as to how the Government and Private sector are looking at incurring fresh capex and implementing new project investments.

Impact on demand has led to production and job cuts

The investment cycle is already depressed and with muted demand, the factory production needs to be cut in many sectors and that may result in job losses which will further aggravate the agony of affected class. Though the GDP already got affected due to demonetisation in second half of financial year 2016-17 (3Q to some extent and 4Q a lot more) and 1Q of FY18, it is very difficult to state that there will not be more impact in the current financial year.

Indian economy was certainly not undergoing a crisis before the announcement of demonetisation was made. But at the same time, it was not firing on all cylinders and there were many concerns,

- very slow growth in manufacturing,
- private sector's unwillingness to do capex because there is a lack of demand,
- struggle of Banks (especially Public Sector Undertakings) with bad loans,
- challenges for Information Technology and Pharma sectors in overseas markets,
- volatile and protectionist world economy.

So, was November 2016 really an opportune time for the Government to carry out a major surgery in the form of demonetisation, we are not very sure.

Job creation[9]

The issue of employment creation is politically important. One of BJP's and Modi's core campaign promises in 2014 election was creating jobs for the youth. And unfortunately the track record of Modi Government does not inspire much confidence on this count as seen from quarterly employment surveys (QES). Though comprehensive and detailed employment data in India is lacking, the quarterly employment surveys (QES) can be used as proxy for the same.

These surveys look at eight sectors;

- Textiles including apparels;
- Metals;

- Gems and Jewellery;
- Automobiles;
- Transport;
- IT/BPO;
- Leather;
- Handloom/ Power loom.

Table 3.24: Net change in employment in eight select industries (Old Series)

	Sector wise estimated change in employment (In Lakhs)
Dec,08 over Sep,08	-4.91
Mar,09 over Dec,08	2.76
Jun,09 over Mar,09	-1.31
Sep,09 over Jun,09	4.97
Dec,09 over Sep,09	6.38
Mar,10 over Dec,09	0.61
June,10 over Mar,10	1.62
Sep,10 over June,10	4.35
Dec,10 over Sep,10	2.07
Mar,11 over Dec,10	1.74
June,11 over Mar,11	2.15
Sep,11 over June,11	3.15
Dec,11 over Sep,11	2.26
Mar,12 over Dec,11	0.81
June,12 over Mar,12	0.73
Dec,12 over Jun,12	1.68
Mar,13 over Dec,12	1.07
Jun,13 over Mar,13	0.86
Sep,13 over June,13	1.43
Dec,13 over Sep,13	0.83
Mar,14 over Dec,13	-0.36

	Sector wise estimated change in employment (In Lakhs)
June,14 over March,14	1.82
Sep,14 over June,14	1.58
Dec,14 over Sep,14	1.17
Mar, 15 over Dec, 14	0.73
June, 15 over Mar, 15	-0.26
Sept, 15 over June, 15	0.31
Dec, 15 over Sept, 15	0.44

Source: Labour Bureau of Ministry of Labour and Employment, Government of India

With a view to generate better quality data on labour market for effective implementation of policies and welfare of labour, Government decided to conduct new series of Quarterly Employment Survey (QES)on a larger scale to assess employment situation in respect of selected sectors of Non-farm Industrial economy of India over successive quarters. The selected 8 sectors are Manufacturing, Construction, Trade, Transport, Education, Health, Accommodation and Restaurants and Information and Technology (IT)/ Business Process Outsourcing (BPO). The revised series data is indicated below. **We don't see much improvement in job creation under the NDA Government.**

Table 3.25: Net change in employment in eight select industries (New Series)

	Sector wise estimated change in employment (In Lakhs)
1st Jul over 1st Apr'16	0.77
1st Oct over 1st Jul'16	0.32
1st Jan'17 over 1st Oct'16	1.22

Source: Labour Bureau of Ministry of Labour and Employment, Government of India

What does this mean for NDA vs. UPA comparison?

If we look at the growth rate of Indian economy over last five years, the trend is as follows;

- For 2012-13, 5.5 percent
- For 2013-14, 6.4 percent
- For 2014-15, 7.5 percent
- For 2015-16, 8.0 percent
- For 2016-17, 7.1 percent.

The Indian economy hit its bottom in 2012-13 and this was UPA-II's worst performance year. This came at a wrong time for UPA and they were punished in 2014 elections. Things started to pick up and got better afterwards but it seems like that the steam has run out now. Since the Modi Government took charge in May 2014, the economy's performance in at least FY14 and some part of FY15 can be attributed to UPA II. It may not have been visible back then but the data suggests that the economy's revival had begun during UPA's tenure.

In FY17, the growth rate is down significantly and if we look at the quarterly data in the previous financial year (FY17), the momentum is building against a big revival as things have slowed down considerably. For example, the latest economic survey that was released in August 2017 and which we discussed earlier in this Chapter, express the fear that the GDP growth rate in 2017-18 is likely to be lower than 2016-17 even in the best case scenario. The surprisingly low GDP growth rate of 5.7 percent in 1Q FY18 has not done much to assuage these concerns and it becomes difficult to claim that NDA government knows it better than UPA on how to make the economy grow faster.

There have been some areas such as inflation control where the Government has been successful with help from low crude oil prices and low food inflation (which has created severe distress in the farming sector). However, on several other fronts such as industrial growth, capacity utilisation, new orders, and creation of new jobs, the NDA Government has not been able to make a positive impact. The failure of demonetisation has given another opportunity to critics of Narendra Modi that while demonetisation didn't address the problem of black money, it led to widespread damage to the Indian economy.

Things we didn't discuss here

There are several other economic factors which we think are important, including;

- How much Foreign Direct Investment the country is able to attract?
- Has the Government been able to control the fiscal deficit?
- How much the Government is spending on healthcare and education?
- How focused the Government is on the infrastructure development?
- How India performed in its peer group and against the set of relevant competitors?

In this chapter, we have not touched upon any of them and the reason is not because we think they are unimportant. We do agree and fully understand that they are relevant but since the scope of this book is largely political, we have only tried to include things which are visible to the voters and could be the immediate reasons for them to feel satisfied or dissatisfied with the performance of the Government. That explains the exclusion of discussion on these factors which have been cited above.

What are the implications for BJP in 2019?

While the track record of Modi Government has been better than how UPA II was doing towards the end of its tenure; this alone will not be a consolation for the general population:

- The Indian economy's performance under UPA II was disappointing and that will not be seen as a benchmark by the voters to assess the performance of NDA Government under Modi. In addition, the ten year track record of UPA I and UPA II combined from 2004 to 2014 was significantly better than the performance of Indian economy in second half of UPA II or the economy's performance under Modi Government.
- In 2014, people voted for Modi and he won a huge mandate because the voters had very high expectations from him. The burden of expectations Modi has been carrying since the time he took over is huge and hence, he needs to deliver a performance which is far superior to what the NDA Government has been able to achieve so far.

We think that unless things improve dramatically in next 12-18 months especially on GDP growth and job creation front, there is a huge risk for BJP that people may not be very happy with the performance of Modi Government. If there is no revival in Indian economy, there could be serious repercussions for BJP in 2019 General Elections.

In the next Chapter

We have seen in this chapter that performance of Modi Government has been at best mixed on several parameters which matter for Indian economy. The Modi report card may not be bad in absolute terms or in comparison of second half of UPA II but people had much higher expectations from him. As things stand today, this will potentially be a big risk for BJP in 2019 elections. In the next Chapter, we will discuss how BJP's victory was heavily concentrated in Northern and Western parts of the country. Despite an expanding footprint across the country and an aggressive leadership in Narendra Modi and Amit Shah, BJP is yet to become a national party in the true sense. There are many states such as Tamil Nadu, Bengal, Kerala and Odisha where BJP still has a long way to go before it becomes a key player in the state politics. This limits the scope for improvement in BJP's tally in 2019 vs. 2014. On the other hand, even a minor slippage in states like Uttar Pradesh, Bihar, Madhya Pradesh, Gujarat and Rajasthan could prove very costly to BJP in 2019. Even in some of smaller states such as Delhi, Jharkhand, Uttarakhand and Himachal Pradesh, small changes in BJP's fortunes could pose a serious challenge for the party in 2019.

4

2014 MANDATE: BJP'S STATISTICAL PEAK?

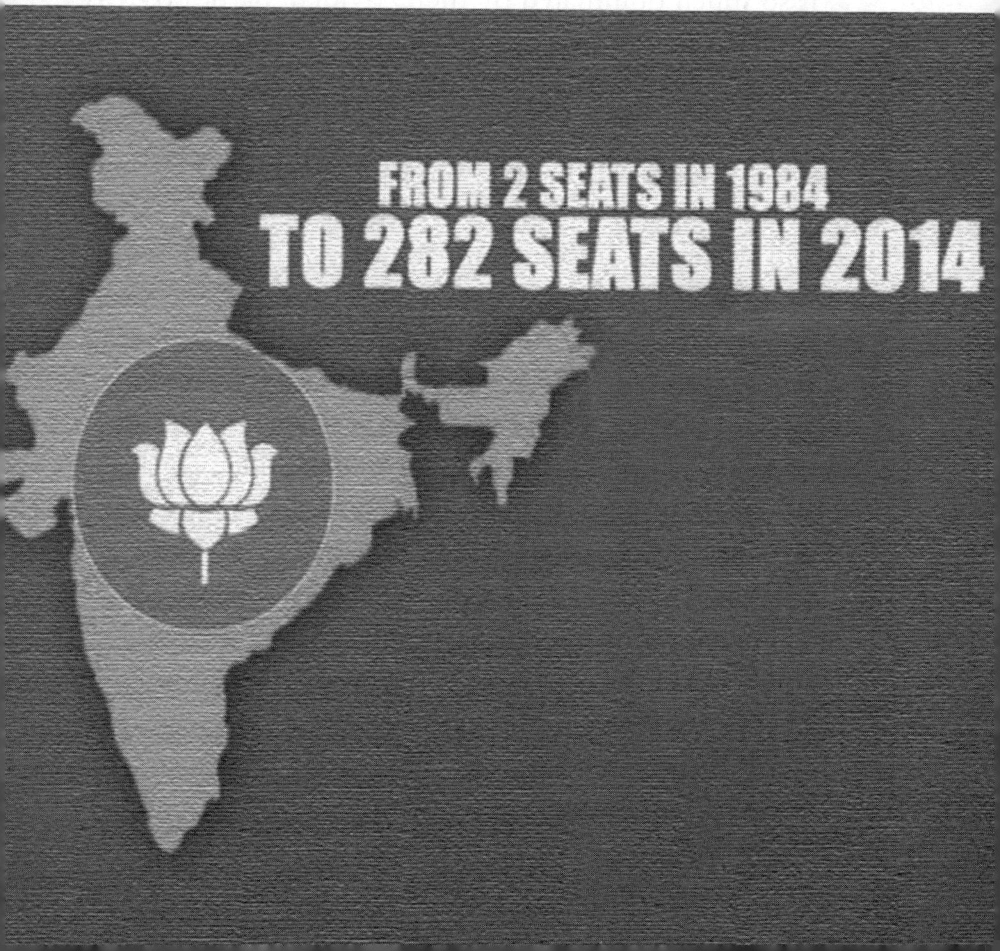

You can observe a lot by just watching.

— Yogi Berra[1]

How many Lok Sabha seats BJP is really contesting?

From the perspective of BJP's strength, there are six categories of *Lok Sabha* constituencies;

- **BJP is largely an inconsequential player** - This group of states include Tamil Nadu (39 seats) and Kerala (20 seats). There are 59 seats in total in these two states and for BJP, both of these states have been a tough nut to crack so far. The Tamil Nadu politics is so much dominated by the Dravidian parties (DMK and AIADMK) that the national parties have not been able to make any impact. Similarly in Kerala, though BJP had 10.5 percent vote share in 2014 *Lok Sabha* elections and again the same percentage of vote share in 2016 Kerala *Vidhan Sabha* elections, the Left front and Congress are so dominant that winning a sizable number of seats is difficult for BJP. In reality, it is really difficult for BJP to win a meaningful number of seats out of these 59 seats in Tamil Nadu and Kerala.
- **BJP matters but the party may not win a large number of seats** – This group of states would include Bengal (42 seats), Andhra Pradesh (25 seats), Odisha (21 seats) and Telangana (17 seats). A total of 105 seats. These are the states where BJP as a party has a reasonably sizable following but it has not been able to cross the required threshold of vote percentage to win a significant number of seats. In Bengal, though the BJP had 17 percent vote share in 2014 *Lok Sabha* elections and 10.2 percent vote share in *Vidhan Sabha* elections, the TMC is dominant

and it is unlikely that BJP can win a large number of seats in Bengal. This is especially true in the light of the fact that between 2014 and 2016, BJP lost its popular appeal and the party's vote share declined by as much as 40 percent (from 17 percent to 10.2 percent). In Andhra Pradesh, Telangana and Odisha, BJP may find it difficult to increase its tally significantly. Odisha is an interesting case and though BJP's performance in local body elections held in the first half of 2017 has been encouraging, it would not be easy for BJP to dislodge BJD in the state.

- **BJP has to share the spoils with a partner** - This set of states would include Punjab (13 seats) and Jammu and Kashmir (6 seats). This is 19 seats in total. BJP has been playing second fiddle to Shiromani Akali Dal (SAD) in Punjab and the party is also a junior partner to PDP in J&K. It is important to note here that we are not talking about Maharashtra and Bihar in this category. Though BJP had a seat sharing pact with Shiv Sena in Maharashtra for 2014 General Elections, things have not been cordial between these two partners afterwards. In the *Vidhan Sabha* Elections of 2014 and recently concluded elections for local bodies, both Shiv Sena and BJP fought the elections separately. Though both BJP and Shiv Sena are partners in the coalition Government at the state, the relationship between these two parties has been nothing short of being turbulent. It would be difficult to predict if BJP and Shiv Sena will be having a pre-poll seat sharing arrangement in Maharashtra for 2019 General Elections. Similarly, in Bihar where BJP has a new partner in Nitish Kumar's JDU, it is difficult at this stage to forecast if BJP and JDU will be having a seat sharing arrangement for 2019 General Elections.

- **BJP is in a multi-polar contest**–These states would include Uttar Pradesh (80 seats), Maharashtra (48 seats), Bihar (40 seats), Karnataka (28 seats), Jharkhand (14 seats), Haryana (10 seats) and Delhi (7 seats). There are 227 seats (42 percent of total 543 in *Lok Sabha*) in this category. These are the seats where either there is a triangular contest or even four parties are vying to grab voter's attention. In these *Lok Sabha* seats, BJP is in direct contest with Congress and regional parties. We can expect that BJP will be a serious contender to win these seats in the elections of 2019.
- **BJP is in a one-on-one fight** – These states would include Madhya Pradesh (29 seats), Gujarat (26 seats), Rajasthan (25 seats), Assam (14 seats), Chhattisgarh (11 seats), Uttarakhand (5 seats) and Himachal Pradesh (4 seats). There are 114 seats (21 percent of the total 543 seats in *Lok Sabha*) in this category. These are the seats where BJP is in direct contest with Congress and hence, we can expect that BJP will have a good chance to win these seats in the elections of 2019.
- **Other states–** In Categories 1 to 5, we have covered 524 *Lok Sabha* seats (more than 96 percent of the total 543). We have not covered some of the smaller states and Union Territories. These are Arunachal Pradesh (2 seats), Goa (2 seats), Manipur (2 seats), Meghalaya (2 seats), Tripura (2 seats), Andaman and Nicobar Islands (1 seat), Chandigarh (1 seat), Dadra and Nagar Haveli (1 seat), Daman and Diu (1 seat), Lakshadweep (1 seat), Mizoram (1 seat), Nagaland (1 seat), Puducherry

(1 seat) and Sikkim (1 seat). There are 19 seats (3.5 percent of the total 543 seats in *Lok Sabha*) in this category. At some of these seats, BJP is in direct contest with Congress or other parties. Hence, we can expect that BJP will have a good chance to win these seats in the elections of 2019.

Table 4.1: How BJP is placed in the electoral contest in states for 2019

	States	Seats	Remarks*
1	Tamil Nadu and Kerala	59	BJP is largely an inconsequential player.
2	Bengal, Andhra Pradesh, Odisha and Telangana	105	BJP matters but may not win huge number of seats.
3	Punjab and Jammu and Kashmir	19	BJP has to share the spoils with a partner.
4	UP, Maharashtra, Bihar, Karnataka, Jharkhand, Haryana and Delhi	227	BJP is in a multi-polar contest.
5	MP, Gujarat, Rajasthan, Assam, Chhattisgarh, Uttarakhand, Himachal Pradesh	114	BJP is in a one-on-one fight.
6	Others (Smaller states and Union Territories)	19	In some cases, BJP is in a one-on-one fight.

*Remarks are based on our assessment which is largely subjective.
Source: Election Commission for states and number of *Lok Sabha* seats.

It is important to note here that category 1, 2 and 3 put together have 183 seats and out of these, BJP had won only 12 in 2014. If there is no drastic change before 2019 elections, it is extremely unlikely that this tally could increase significantly. The direct implication is that in 2019, BJP needs to score big in the rest of the country as it did in 2014 General Elections. This is in category 4, 5 and 6 where BJP is comparatively stronger.

In 2014, BJP had 270 MPs from the 360 Lok Sabha seats
Once we exclude the 183 seats (Bengal, Tamil Nadu, Andhra Pradesh, Odisha, Kerala, Telangana, Punjab, Jammu and Kashmir) where BJP had only won 12 seats and the party may not be a very serious contender at least at this point, the number of seats left is 360 or approximately 2/3rd of the total members in *Lok Sabha*. BJP had won 270 or 75 percent of these seats in 2014.

These 360 seats can be further divided into two categories; a) More than 200 seats (207 to be precise) where BJP had done exceptionally well and the party had more than 90 percent success rate in 2014 elections winning 193 seats, b) Other approximately 150 seats where BJP had won about 50 percent or 77 seats.

Let us take a look at the first category. These are 200+ seats where BJP was highly successful, winning 90 percent plus from the available number of seats. This can be further sub-divided into two distinct categories;

- **Winning 100 percent of the seats in a state** – In 2014, BJP had 100 percent success rate in Gujarat (26 seats), Rajasthan (25 seats), Delhi (7 seats), Uttarakhand (5 seats), Himachal Pradesh (4 seats), Goa (2 seats) and Andaman and Nicobar Islands, Chandigarh, Dadra and Nagar Haveli and Daman and Diu (1 seat each). There are 73 *Lok Sabha* seats in these States and Union Territories and BJP had won all 73 seats in 2014. These are the states where BJP has absolutely zero chance to increase its tally even theoretically and the repeat of 2014 performance is going to be a challenging task for BJP in 2019, if not impossible.

- **Winning more than 80 percent of total seats in a state** –BJP had a very good record in many other states where the win ratio was in excess of 80 percent. The most important among these states was Uttar Pradesh where BJP won 71 out of 80 seats and if we include the seats won by NDA (including BJP's allies); BJP's success rate was more than 90 percent in UP. The other states are Madhya Pradesh (27 out of 29 seats, 93 percent), Jharkhand (12 out of 14 seats, 86 percent) and Chhattisgarh (10 out of 11 seats, 91percent). There are 134 *Lok Sabha* seats in UP, MP, Jharkhand and Chhattisgarh combined and BJP had won 120 of these seats with an overall success rate of 90 percent. Please note that we have calculated the win ratio by using the total number of seats and only considered the seats won by BJP. But, in some of the seats in these states, BJP didn't field a candidate because the seats were given to the smaller allies and hence, the win ratio was actually higher for BJP on a standalone basis. For example, BJP had allocated two seats for Apna Dal candidates in UP. These are the states where BJP has practically little chance to increase its tally.

Of the 207 (73 seats with 100 percent success rate and 134 seats with 90 percent success rate), BJP had won 193 seats in 2014. It shows an excessive dependence for BJP on these states. Borrowing from an analogy from Cricket once more, it was said about the Indian cricket team in 1970s and early 80s that if a bowling team gets either Sunil Gavaskar[2] or Gundappa Vishwanath[3], half the Indian team is out and if you get both, the entire Indian team is out.

This may be an oversimplification but there is no denying the fact that the Indian batting in those days was excessively dependent on Gavaskar and Vishwanath. For the relatively younger generation, the same example could work very well with Sachin Tendulkar[4]. Once Sachin got out, many of us used to switch off our TV sets. The situation for BJP is similar as the party is heavily dependent on incredibly good performance in these states to do well in 2019.

It would be a challenge for BJP to repeat similar performance again in 2019 as the changed poll dynamics (factors such as Opposition putting up a united front) would also play an important role. BJP may perform very well in vote share again in 2019, but the end result will also depend on how the opposition parties are aligned.

70 percent of BJP's MPs came from only six states

There is another way to look at BJP's excessive dependence on certain pockets. In BJP's tally of 282 MPs in 2014 elections, a massive 69 percent contribution came from six states i.e. 194 out of 282 MPs of BJP were elected from Uttar Pradesh, Madhya Pradesh, Gujarat, Rajasthan, Maharashtra and Bihar. Interestingly, these six states only contribute 46 percent of the total seats in *Lok Sabha*. In other words, 194 BJP MPs came from the states which elect only 248 members for *Lok Sabha*.

Table 4.2: BJP's performance in UP, MP, Gujarat, Rajasthan, Maharashtra and Bihar

State	Seats won by BJP and total seats in the state	Contribution in BJP tally
Bihar	22 (40)	8 percent
Gujarat	26 (26)	9 percent
Madhya Pradesh	27 (29)	10 percent
Maharashtra	23 (48)	8 percent
Rajasthan	25 (25)	9 percent
Uttar Pradesh	71 (80)	25 percent
Total	194 (248)	69 percent

Note: The states are in an alphabetical order.
Source: Election Commission of India

From the remaining 295 seats, BJP was only able to win less than one-third i.e. 88 seats (30 percent success rate). It can be stated that there are many seats out of these 295 where BJP either didn't have its candidates or was not in the contest effectively and including those seats which artificially lower the success rate is only the manipulation of available data. However, this is a point worth noting. Why?

When we are saying that BJP did exceptionally well by winning more than 272 out of 543 *Lok Sabha* seats in 2014, we are underestimating the extent of BJP's victory in 2014. BJP had won 282 seats not really out of 543 but the party has won this number from approximately 360-370 odd seats, which is a much smaller and a 30 percent less number than 543.

In reality, the 2014 mandate for BJP was much more impressive than how we analysed it taking into account total number of seats. In 2014, BJP's victory was as massive (or even much bigger in some sense) as 1984 mandate for Congress. While Congress had won 400 plus seats out of 543 which is about 75 percent success ratio in 1984, BJPs' success ratio was almost 80 percent as the party won 282 effectively from not more than 360-370 odd seats because in all other seats, BJP didn't have a realistic chance to win. This performance is once-in-a-lifetime event and even for someone as politically astute and popular as Modi, the repetition is going to be a daunting task.

There is a huge concentration risk for BJP because the success of the party in 2014 was mostly derived from North and Western India. These geographical areas have been very fickle in changing their political preferences and most of the massive changes seen in *Lok Sabha* elections historically have happened because the voters in these areas changed their mind.

For example, a) Defeat of Indira Gandhi in 1977, b) Defeat of Janata Party in 1980, c) Defeat of Rajiv Gandhi in 1989, d) Defeat of NDA in 2004, and finally, e) the defeat of UPA in 2014. Would North and West change their mind again in 2019?

2009 to 2014: Bharatiya Janata Party's Gain = Loss for Congress

Most of the gains BJP made in 2014 came at the expense of Congress. From 206 seats in 2009, Congress was down by 162 seats to 44 seats in 2014. Interestingly, the BJP increased its tally from 116 seats in 2009 to 282 seats, a gain of 166 seats. This means that the combined strength of BJP and Congress was 322 (206 of Congress and 116 of BJP) in 2009 and that number remained almost the same in 2014 (326 including 282 of BJP and 44 of Congress). This is different in comparison of the change in 2009 vs. 2004. In 2004, the combined strength of BJP and Congress was much lower at 283 (145 for Congress and 138 of BJP).

What does this indicate? It means that the other parties (excluding BJP and Congress) were at 221 seats in 2009 and that number declined only marginally to 217 in 2014. Effectively, the non-BJP and non-Congress parties had 40 percent strength in 15th and 16th *Lok Sabha*. All the gains made by BJP came at the expense of Congress and the weakening of 'Grand Old Party' contributed in the rise of BJP.

The regional parties have remained as strong in 2014 as they were in 2009. We think this is not a good sign for the national parties. If for some reason BJP doesn't do well in 2019, the regional and smaller parties may emerge more powerful and stronger. At this stage, it doesn't look very likely that Congress will benefit from BJP's loss if that happens in 2019. However, even a small revival for Congress or the regional parties in 2019 *Lok Sabha* Elections or a small anti-BJP sentiment in some pockets would be enough to hit BJP's tally in 2019 meaningfully.

The winners and the candidates who finish second best

If we look at BJP candidates who didn't win but at the same time, didn't lose badly in the 2014 elections vs. Congress, there is a huge difference. First of all, why does it even matter? This is important because at least a Top 3 finish implies that you are in the game and given more favourable conditions next time, you stand a chance to win. It is not essential that this may necessarily happen but there is a possibility.

However, if you are not in even Top 3, the task is almost impossible to win next time. For example, when we say that Congress is not in the reckoning in UP or Bihar, we highlight that how many candidates of the party were not in even Top 3 and how many of them had to forfeit their deposits. This means that the strong candidates will not prefer or want Congress tickets in UP and Bihar. Unless they are denied a ticket from three leading parties (BJP, SP and BSP in UP or BJP, RJD and JDU in Bihar), they will not look at Congress party ticket as an option to contest elections and that becomes a key challenge for Congress to find good candidates. Victory or defeat depends on so many variables but if a majority of a party's candidates are not finishing in Top 3, the revival would only remain a pipe dream.

Table 4.3: BJP and Congress in 2014
(candidates who had to forfeit their deposits)

Party	Seats contested	Seats won	Deposit Forfeited	Votes Secured	Percent Over Total votes
Bharatiya Janata Party	428	282	62	171,660,230	31.34
Congress	464	44	178	106,935,942	19.52

Source: Election Commission of India

If we look at the number of seats BJP contested and exclude the ones where the party's candidates had to forfeit their deposits because they didn't get the minimum stipulated number of votes, BJP candidates were in the fray at 366 seats. We think that you may not fail to notice that this number is very close to the 2/3rd strength of *Lok Sabha* and as we have discussed earlier that in practical terms, BJP was in the fray in only about 360-370 of total seats.

The 282 MPs in 16th *Lok Sabha* effectively means that 77 percent of BJP candidates (282 out of 366) were successful. More than 3/4th is a very high success ratio and this does not happen every day. So we think in comparison of 2014, the possible downside is much more for BJP in 2019. If law of averages catches up with BJP or the Opposition gets smarter, there exists a huge risk for BJP.

Similarly, Congress candidates were in the fray at only 286 seats (464 – 178). Only 44 Congress MPs in 16th *Lok Sabha* effectively means that only 15 percent of Congress candidates (44 out of 286) among serious contenders were successful. This is an abysmally low success rate and hopefully for Congress, should not happen every day.

In the next Chapter

We have seen in this chapter that a repeat of 2014 for BJP is difficult as the party already has a very high success ratio at the seats where it was practically in contest. In the next Chapter, we will take a look at examples from India's political history that how staying at the top is more difficult than reaching there. Usually very strong mandates (as it was in favour of Modi in 2014) are followed by a dip in popularity and that may potentially be a serious threat for BJP in 2019.

5

MODI'S PINNACLE: WAS IT 2014 OR WILL IT BE 2019?

It is more difficult to stay on top than to get there.
— Mia Hamm[1]

Cricket or Politics: Defending the 'Top Slot' is more difficult than winning it

Indian cricketer Yuvraj Singh[2] played his 300th One Day International in June 2017 during ICC Champions Trophy in England and Wales. A cancer survivor, Yuvraj has seen many ups and downs during his 17 year long cricketing career and when he was interviewed before his milestone match, he said that while it is not difficult to play for India, sustaining the level of performance is tough and it requires determination and self-belief. Effectively, perhaps what Yuvraj meant was that getting into the national cricket team is difficult but keeping your place in the side is an even more difficult part.

This applies to not just cricket but remains true for everything. Winning is tough but keep winning is even tougher. In the last 40 years of political history in India, exceptionally strong showing in elections by a political party was invariably followed by a huge dip in performance. We are deliberately excluding the first thirty year period post-Independence because in 1951, 1957, 1962, 1967 and 1971, there was no serious threat to Congress.

There was a kind of *status quo* as Congress was getting reelected again and again. All of that changed in 1977 onwards as the electorate's patience levels with politicians went down. In last 40 years, the common experience has been that it is difficult to hold on to popularity for any leader and usually, the bigger they are, the harder they fall. This has happened to the most popular and powerful among them; Mrs. Indira Gandhi, Rajiv Gandhi, Atal Bihari Vajpayee are only a few examples.

How India's political scene evolved during 1970s and later

Mrs. Indira Gandhi was riding high on her popularity in 1971 and her catchy slogan of *Garibi Hatao* (Abolish poverty) helped Congress in securing a comfortable majority in those elections. Soon after, she reached the pinnacle of her career with an emphatic victory over Pakistan and creation of a new country, Bangladesh. However, things started to go downhill very quickly and just four years later, imposition of *Emergency* was one of the biggest mistakes she made.

The 1977 election verdict was strongly influenced by popular sentiment against *Emergency* and at least in the North India, people were only voting against Mrs. Indira Gandhi (and her son, Sanjay Gandhi) in those elections. Since the Opposition was united, the anti-Congress vote didn't split and the result was that she lost to Janata Party. Subsequently, people got tired of Janata Party very quickly because of continuous infighting among its leaders.

In 1980, Congress returned to power. Then in 1984, the sympathy wave in favour of Congress post the brutal assassination of Mrs. Indira Gandhi helped the party win the General Elections. The 1984 mandate was unprecedented, both in terms of vote percentage and number of seats.

The more interesting period is from 1989 and onwards because this is the phase when Congress started to lose its core vote banks and other parties emerged on the horizon e.g. the growth of BJP at the national level and emergence of Bahujan Samaj Party (BSP) in UP. Similarly, the splinter groups from the erstwhile Janata Dal became key players in several states. Some of the more prominent names among these parties include Samajwadi Party in Uttar Pradesh, Rashtriya Janata Dal and Janata Dal United in Bihar and Biju Janata Dal in Odisha.

1990s and the following decades witnessed the emergence of many powerful regional satraps in Congress and they also started to explore options to become independent and formed their regional outfits. Some of the more successful ones among them are, a) G K Moopanar of Tamil Maanila Congress[3] in Tamil Nadu, b) Sharad Pawar of Nationalist Congress Party in Maharashtra, c) Mamata Banerjee of All India Trinamool Congress in Bengal and, d) Jagan Mohan Reddy of YSR Congress[4] in Andhra Pradesh.

The favorable mandate is invariably followed by dip in popularity

When we are talking about a massive decline in a leader's popularity post a very strong showing in an election, it would also be important to exclude:

- **1984 after 1980** – The 1984 election revolved around the sympathy wave in favour of Congress and 1980 election lost its relevance from the perspective of people's voting behaviour.
- **1998 after 1996** –The vote was massively fragmented in 1996 and there was no party a huge winner in 1996 and as such there was no clear winner in 1998 as well.
- **1999 after 1998** - The era of coalition politics had already begun and the mandate of 1998 itself was not very clear. BJP emerged the single largest party but by no means, it was a huge victory in party's favour.

- **2009 after 2004** -NDA was ousted in 2004 but Congress didn't really win that big. Though the number of seats Congress and BJP had won was not very different, Congress was able to form the Government because it was more acceptable to some of the important non-Congress and non-BJP parties.

Post 1977, other than the above mentioned elections of 1984, 1998, 1999 and 2009; all other elections are examples of strong mandates which were followed by a drastic dip in popularity. Let us take a look at them one by one.

1980 – Janata Party ousted unceremoniously

The Janata Party came to power after the elections held in 1977 mainly because of the public anger against the Congress. After the massive mandate Janata Party had won in 1977 elections, the various factions of this combine started squabbling and bickering with each other almost immediately after the Government formation. The coalition itself was unnatural and there were huge inconsistencies and contradictions[5].

Two prominent leaders of Janata Party Government, Bharatiya Lok Dal leader Chaudhary Charan Singh[5] and Babu Jagjivan Ram[6], who had quit the Congress, were almost always at loggerheads with Prime Minister Morarji Desai[7]. The general public soon got fed up with this rag-tag coalition. In 1980, Janata Party lost so badly that even all the factions put together could not reach 100 seats. On the other hand, it was not really a surprise that Indira Gandhi made a spectacular comeback with Congress winning more than 350 seats in 1980 *Lok Sabha* Elections.

1989 – Congress lost 10 percent vote and more than half the seats it won in 1984

After the assassination of Indira Gandhi in October 1984, Congress under the leadership of Rajiv Gandhi tasted "never before and never again" electoral success. The party's vote share was close to 50 percent and the party won more than 400 seats in *Lok Sabha* in 1984 elections. With 400 plus seats, Rajiv Gandhi was able to achieve something which eluded even his illustrious grandfather, the first Prime Minister of India, Pandit Jawaharlal Nehru and Rajiv's mother, Mrs. Indira Gandhi.

But, a lot had changed between 1984 and 1989. Rajiv Gandhi was not a very experienced politician. He had entered active politics only after the death of his younger brother, Sanjay Gandhi in June 1980 and at the insistence of their mother, then Prime Minister, Mrs. Indira Gandhi. There were also serious charges of corruption against his Government and almost the entire Opposition once again came together to fight Congress in 1989 *Lok Sabha* Elections. The result was a huge defeat for Rajiv Gandhi. Congress won less than 200 seats and less than 40 percent vote share. This was the worst ever performance till then for Congress, except for the drubbing it had received in 1977. Rajiv Gandhi lost power despite the fact that Congress was the single largest party in *Lok Sabha*. Neither there was support available from other political parties to form a Government nor was Congress itself too keen as it had never run a coalition government till then. Rajiv Gandhi was assassinated in May 1991 and he could never become PM again.

1991 – V P Singh became a leader with no followers

The star of Indian politics in 1989 was Vishwanath Pratap Singh or V P Singh, a man who became the symbol of honesty in the dirty world of Indian politics. He sacrificed his post as an important Minister in Rajiv Gandhi's Government and quit the Congress party; he also became the centre of anti-Congress campaign in 1989, the main plank of which was corruption at the top level of decision making in the Government. The people from that generation may still be able to recall slogans like *Raja nahin fakir hai, desh ki taqdeer hai* (he is not a prince, he is an ascetic; he is the destiny of this country) from 1989 elections.

V P Singh's party Janata Dal was not as successful as Janata Party in 1977 because learning from the previous experience, many constituents of erstwhile Janata Party stayed away and didn't directly become the part of Janata Dal. However, because of smart pre-poll seat sharing arrangements with Bharatiya Janata Party, Janata Dal was able to win 143 seats. Though Janata Dal was well short of half way mark in *Lok Sabha*, V P Singh became the Prime Minister with the support of BJP and Left parties. However, this bonhomie was short lived.

V P Singh not only lost his chair after BJP withdrew its support, he also became the villain for upper castes and a large section of Indian middle class population when he launched the Government initiative to implement the recommendations of 27 percent reservation for Other Backward Classes by Mandal Commission[8]. V P Singh was Prime Minister for less than a year and a breakaway faction of Janata Dal which was led by Chandra Shekhar formed the next Government with the outside support from Congress.

When the mid-term elections were held in the summer of 1991, V P Singh's party lost badly (down by more than 50 percent plus seats) and slowly, most of his lieutenants deserted him. Though he remained politically active for many years, V P Singh could never become the same force in Indian Politics again.

1996 – Congress succeeded in reviving the economy but failed politically

The coalition experiment of 1989 had failed miserably and there was also sympathy for Congress after Rajiv Gandhi was assassinated. As a result, Congress was able to improve its position from 197 seats in 1989 to 244 in 1991 though its vote share came down further. After 1991 elections, P V Narasimha Rao[9] of Congress became the Prime Minister and he proved to be an extremely successful administrator. Not only the launch of economic reforms was a key highlight of his tenure, he also did well on foreign policy front.

In many ways, he was one of the most successful Prime Ministers India has ever seen. However, there were several scandals during his term and many senior Ministers faced charges of corruption. There were also serious internal conflicts in Congress where Narasimha Rao had to deal with rebellion from senior colleagues. As a result, Congress for the first time was down to less than 30 percent vote share in 1996 and in these elections, the party could not even become the single largest party. It can be argued that though Congress lost in 1996 *Lok Sabha* Elections, even the 1991 verdict in favour of the party was not really indicative of any major wave in the party's favour.

Still, the loss in 1996 was huge for the Congress party. 1996 election result was significant for two reasons, a) the country would not see a single party rule for almost two decades after this, b) 3-4 years immediately after these elections and till 1999 was a period of massive political instability in India as the country saw two successive mid-term elections in 1998 and 1999.

2004 – The most unexpected result

After the one vote loss for NDA Government during no-confidence motion in *Lok Sabha* in April 1999, the Atal Bihari Vajapyee led alliance got reelected in elections of September/October 1999. In 1999, BJP won 182 seats and managed to reach the required majority with the help of its allies. Not because of a huge mandate in 1999, but because of NDA's good performance in running a coalition Government from 1999 to 2004, it was expected that NDA will win in 2004 elections. Prime Minister Atal Bihari Vajpayee was reasonably popular and NDA seemed to have done a good enough job to receive the popular mandate one more time.

Even BJP was so confident of its victory that it advanced the general elections by a few months. As such, the victory of NDA was a foregone conclusion and the only subject of interest was the victory margin. However, the result of 2004 General Elections in India is a classic example of when almost everyone got the understanding of popular sentiment completely wrong. In these elections, the NDA suffered a shocking defeat and Congress made a comeback.

Before the elections, Congress was in complete disarray. The party had also failed in highlighting the failures of

NDA Government. So, this was a completely unexpected election result for the media and to a large extent, the entire country. BJP could not even become the single largest party in these elections and the party's seat count was down to 138 from 182.

2014 – Loss of power and loss of face for Congress

From 2004-2009, Congress though didn't have a large number of seats in *Lok Sabha*, the party did very well because of successful use of populist measures and huge support from a buoyant global economy. As a result, in 2009 elections, Congress did spectacularly well and crossed the 200 seats mark in *Lok Sabha* after almost twenty years (first time after 1991). BJP slid further with the party being reduced to 116 seats in *Lok Sabha*. After the 2009 General Elections, Congress had a comfortable majority in *Lok Sabha* with the help of its allies and wasn't excessively dependant on any single political entity.

As we have seen earlier, Congress squandered this huge political advantage because of many reasons including; a) the charges of Corruption against UPA, b) Policy Paralysis and a crumbling Economy, c) Dual Power Centers in the Party and the Government, d) the Unruly Allies and, e) Excessive dependence on Populist Measures. The 2014 *Lok Sabha* election result proved to be disastrous for Congress. For the first time ever in the history, Congress didn't even reach a three figure mark or rather the party got the number of seats much more befitting for a one-state regional party. Congress didn't even have the sufficient number of seats to become the principal Opposition Party officially.

But, Modi wave is still strong and there are no challengers to him

Except for the extraordinary circumstances, it is unlikely that a wave can sustain itself in Indian Politics for a long time of five years between two general elections. It has never happened in last forty years. And there is no doubt that 2014 General Elections result was a strong Modi wave. The way BJP swept the regions where it was strong or had decent presence, increased its influence where it was barely present and expanded its frontiers to the territories previously unchartered, the 2014 election result was a stupendous success for the BJP. Of course, it helped the party that the people were extremely angry with UPA in 2014.

Narendra Modi delivered a result for BJP, which was far superior to even the best of the expectations. In terms of popularity in the history of independent India, no one could come close to Modi other than Pandit Nehru or Mrs. Indira Gandhi. However, the achievement of Narendra Modi is much more creditworthy because both Nehru and Indira had a huge advantage when they had begun their respective campaigns to become the Prime Minister of India. Nehru was one of the most popular leaders of Congress even before 1947 and in 1966, when Indira took charge; she had an advantage of being the daughter of an illustrious father and she also had hands-on experience in Congress organisation and in the Government.

However, can the Modi wave sustain itself till 2019? Would people vote for him with the same enthusiasm once more? Or, it would be the same story again where people would get disenchanted with him. At this point, Modi looks comfortably placed which in itself is huge achievement because it has been more than three years since he took charge. There is no visible anger against him and he enjoys considerable goodwill and popularity among masses.

Also, the performance of Modi administration is largely acceptable and we have not seen any big instances of financial impropriety from Modi's Ministers and bureaucrats. Here, it is also important that people don't in general see Modi as someone who extends favours to his family or coterie of favorite industrialists. As a result, people still see him as clean and honest. There have also been several famous stories on how Modi maintains a punishing schedule for himself as the Prime Minister and is working very hard to take India to greater heights.

Another important factor is that so far, the Opposition has not been able to find any big and important issue which they can use to target Modi. Also, there is not even one leader in Opposition who can challenge Modi effectively:

- Rahul Gandhi despite making efforts (which many people see as inconsistent efforts and only coming in bursts) has not been able to put up a serious challenge to Modi. Several people and a large section of media don't see Rahul Gandhi as a full-time and sincere politician.
- Arvind Kejriwal has lost his sheen and many people don't really see him as an unconventional and different politician anymore. After the losses in Assembly Elections in Punjab and Goa and a disastrous performance in municipal elections in Delhi, Kejriwal may be experiencing a serious existential crisis at this stage.
- Mamata Banerjee is still far away from being seen as a credible alternative at the national level. She is doing

very well politically in Bengal but she would face serious difficulties in gaining acceptability as an alternative for the post of Prime Minister.

- Before he aligned himself with BJP in July 2017, Nitish Kumar was not being seen anymore as an independent and upright politician because he had an alliance with Lalu Prasad Yadav. That may have worked in Bihar but it posed a serious hurdle for his national ambitions. Now, when he has accepted the role of only a regional leader and is back in NDA fold, he has also accepted Modi as the leader of NDA. Under the circumstances, Nitish Kumar cannot be the face of Opposition. Even if we argue that he may ditch NDA just before the elections in 2019, it is unlikely that he will be acceptable to Congress and other Opposition parties.
- The old guard such as Sharad Pawar and Mulayam Singh Yadav are not the same force as they were 5-10 years earlier and they may not be in the reckoning for the chair of PM in 2019. Their age will also work against them.
- Other big regional leaders such as Naveen Patnaik[10] of BJD in Odisha or N Chandrababu Naidu[11] of TDP in Andhra Pradesh would be preoccupied in their respective states and it is unlikely that they would be able to afford having any political ambitions at the national level.
- Some of the candidates, who are not in the race for "Prime Minister in 2019" as of today but could prove to be a dark horse, may come from Congress. We think that it may be difficult to build consensus on their names and it is also doubtful if Mrs. Sonia Gandhi will be willing to consider those possibilities, but someone like Shashi Tharoor or P Chidambaram or Jyotiraditya

Scindia could prove to be much more formidable competitor to Modi. Akhikesh Yadav is not the CM of UP anymore, otherwise; he could also be an option for non-Congress political forces.

The conclusion is that it has been more than three years since Narendra Modi was elected as the Prime Minister and three important factors still work for him,

- Modi has been able to maintain his image as a no non-sense, strong, decisive, incorruptible and hardworking Prime Minister and this is in general the perception about him.
- Modi is not facing any serious competition from Opposition parties and there is no strong leader who can offer any credible alternative. In other words, the position of Modi has become stronger.
- The Modi factor is still much bigger than the combined might of BJP and RSS put together and there is virtually zero risk of an internal threat to him from within the party and this is because the old guard is no longer active and Modi's other competitors in the party have accepted him as the face of BJP.

So, will the history repeat itself in 2019?

The Modi factor is still strong which means that the powerful sentiment in BJP's favour may sustain till next elections. However, there are certainly things which could be different in 2019. The first and foremost factor is time. Things are never static in politics and even some of the innocuous or seemingly trivial things could change the direction of which way the people are going to vote.

Onions and BJP's loss in Delhi Assembly Elections in 1998

Onions and Mrs. Sheila Dixit[12] have a deep connection. She ruled for 15 years and in the process, became one of the longest serving Chief Ministers of Delhi. But, her election as the CM of Delhi could be attributed to something as trivial as onions. Before 1998 Assembly Elections in Delhi, BJP had a comfortable majority in Delhi *Vidhan Sabha* and both Madan Lal Khurana[13] and Sahib Singh Verma[14] as the Chief Minister had done a decent job for the party. There was apparently no big issue for people to feel unhappy with the Government. As late as the end of first half of the year 1998, it was expected that the upcoming Assembly Elections in Delhi will see a good contest between BJP and Congress. So, BJP had a fair chance to get reelected for another term.

Then, something strange happened with the prices of onions in Delhi. Because of multiple reasons including lower production linked with unsuitable weather and unfair manipulation by traders, the prices of onions sky rocketed. The commodity which was available at Rs10-12 per kg a few months earlier was not even available at Rs 60 to Rs 80 per kg. There was a severe rationing and even theft of onions was reported to the police. To cut the long story short, the unavailability and high prices of onions made people very angry with the local Government which of course was guilty of mismanagement but in no way was directly responsible for other factors such as low production, insufficient arrival from other states etc.

The result was a huge loss for BJP in Delhi. Compared to Congress which had won in more than 50 seats out of total 70, BJP was down to 15 seats in Delhi Assembly. The key reason for BJP's loss was onions and even BJP leaders knew this well. Interestingly, even while BJP was successful in all seven *Lok Sabha* seats in Delhi in 2014 elections, the wait for return to power in the state still continues for BJP in Delhi even after almost 20 years of that onion induced debacle. Indeed, Mrs. Sheila Dixit would be forever indebted to this humble vegetable.

And this was not the first time either. Onions have been important in politics and for elections earlier as well. In 1980 elections, the Opposition led by Indira Gandhi prominently highlighted the fact that high onion prices have made the vegetable out of reach for ordinary people. The prices had escalated to more than Rs 5 per kg then and it was attributed to then in power, Janata Party's callous attitude. Not only this, it is almost a very regular occurrence. Every few years, onions would become unaffordable for weeks and sometimes even for months and that becomes a huge political issue. To some extent, this happens with tomatoes as well but the difference is that while onions are considered a necessity, tomatoes can be termed as luxury when unaffordable.

What can go wrong for BJP in 2019?

We are only speculating but there are many issues which could prove to be difficult for the NDA Government to handle in 2019, a) the state of economy is still not in perfect health, b) job creation has not been sufficient, c) the situation in Jammu and Kashmir has significantly worsened, d) the fringe elements from aggressive Hindu organisations have become more violent.

We don't know if any of these issues could become powerful enough to change the public opinion on Modi.

Or there could be something else which could come up between now and 2019 elections. As they say, "a week is a long time in Indian politics" and we still have more than a year to go before the 2019 elections. It is possible that Modi may remain as popular as he was in 2014 but that is not a certainty.

In the next Chapter

We have seen in this chapter that more often than not, a very strong mandate for a political leader is followed by a serious dip in popularity five years later. And, this makes the task for Narendra Modi difficult in 2019. Thankfully for him and BJP, he is extremely popular even after more than three years since he took over. But, there is still some way to go before 2019 elections. In the next Chapter, we will take a look at how anti-incumbency against state governments and local representatives affect voters' choices. There are enough instances when people remain happy with the central leadership of a party but still don't vote for the party because they are not satisfied with the state Government run by the same party or the local representatives have not performed up to the expectations. Modi and his team need to be careful about this. They would be required to select the party candidates judiciously, if they don't want to receive any negative surprises in 2019.

6

ANTI INCUMBENCY AGAINST STATE GOVERNMENTS

> People don't leave bad companies, they leave bad managers.
>
> — Marcus Buckingham[1]

Is strong liking for party leadership same as liking your local representative?

Before we start discussing the importance of popularity of local elected representatives (the MLAs, MPs, representatives in local bodies such as municipal corporations and other elected officials) and respective state Governments and the role this could play in 2019, it would be worthwhile to draw an analogy from the corporate world. It is often said that in respect of employee attrition, the most important role is being played by the manager of the concerned employee.

This happens because the immediate boss or reporting manager is the most important representative of the firm for an employee. This employee's decision to join the organisation may have been driven by various factors such as, a) salary, b) brand name, c) job profile, d) location, or simply the fact that this was the best available opportunity at that point of time. However, once the employee is in the job, the single most important factor for him/her to feel comfortable, nurtured, appreciated and in general taken care of is how the reporting manager is behaving with him or her.

Does the employee feel threatened, is the manager abusive, does the manager always take credit for good things and puts the blame on subordinates when things go wrong are some of the characteristics which will negatively impact the relationship between a manager and his/her directly reporting employees. No matter how good the CEO of a company is, it is their reporting manager, people will have to deal with on a day to day basis.

It is not really a surprise that despite everything else being good or acceptable, people leave their jobs because they don't get along very well with their bosses. Similarly, there are many cases when employees do not just stay longer in their jobs but also give more than hundred percent despite not being too happy with other aspects only because they love to work with their bosses.

This analogy is appropriate in the case of elections too. Even when people remain fully satisfied with NDA Government and Modi's performance as the Prime Minister, they may still not vote for BJP if they are not happy with their MP who is contesting again or they are not satisfied with the choice of the candidate the party has made in their respective constituencies. Or, these voters may abstain from voting.

The performance of local state Governments also has link with the voters' preferences in *Lok Sabha* elections. If the general dissatisfaction is high with the state Government's performance, this anger also gets reflected in the *Lok Sabha* elections despite the fact that *Vidhan Sabha* elections is the right channel to vent this anger out.

We have seen enough examples that whenever *Lok Sabha* and *Vidhan Sabha* elections are held simultaneously, the performances of political parties more or less remain similar at both these levels. This is not just a coincidence. On a day to day basis, things which affect the citizens more (for example; the availability and regularity of electric supply, law and order situation, visible and gross misuse of power by elected representatives, corruption and illicit wealth accumulation by local politicians etc.) have no direct role of the Central Government and they are more dependent on how the state Government and local bodies are performing.

This is why when the same party is in power, people punish the Central Government for the non-performance of state Government. We think this could pose a serious problem for BJP in 2019 because now, BJP is in power in several states and it is possible that in some states people would not be happy with the state government's performance.

Anti-incumbency against local State Governments is a Major factor

There are several states where the election verdict keeps changing between the two major parties. These states would include Tamil Nadu (except for the last Assembly Elections when AIADMK got reelected; for several years, the DMK and AIADMK were taking turns to win the Assembly Elections and form the Government in the state) and Kerala (for last several elections, the Left Front and Congress led coalition are winning alternately, one followed by another). But, from the perspective of BJP, the more important states are the ones which keep changing parties which rule between Congress and BJP.

Karnataka

In several previous Assembly Elections, the people of Karnataka have been voting against the incumbent Government. Since 1989, the six Assembly Elections have mostly witnessed a vote against incumbents. Though the number of seats won by parties kept changing, the broad result was always against the incumbent Government.

Table 6.1: Results of Assembly Elections for Karnataka

Assembly Elections	Winner
1989	Congress
1994	Janata Dal
1999	Congress
2004	Congress and JD (S)
2008	BJP
2013	Congress

Note: In 2004, Congress and JD (S) formed the Government though BJP was the single largest party.
Source: Election Commission of India

The *Lok Sabha* results from Karnataka are very interesting. Despite the fact that BJP has been a dominant party in the state in terms of seats won in the last three *Lok Sabha* elections; Karnataka is the only state where BJP had actually won a lesser number of seats in 2014 as compared to both 2004 and 2009 elections.

How things will develop in 2019 also depends on the outcome in 2018 Assembly Elections. It is possible that because of anti-incumbency against Congress, BJP may do well in the *Vidhan Sabha* elections and if they can sustain this momentum a bit longer, a marginal increase in BJP's tally from the state is possible in 2019. However, potential increase would not be huge because BJP already has 17 out of 28 seats in the state.

Table 6.2: Karnataka - Number of seats won in the *Lok Sabha* Elections

Lok Sabha Elections	BJP	Congress
1998	13	9
1999	7	18
2004	18	8
2009	19	6
2014	17	9

Source: Election Commission of India

Rajasthan

Since 1993, the five Assembly Elections in Rajasthan have always seen a change in regime from the BJP to Congress and then again from Congress to BJP. The change also reflects in the results of *Lok Sabha* elections.

Table 6.3: Results of Assembly Elections for Rajasthan

Assembly Elections	Winner
1993	Bharatiya Janata Party
1998	Congress
2003	Bharatiya Janata Party
2008	Congress
2013	Bharatiya Janata Party

Source: Election Commission of India

Table 6.4: Rajasthan - Number of seats won in the *Lok Sabha* Elections

Lok Sabha Elections	BJP	Congress
1998	5	19
1999	16	9
2004	21	4
2009	4	20
2014	25	0

Source: Election Commission of India

The scenario in 2019 should be largely in-line with the outcome of the 2018 Assembly Elections in Rajasthan. It is possible that because of anti-incumbency against the Vasundhara Raje[2] led BJP Government, Congress may do well in the *Vidhan Sabha* elections. In that case, a drastic decline in BJP's tally is likely in 2019. Even in a scenario which is more benign from BJP's perspective, it would be reasonable to expect that a reduction in BJP's tally is possible.

Haryana

Except for 2009 when Congress Government got reelected, Haryana has been voting against the incumbent Governments in last several Assembly Elections.

Table 6.5: Results of Assembly Elections for Haryana

Assembly Elections	Winner
1991	Congress
1996	Haryana Vikas Party
2000	Indian National Lok Dal
2005	Congress
2009	Congress
2014	Bharatiya Janata Party

Source: Election Commission of India

1987 – Devi Lal[3] trumped Congress in Haryana and the downfall of Rajiv Gandhi began

In 1982, the Assembly Election was a close fight in Haryana but finally, Congress formed the Government in the state. For the supporters of Chaudhary Devi Lal and some neutral observers as well, it was a clear case of Central Government trying to unfairly influence the Government formation in the state. However, the 1984 *Lok Sabha* election was a pure 'Congress Only' outcome and the party made a clean sweep by winning all the ten *Lok Sabha* seats in the state. The sympathy wave in favour of Congress was just too strong after Indira Gandhi's assassination and people voted for Congress *en masse*.

In Northern region of the country, the first important evenly contested state Assembly Election after Rajiv Gandhi came to power was Haryana in 1987. The elections which were held only about two and a half years of the previous General Elections were not just humiliating for Congress as they resulted in a massive defeat for the party; this result was also a precursor of what was to happen with Congress in 1989.

In 1987 Haryana Assembly Elections, Devi Lal was leading Lok Dal and he also had a pre-poll alliance with BJP. There are total 90 seats in Haryana Legislative Assembly and while Lok Dal won 60 seats, BJP won 16. The Congress was down to 5 seats and even the number of independent candidates who got elected was more than the tally of Congress. The victory of Lok Dal-BJP combine and defeat of Congress was much more noteworthy for the reason that it came at a time when the Rajiv Gandhi Government had not even completed three years of its full term and Haryana is a neighboring state of Delhi.

Haryana is a very small state and sends only ten Members in *Lok Sabha*. But, this result in Haryana Assembly Elections and the pre-poll alliance experiment was important for three reasons;

- This provided an indication that people have become disenchanted with Congress and there is a need for Opposition parties to channelise this anger.

- This election provided the template of political alignment required to defeat Congress. This strategy was replicated in 1989 across many Northern and Western states in the country.
- This result was a major morale booster for the Opposition which received a shot in the arm and realised that despite having 400+ MPs in *Lok Sabha*, Congress was not really invincible.

Coming back to quick changes in Haryana election results, this trend reflects in the popular verdict in *Lok Sabha* elections too. For example, the Congress was down from 9 seats in 2009 elections to winning only one seat in 2014.

Table 6.6: Haryana - Number of seats won in the *Lok Sabha* Elections

***Lok Sabha* Elections**	**BJP**	**Congress**
1996	4	2
1998	1	3
1999	5	0
2004	1	9
2009	0	9
2014	7	1

Source: Election Commission of India

The scenario for BJP in 2019 depends on how well the Manohar Lal Khattar[4] led BJP Government in the state performs. It is possible that because of anti-incumbency against the local BJP Government in the state, Congress may do well in the state in *Lok Sabha* Elections in 2019. In any case, a major increase in BJP's tally is unlikely as BJP already has 7 out of 10 seats in the state.

Uttarakhand

Since the formation of Uttarakhand state, the four Assembly Elections have always seen a change in regime from BJP to Congress and then again from Congress to BJP. This applies to *Lok Sabha* election results too. For example, Congress had won all the five seats in the state in the 2009 elections and in 2014, the result was same but in BJP's favour.

Table 6.7: Results of Assembly Elections for Uttarakhand

Assembly Elections	Winner
2002	Congress
2007	Bharatiya Janata Party
2012	Congress
2017	Bharatiya Janata Party

Source: Election Commission of India

Table 6.8: Uttarakhand - Number of seats won in the *Lok Sabha* Elections

Lok Sabha Elections	BJP	Congress
2004	3	1
2009	0	5
2014	5	0

Source: Election Commission of India

BJP led state Government will be two years old by 2019 and even in a best case scenario, retaining all 5 seats in the state will be a challenge for BJP.

Himachal Pradesh

Just like Uttarkhand, the people of Himachal Pradesh have also been voting against the incumbent state government in previous several elections. Since 1985, the seven Assembly Elections have always seen a change in regime from the Congress to BJP and then again from BJP to Congress.

Table 6.9: Results of Assembly Elections for Himachal Pradesh

Assembly Elections	Winner
1985	Congress
1990	Bharatiya Janata Party
1993	Congress
1998	Bharatiya Janata Party
2003	Congress
2007	Bharatiya Janata Party
2012	Congress

Source: Election Commission of India

The performance of Bharatiya Janata Party in *Lok Sabha* elections has been better than Congress in Himachal Pradesh. Except for 2004, BJP has done consistently better than Congress in *Lok Sabha* elections in the state.

Table 6.10: Himachal Pradesh - Number of seats won in the *Lok Sabha* Elections

Lok Sabha Elections	BJP	Congress
1998	3	1
1999	3	0
2004	1	3
2009	3	1
2014	4	0

Source: Election Commission of India

In a best case scenario for BJP in 2019, it is possible that BJP will be able to retain all the four seats the party currently holds in the state.

The Safer States for BJP – The risk lies in the tally of seats for2019 vs. 2014

We have looked at some of the states where anti-incumbency against local state Governments plays a key role and the prominent among them is Rajasthan from the point of view of a possible decline in BJP's tally in 2019 *Lok Sabha* elections.

However, there are some states where BJP has been in power for a long time and the party has won at least three consecutive *Vidhan Sabha* elections. These are Gujarat, Madhya Pradesh and Chhattisgarh and though BJP remains strong in these states, the task before BJP is an uphill one for 2019. Of the 66 *Lok Sabha* seats in these three states, BJP currently has 63 and it is likely to be difficult for BJP to repeat this performance in 2019 *Lok Sabha* elections.

Gujarat

In last several Assembly Elections, Gujarat has been voting for BJP. Since 1995, the five Assembly Elections have always seen a BJP victory and the last time Congress had won in the state was way back in 1985.

Table 6.11: Results of Assembly Elections for Gujarat

Assembly Elections	Winner
1995	Bharatiya Janata Party
1998	Bharatiya Janata Party
2002	Bharatiya Janata Party
2007	Bharatiya Janata Party
2012	Bharatiya Janata Party

Source: Election Commission of India

However, the more interesting part is that the results in *Lok Sabha* elections have never been that lopsided except for 2014 General Elections.

Table 6.12: Gujarat - Number of seats won in the *Lok Sabha* Elections

Lok Sabha Elections	BJP	Congress
1991	20	5
1996	16	10
1998	19	7
1999	20	6
2004	14	12
2009	15	11
2014	26	0

Source: Election Commission of India

In the absence of Narendra Modi leading the state as its Chief Minister, it is possible that BJP may find it difficult to repeat the good performance of 2014 *Lok Sabha* elections. What will actually happen in 2019, the first indications of which will be visible in the Assembly Elections due by the end of 2017.

Madhya Pradesh

Madhya Pradesh is an absolutely critical state for BJP. After UP, the party had won the highest number of seats in 2014 elections from this state. In the last three Assembly Elections, Madhya Pradesh has been voting for BJP.

Table 6.13: Results of Assembly Elections for Madhya Pradesh

Assembly Elections	Winner
1985	Congress
1990	Bharatiya Janata Party
1993	Congress
1998	Congress
2003	Bharatiya Janata Party
2008	Bharatiya Janata Party
2013	Bharatiya Janata Party

Source: Election Commission of India

However, the performance of Congress was better in 2009 *Lok Sabha* Elections before BJP won 27 out of 29 seats in *Lok Sabha* in 2014.

Table 6.14: Madhya Pradesh - Number of seats won in the *Lok Sabha* Elections

***Lok Sabha* Elections**	**BJP**	**Congress**
1984	0	40
1989	27	8
1991	12	27
1996	27	8
1998	30	10
1999	29	11
2004	25	4
2009	16	12
2014	27	2

Note: Till 1999 general elections, Madhya Pradesh had 40 *Lok Sabha* Constituencies. After Chhattisgarh was carved out, the number of seats went down to 29 as Chhattisgarh got 11 seats.
Source: Election Commission of India

BJP has 27 out of 29 Members in *Lok Sabha* from the state and this was the best ever performances for the party in the state. The two *Lok Sabha* seats where Congress was victorious in 2014 were Chhindwara and Guna. While anything is possible in elections, these two are very difficult for BJP to wrest from Congress. This is because of the clout of incumbent Congress MPs in these two constituencies.

Guna and Chhindwara: The stronghold of Congress

What is so special about these two *Lok Sabha* constituencies in Madhya Pradesh?

- These are the only two *Lok Sabha* seats in Madhya Pradesh from where Congress candidates got elected in 2014.

- The winning candidates defeated their nearest BJP rivals by a difference of more than 100,000 votes.
- The winning candidates received more than 50 percent of total votes polled in their respective constituencies. This was something even Rahul Gandhi could not achieve in Amethi in 2014.

And all of this happened when the Modi wave swept through the entire North India.

Jyotiraditya Scindia[5] represents Guna constituency in 16th *Lok Sabha*. He is a senior leader of Congress and has also been a Minister in the UPA Government headed by Dr. Manmohan Singh. Just like his father, late Shri Madhav Rao Scindia[6], he has remained undefeated so far in all the *Lok Sabha* elections he contested. The first was 2002 by-election after the untimely death of Madhav Rao Scindia and the victory in 2002 was followed by the same result in 2004, 2009 and 2014. Jyotiraditya continues to represent Guna which was earlier a part of the State of Gwalior ruled by the Scindias. His connect with the electorate in the constituency is very powerful because of his lineage and though BJP fielded a strong candidate in 2014, that didn't really make a difference in the final outcome.

Kamal Nath[7] represents the Chhindwara constituency. He has close ties with Gandhi family and is a senior leader of Congress. He has served in the Government and also in the organisation for Congress Party. He entered active politics at a very young age and got elected to *Lok Sabha* for the first time in 1980. In last more than 35 years of his life as an active politician, he has been elected repeatedly from

Chhindwara except once. Just like Scindia, he also remains a very difficult candidate to defeat for BJP.

Coming back to Madhya Pradesh in 2019 elections, there is a reasonable anti-incumbency against Shivraj Singh Chouhan[8] led BJP government and if Congress is able to tap that sentiment well, BJP may find it really difficult to repeat the good performance of 2014 again in 2019. Whether a Congress revival will actually happen in 2019, the indications will be visible in the Assembly Elections due in 2018.

Farmer Unrest and Popular Sentiment in Madhya Pradesh

Madhya Pradesh is a state in central India. In terms of geographical area, it is the second-largest state in the country after Rajasthan and it is also the fifth-largest state in India by population. The state has 29 representatives in *Lok Sabha*. BJP has 27 MPs from Madhya Pradesh, accounting for 10 percent of party's current strength in *Lok Sabha*.

The state government is struggling with serious farmer unrest currently. For example, in Mandsaur, which is a small town in MP, farmers went on a rampage destroying public property and pelting stones at the police after five farmers were killed by police gunfire on June 6, 2017. We think there are several other issues which will play an important role in 2018 Assembly Elections in Madhya Pradesh.

The Good part:

- The people are in general happy with the law and order situation. Even historically, the state has remained relatively more peaceful than its peers in Northern India. This is a strong Unique Selling Proposition (USP) of BJP Government in the state.

- The state has done very well on welfare measures. The BJP Government launched many new schemes such as no-cost religious pilgrimage for elderly people and financial support for girl child. These schemes have helped in creating goodwill for Shivraj Singh Chouhan.
- The people are in general satisfied with the development work undertaken by the state government and they think that Government has been doing a reasonable job.

The Bad part:

- There is huge pent-up anger among farmers and this is mainly because they believe that they do not receive a reasonable price for their produce. The primary reasons are,
  a) the MSP (Minimum Support Price) for crops have not been increased in-line with increase in input costs,
  b) the prices received by farmers are extremely volatile and hence unpredictable, and,
  c) the farmers also have complaints about massive corruption at local APMCs (Agriculture Produce Marketing Committees).
- People think that Prime Minister Narendra Modi and the Chief Minister are not on the same page. People are apprehensive that the central leadership of BJP does not like strong regional leaders and there is a trust deficit between PM and CM. This could work against the state Government.
- People think that the *Vyapam* Scam (irregularities in appointments and exams conducted by Professional Examination Board of MP) has not been investigated

thoroughly and there are people from the very top involved.

Chhattisgarh

Since 2003, the three Assembly Elections in this state which was carved out of Madhya Pradesh have always seen a BJP victory.

Table 6.15: Results of Assembly Elections for Chhattisgarh

Assembly Elections	Winner
2003	Bharatiya Janata Party
2008	Bharatiya Janata Party
2013	Bharatiya Janata Party

Source: Election Commission of India

The results in *Lok Sabha* elections have also been one sided though the contest in Assembly Elections have been more even and BJP was only marginally ahead of Congress in *Vidhan Sabha* results.

Table 6.16: Number of seats won in the *Lok Sabha* Elections

Lok Sabha **Elections**	**BJP**	**Congress**
2004	10	1
2009	10	1
2014	10	1

Source: Election Commission of India

In Assembly Elections, the difference in vote share between the BJP and Congress in Chhattisgarh has been very slim. Despite its three consecutive defeats, Congress remains a serious contender to wrest power from BJP and dislodge Raman Singh[9] in 2018 unless the Ajit Jogi[10] led outfit harms the prospects of Congress. While it is difficult to forecast 2019 verdict in this tribal state, BJP has everything to lose and Congress has everything to gain in Chhattisgarh.

Across the country: the variance between 2014 general elections and subsequent Assembly Elections

Between the period from 2014 General Election and 2015 Assembly Election, we have discussed the contrast in results in Bihar in ***Chapter 1, The Opposition will be better prepared for Modi***. But, Bihar is not an exception. There are other states as well where Assembly Elections took place in last three years and often, BJP's vote share has dipped in comparison to 2014 General Elections. In most situations, BJP's vote share in Assembly Elections held after 2014 is lesser than the party's vote share in 2014 *Lok Sabha* Elections.

The results of Assembly Elections in 2017 vs. General Elections in 2014

Uttar Pradesh

In the Assembly Elections of 2017, BJP had 39.7 percent vote share and won 312 seats in a house of 403 (about 77 percent of total). This was lower than 42.6 percent vote share the party had won in 2014 General Elections and 71 seats out of 80 (about 89 percent of total).

Uttarakhand

In the Assembly Elections of 2017, BJP had 46.5 percent vote share and won 57 seats in a house of 70 (about 81 percent of total). This was lower than 55.9 percent vote share the party had won in 2014 General Elections and 5 seats out of 5 in *Lok Sabha* from the state (100 percent of total).

Punjab

In the Assembly Elections of 2017, BJP had 5.4 percent vote share and won 3 seats in a house of 117 (about 3 percent of total). This was lower than 8.8 percent vote share the party had won in 2014 General Elections and 2 seats out of 13 from the state (15 percent of total).

Goa

In the Assembly Elections of 2017, BJP had 32.5 percent vote share and won 13 seats in a house of 40 (about 33 percent of total). This was lower than 54.1 percent vote share the party had won in 2014 General Elections and 2 seats out of 2 from the state (100 percent of total).

Manipur

Manipur was an exception as BJP's vote share increased in 2017 vs. 2014. In the Assembly Elections of 2017, BJP had 36.3 percent vote share and won 21 seats in a house of 60 (about 35 percent of total). This was higher than 12.0 percent vote share the party had won in 2014 General Elections and zero seats out of 2 from the state (0 percent of total).

The results of Assembly Elections in 2016 vs. General Elections in 2014

Bengal

In the Assembly Elections of 2016, BJP had 10.2 percent vote share and won 3 seats in a house of 294 (about 1 percent of total). This was significantly lower than 17.0 percent vote share the party had won in 2014 General Elections and 2 seats out of 42 from the state (about 5 percent of total).

Tamil Nadu

In the Assembly Elections of 2016, BJP had 2.8 percent vote share and didn't win any seats in a house of 234. This was lower than 5.6 percent vote share the party had won in 2014 General Elections and 1 seat out of 39 from the state (about 2.5 percent of total).

Puducherry

In the Assembly Elections of 2016, BJP had 2.4 percent vote share and didn't win any seats in a house of 30. BJP had not contested from Puducherry in 2014 *Lok Sabha* Elections.

Kerala

In the Assembly Elections of 2016, BJP had 10.5 percent vote share and won 1 seat in a house of 140. This was same as the 10.5 percent vote share the party had won in 2014 General Elections. In Kerala, BJP had not won any *Lok Sabha* seats out of 20 in 2014.

Assam

In the Assembly Elections of 2016, BJP had 29.5 percent vote share and won 60 seats in a house of 126 (about 48 percent of total). This was lower than 36.9 percent vote share the party had won in 2014 General Elections and 7 seats out of 14 from the state (50 percent of total).

The results of Assembly Elections in 2015 vs. General Elections in 2014

Bihar

In the Assembly Elections of 2015, BJP had 24.8 percent vote share (37.5 percent in the seats the party contested) and won 53 seats in a house of 243 (about 22 percent of total). This was lower than 29.9 percent vote share the party had won in 2014 General Elections and 22 seats from the state (55 percent of total).

Delhi

In the Assembly Elections of 2015, BJP had 32.2 percent vote share and won only 3 seats in a house of 70 (about 5 percent of total). This was lower than 46.6 percent vote share the party had won in 2014 General Elections and BJP had won all seven seats in Delhi (100 percent of total) in 2014 *Lok Sabha* Elections.

The results of Assembly Elections in 2014 vs. General Elections in 2014

In the year 2014, the elections for State Legislative Assemblies of Andhra Pradesh, Telangana, Arunachal Pradesh, Haryana, Jammu and Kashmir, Maharashtra, Odisha, Jharkhand and Sikkim were held. Of these, the Assembly Elections in Andhra Pradesh, Telangana, Arunachal Pradesh, Odisha and Sikkim were held along with the General Elections. So, we would focus on the other states where elections were held after the General Elections.

Maharashtra

In the Assembly Elections of October 2014, BJP had 27.8 percent vote share and won 122 seats in a house of 288 (about 42 percent of total). In comparison, 27.6 percent was vote share of the party in 2014 General Elections and BJP had won 23 seats out of 48 from the state (48 percent of total). The difference between Assembly Elections of October 2014 and General Elections in May 2014 was that Shiv Sena and BJP had a tie up at the time of General Elections while they fought the Assembly Elections separately.

Haryana

In the Assembly Elections of 2014, BJP had 33.2 percent vote share and won 47 seats in a house of 90 (about 52 percent of total). This was lower than 34.8 percent vote share the party had won in 2014 General Elections and 7 seats out of 10 from the state (70 percent of total).

Jharkhand

In the Assembly Elections of 2014, BJP had 31.3 percent vote share and won 37 seats in a house of 81 (about 46 percent of total). This was lower than 40.7 percent vote share the party had won in 2014 General Elections and 12 out of 14 MPs were elected from the state (85 percent of total).

Jammu and Kashmir

In the Assembly Elections of 2014, BJP had 23.0 percent vote share and won 25 seats in a house of 87 (about 29 percent of total). This was lower than 32.7 percent vote share the party had won in 2014 General Elections and 3 seats out of 6 from the state (50 percent of total).

Anti-incumbency against local elected representatives also plays a role

It is a fact that in any sport, staying at top is more difficult than reaching there. Not to take anything away from the winners because it requires a lot of effort and single minded focus to reach the top spot, but to do well consistently in all conditions and against every opponent is much more difficult.

There is not just burden of expectations but also you need to be in the top form always. Moreover, a victory for a winner is never a surprise and never a great story. On the other hand, a loss for a champion makes far better headlines. So, the psychological pressure under which the champions have to play is immense. They always need to be tough with the mind and with the body.

How does this work in politics? In elections, people may give someone new a chance because of a wave and faith in the national leader of a party. But, getting reelected is a different ball game altogether. The candidate has to work tirelessly and has to deliver consistently.

A national leader of a party can't really fill for the local representatives. The proactive approach of an elected representative can't be enforced from the party head quarters. For example, just look at how regular BJP MPs have been in attending the Parliament despite getting reprimanded by the Prime Minister and the BJP President. Some of them may have complied but not everyone. This is the case with each and every political party and BJP's situation would not be any different. Modi can help someone win an election but for that person to get reelected, the person needs to work hard or to make Modi magic work again; a new candidate needs to be found and given ticket to contest.

Assuming in the most natural situation that some leaders on the ground for BJP are good and some will not be so good, this could pose a potential problem for BJP in 2019. Almost at every place where BJP candidates were victorious in 2014, there is need for a critical evaluation before awarding the party nomination in 2019. This implies that some of the incumbents would lose the party symbol to contest.

This has two major issues. First, it is not an easy task to reliably understand the undercurrent for or against an elected representative. Of course, BJP and RSS have a very strong feedback mechanism to identify these trends but this is still a subjective exercise. Even if BJP is able to deny the party tickets to some of its MPs in 2019, there is a possibility that, a) some unpopular MPs would still be able to retain their party nomination, and, b) some of the genuinely popular MPs would get dropped.

Second, even if a party is able to make the correct assessment on who among the incumbents remain popular, the incumbent is the first claimant to the party ticket in the subsequent elections. If their claims are ignored in ticket distribution, they may become rebel candidates. Not many of them would be able to win as an independent candidate or from a different party; some of them may still be strong enough to create difficulties for official BJP candidate. It is a realistic possibility that these rebel candidates may become the reason for the loss of official candidates of BJP in certain constituencies.

In 2014, BJP never had this issue because in many areas where the party had big wins in 2014, the number of elected BJP representatives from 2009 was not very high. For example, BJP only had 10 MPs from 80 seats in

Uttar Pradesh and this provided more flexibility to central leadership in nominating official candidates.

In 2019, the BJP will have a problem of plenty and there would be many new claimants to party tickets in addition to Members of Parliament who are representing these constituencies at present. It is scientifically proven that there are times when the problem of plenty compromises the quality of decision making as the chances of making a wrong choice increases significantly beyond a certain number for choices available.

In 2014 General Elections, it was almost as if everything fell in place and BJP won wherever it had a realistic or even an outside chance. Now, the margin of error is really small. Even if BJP suffers some small reversals because of either wrong selection of candidates or because of ignoring anti-incumbency against incumbent MPs or the anti-incumbency against state governments, it may negatively impact the number of seats BJP will win in 2019.

In the next Chapter

We have seen in this chapter that a powerful anti-incumbency against the state governments where BJP is in power or dissatisfaction with local BJP MPs could become a serious obstacle for the party in 2019. This is another important reason why we think that repeating the performance of 2014 will not be easy for BJP. In the next Chapter, we will take a look at how whatever we have discussed so far from Chapter 1 to Chapter 6 will affect the prospects of BJP in the next *Lok Sabha* Elections. We will also analyse the different scenarios to be expected in 2019. But, a quick recap will help before we move forward.

What have we discussed so far – A quick recap

Before we move on to the next chapter, let us see what the discussion so far means for 2019 election results:

- In ***Chapter 1, The Opposition will be better prepared for Modi***, we have seen that there is a very high probability that the entire opposition will gang up against Modi and BJP will not benefit from the split in Opposition vote as it did in 2014. In 2019, the Opposition parties will surely not underestimate the 'Modi Wave'.
- In ***Chapter 2, 2014 Mandate: UPA - The Story of Self Goals***, we looked at how UPA II was plagued with serious charges of corruption and indecisiveness and this created a strong anti-incumbency against UPA. It worked as a strong tail wind for Modi and BJP in 2014. However, this strong support for BJP will be missing in 2019.
- In ***Chapter 3, The Role of Economy in Elections,*** We have highlighted that the role played by the state of economy was a key reason why people were so unhappy with UPA II in 2014. The policy paralysis under Dr. Manmohan Singh's Government and how Modi will be different made a significant contribution in enhancing his appeal among voters. The record of Modi administration is at best mixed so far and that may become a serious obstacle for BJP in 2019. In areas such as GDP growth rate, industrial production and job creation, track record of Modi Government is not necessarily better than UPA.
- In ***Chapter 4, 2014 Mandate: BJP's Statistical Peak?,*** we discussed how in 2014, BJP enjoyed a success rate which was unprecedented. Practically speaking, BJP

was contesting not more than around 360-370 seats in 2014 and it won more than 75 percent of them. For BJP, the scope for losses in 2019 is much larger than the possibility of gains.

- In ***Chapter 5, Modi's Pinnacle: Was it 2014 or Will it be 2019?,*** we went through some of the relevant examples of Indian elections to conclude that the voter preferences are fickle especially in Northern India as seen more in 1980, 1989, 2004 and 2014. History doesn't repeat itself always but the odds will certainly be against Modi in 2019.
- In ***Chapter 6, Anti-Incumbency Against State Governments,*** we looked at the influence of performance of state governments and local elected representatives on voters' choices in *Lok Sabha* Elections. Now, BJP has been running the state governments in many states and also has 282 MPs in *Lok Sabha* which is a never before experience for the party. Not all the state governments or MPs would perform badly but if some of them do, that will become a big obstacle for Modi in 2019.

7

THE IMPLICATIONS FOR 2019

> Leadership is not about the next election, it's about the next generation.
>
> — Simon Sinek[1]

So far, we have discussed how it would be difficult for BJP to replicate its performance of 2014 elections in 2019. In this Chapter, we will take a look at the more likely scenarios in totality for the entire country in 2019. But before that, we will take a look at the possibility if BJP can do better in some of the states taking into account how it performed in 2014.

Let us put the conclusion upfront. Yes, there is a realistic chance that BJP can improve its tally in 2019 as compared to 2014 in some of these states.

Can BJP gain in 2019 vs. 2014 in any of the states?

Maharashtra

Except for the scenario where there is a strong alliance among Congress-Shiv Sena-Nationalist Congress Party with a seat sharing agreement against BJP, it is possible that BJP may do better in 2014. BJP had a seat sharing arrangement with Shiv Sena in 2014 but in all likelihood, will go alone next time.

The best chances for BJP would be when all four major parties in the state (BJP, Congress, Shiv Sena and Nationalist Congress Party) fight separately and there is a four cornered contest. If there is no pre-poll alliance between either NCP-Congress or NCP-Shiv Sena or NCP-Congress-Shiv Sena, there is a good chance of BJP being able to enhance its tally of *Lok Sabha* seats from the state. Maharashtra is a large state and sends 48 MPs in *Lok Sabha*. In 2014, BJP had a seat sharing arrangement with Shiv Sena (SS) and the party currently has 23 MPs from the state. In the Assembly Elections in 2014, both Shiv Sena and BJP fought separately and BJP emerged as the single largest party after being the junior partner to Shiv Sena in the state for several years.

BJP is now leading the state Government and Mr. Devendra Fadnavis[2] is heading the BJP-SS coalition Government as its Chief Minister. This BJP-SS coalition Government was a post poll arrangement after BJP fell short of the half-way mark and Shiv Sena also pragmatically realised that it may be better to be in power. However, this has been an uneasy partnership with both sides putting up with each other only out of necessity.

BJP had only contested 24 seats in Maharashtra in 2014 and had won 23. If the situation remains favourable for the party in 2019, improvement in BJP's tally is a realistic possibility. The recent results in the elections for local bodies indicate that BJP has been able to gain at the expense of other parties especially Congress and NCP. So, Maharashtra is certainly one of the important states where BJP can do better in 2019.

Odisha

Odisha has been under the rule of Biju Janata Dal (BJD) for many years and Naveen Patnaik has been heading the state Government. He has an advantage of clean image despite being in power for a very long period. There are also not any widely held perceptions among people that he is hand-in-gloves with industrialists only interested in exploiting the mineral wealth of the state, which is important because Odisha is a mineral rich state and mining has been a contentious issue in the past.

The Opposition in Odisha has also been listless for a while because the primary Opposition party, Congress has not been able to effectively challenge BJD and Naveen Patnaik's leadership. Congress has been losing support consistently in the state. Naveen Patnaik remains the most popular leader from the state. However, if the results in local bodies' election held in first half of 2017 are any indication, it seems that BJD's iron grip on the state is getting weaker.

Odisha sends 21 MPs in *Lok Sabha* and in 2014, BJD had won 20 seats. Though BJP is still way behind in terms of vote percentage, improvement in its tally is a realistic possibility at least theoretically. It may not be easy as there are two conditions that need to be fulfilled for this to happen,

- BJD and CM Patnaik are not able to reverse the slide and continue to lose support which would mean that people in the state are willing to explore the alternatives available,
- Congress doesn't benefit from this anti-incumbency and BJP is able to capitalise on this sentiment better.

Nevertheless, Odisha is certainly one of the important states where BJP can do better in 2019 than how it did in 2014.

Other States

In a few other states such as Tamil Nadu, West Bengal and Kerala, BJP was not very successful in 2014. However, at least as of now, it doesn't look very likely that a major increase in its tally of *Lok Sabha* seats is on the cards from these states. Primarily because BJP is still nowhere close to breaching the threshold which needs to be crossed to win a significant number of seats. For example, the 2016 Assembly Elections in Tamil Nadu was an extremely disappointing result for BJP as the party's vote share declined in comparison of 2014. In Kerala, BJP's vote share has not really grown meaningfully over many elections. The case of Bengal is even more interesting. In Bengal, the BJP suffered a serious decline in its vote share during Assembly Elections in 2016 as compared to the party's vote share in 2014 *Lok Sabha* Elections.

There are some other states such as Karnataka, Punjab, Andhra Pradesh and Telangana where it can be theoretically indicated that BJP can better its 2014 performance. However, we think that it will be a tall order and though minor changes are possible, there is unlikely to be a big difference in the number of seats BJP can win in 2019 General Elections vs. 2014 from these states.

Merger of Two AIADMK Factions in Tamil Nadu: Is this an Opportunity for BJP to Get a Foothold?

All India Anna Dravida Munnetra Kazhagam (AIADMK) leader and Tamil Nadu's Chief Minister J Jayalalithaa's death in December 2016 sparked a political turmoil in the state. After Ms. Jayalalithaa passed away, there was a fierce battle between two rival groups of AIADMK to claim her political legacy and to gain control of AIADMK.

These two factions were led by E Palaniswami (the current Chief Minister who was supported by politically powerful close associate of Jayalalithaa, V K Sasikala and Sasikala's nephew, T T V Dinakaran) and O Paneerselvam (the ex-chief minister). However, in a development which was in works for a few months, both E Palaniswami (EPS) and O Paneerselvam (OPS) decided to bury the hatchet and merged their political groups in August 2017.

Is this an opportunity for BJP to make an impact in Tamil Nadu? The political importance of Tamil Nadu for BJP lies in the fact that the state could be one of the key growth areas for the party and NDA in 2019. There also have been speculations that BJP played a key role in brokering peace between the OPS and EPS factions. The party is making a serious attempt a get a foothold in the state.

However, we think that the recent political development in Tamil Nadu, though somewhat positive for BJP, isn't enough for the party. Despite a rising tide in BJP's favour in several other states, we don't see any meaningful opportunity for BJP to make an impact in Tamil Nadu. BJP may have played a behind-the-scenes role but, the party is unlikely to become an important player in the state politics at least in the near term. It is unlikely that there will be a big change in BJP's tally from the state in 2019.

The gains may not be sufficient to compensate for losses elsewhere for BJP

For BJP, some gains in a few of the states are possible especially in Maharashtra and Odisha as we discussed earlier. A small gain is also theoretically possible in Karnataka and Assam. However, we also think that these gains put together even in the best case scenario would not be sufficient to compensate for the possible losses elsewhere. There is a huge concentration risk BJP is carrying and even small losses in any of the large states could threaten the BJP's tally of seats in 2019.

These states are Uttar Pradesh, Madhya Pradesh, Gujarat, Rajasthan and Bihar. Despite how it is being projected, BJP's footprint has not really expanded that much post 2014 General Elections. Irrespective of the favorable or unfavorable outcome of several Assembly Elections since 2014, there is a realistic possibility that in 2019, BJP may lose ground in the number of seats won.

What would be the most likely outcome for 2019?

PM Narendra Modi is at the peak of his political career. His popularity may remain intact but there are extraneous factors which can influence the outcome of next election. At this stage, there is not much to choose between if there would be a non-BJP coalition Government post 2019 elections or if BJP albeit with the need for much larger support from its allies would be able to form the Government once again.

We think there is a very high likelihood that BJP would find it difficult to repeat the performance of 2014 and may not be able to reach the 272+ or a close enough mark on its own in 2019 General Elections. This is the most probable outcome even when we assume that there won't be any significant decline in BJP's vote share vs. previous elections. The major contributing factors to play a role in this could be,

- A united and much stronger opposition which may stop the repeat of 2014 when BJP was able to win 282 seats with only 31 percent vote share,

- The lack of a phenomenal wave of support for Modi which was there because of massive resentment against UPA II,
- Possible anti-incumbency against local elected representatives of the party and BJP state Governments,
- BJP's excessive dependence on six key states that contributed almost 70 percent of BJP's strength in 16th *Lok Sabha*,
- Some of the possible gains in states like Maharashtra and Odisha would not be sufficient to make up for the possible losses elsewhere.

Can we make a realistic state by state assessment of BJP's chances in 2019?
To keep this exercise simple, we have only put the states/ UTs in three buckets, a) Increment possible, b) likely to remain largely similar, and, c) there is high possibility of a decline in tally.

Increment possible in 2019 general elections
Among the larger states, these could be,

- **Maharashtra** – If BJP decides to go solo in 2019 elections and all other major parties (Shiv Sena, Congress and Nationalist Congress Party) don't have a pre-poll alliance, the BJP stands a good chance of improving its tally from current 23 out of total 48 seats in the state.
- **Karnataka** –This is a unique state because it was the only one where BJP's tally had actually declined in 2014 vs. 2009 though the party had done well in absolute terms by winning 17 seats out of total 28. Unless something goes drastically wrong for the party, the BJP could improve its tally in the state.

- **Odisha** –If the elections held in first half of June 2017 for local bodies are any indication, BJP could increase its tally from currently 1 out of total 21 seats in the state. Though BJP is still not the clear principal opposition party in the state against BJD, there is a possibility that BJP may be able to do better in 2019.
- **Punjab** – This may sound like a completely misplaced expectation today when SAD-BJP combine has suffered a humiliating defeat very recently in Punjab Assembly Elections. However, if BJP reconsiders its ties with SAD and/or if there is anti-incumbency against Captain Amarinder Singh[3], this possibility may not look as unrealistic as it appears today.

There is also Manipur where it is possible that BJP could perhaps win more in 2019 elections. This is where BJP has formed the state Government recently and didn't have any MPs in 2014.

BJP's tally likely to remain more or less same

There are some states where more or less similar result is expected in 2019 as compared to 2014.

- **Bengal** –BJP's vote share suffered a substantial decline in 2016 Assembly Elections vs. 2014 and the party's influence in the state is limited. Hence, it is unlikely that there will be any big change in BJP's tally from 2 out of 42 seats in the state.
- **Tamil Nadu** –2016 Assembly Elections vote percentage actually indicated a decline in the state for the party. We think it is unlikely that there will be any big change in BJP's tally from 1 out of 39 seats in the state.

- **Andhra Pradesh** –BJP has a decent presence in the state but the party is still a junior partner to Telugu Desam Party of N Chandrababu Naidu and it is unlikely that there will be any big change in BJP's tally from 2 out of 25 seats in the state.
- **Kerala** – The BJP's vote percentage has not increased significantly despite making huge effort in this Southern state and it is unlikely that there will be any big change in BJP's tally from current 0 out of 20 seats in the state.
- **Telangana** – This is an interesting case and there is a possibility that TRS will have to face some anti-incumbency in the state. But, it is not certain if BJP will be the primary beneficiary. BJP is still below the threshold level in vote percentage to convert it into a large number of seats, it is unlikely that there will be any big change in BJP's tally from current 1 out of 17 seats in the state.
- **Assam** – BJP already has 7 out of 14 seats in the state and also leading the Government in state. So, apart from minor variations, it is unlikely that there will be any big change in BJP's tally.

There are also some states where BJP had done exceedingly well in 2014 such as Himachal Pradesh and Goa. Though there is a theoretical possibility of a decline in number of seats BJP has in these states, we think the change is unlikely to be big. And even if that happens in some of these smaller states, it won't change the overall picture much at the national level.

High possibility of a decline in BJP's tally in 2019 General Elections

Now, we come to the more important part. Among the larger states, we think there are some areas where the decline in BJP's tally is either likely or possible.

- **Uttar Pradesh**–Just like Punjab which we discussed in one of the previous sections, it may look impossible after a sensational victory in UP Assembly Elections. But 73 out of 80 seats are with NDA today (BJP has 71) and in addition, the BJP state Government would be two years old by that time and anti-incumbency against Yogi Adityanath[4] administration could be likely. UP will be the most critical for BJP and retaining 71 seats would be a challenge.
- **Bihar** – With BJP-Nitish coalition in power now, BJP is unlikely to do as well as it did in 2014 because JDU would ask for a respectable number at the time of seats' allotment in a pre-poll alliance. It is highly likely that BJP's tally would decline from 22 out of 40 in the state though NDA has a chance to increase from 31 to a higher number.
- **Gujarat** – All 26 seats are with BJP and the CMs who succeeded Modi have not been as successful. There is also a simmering anger in the Patidar community which is numerically important in the state. Overall, 26/26 result looks difficult in the state despite the fact that Congress is still lying comatose in the state and has weakened further after Shankar Singh Vaghela's exit and the other opposition party (AAP) has not been able to make any significant impact in the state politics.

- **Rajasthan** – All 25 seats are with BJP today and the anti-incumbency against Vasundhara Raje Government is likely to be the key. Power has been a game of musical chairs in the state and usually, the incumbents find it really hard to remain popular. The success of 2014 is going to be difficult for BJP to replicate in 2019.
- **Madhya Pradesh** – BJP had won 27 out of 29 seats in 2014 and after UP, the second largest contingent of BJP MPs in 16th *Lok Sabha* came from this state. However, a fatigue is creeping in against the state Government led by Shivraj Singh Chouhan. For BJP, it would not be easy to achieve the performance of 2014 again in 2019.

There are some other smaller states such as Jharkhand, Chhattisgarh, Haryana, Delhi and Uttarakhand where one or more factors such as, a) BJP has very high proportion of seats, b) the BJP is in state Government, c) the Assembly Elections post 2014 in the respective states have seen a dip in BJP's vote share, could be responsible for a decline in BJP's tally in 2019.

In the following table with states and Union Territories in an alphabetical order, we have put the total number of *Lok Sabha* seats and BJP's tally in 2009 and 2014. On the basis of our discussion so far, we have also made a qualitative assessment as to how BJP is likely to perform in 2019. To keep it simple, we have only put the states/UTs in three buckets, a) Increment possible, b) likely to remain largely similar, and, c) there is high possibility of a decline in BJP's tally of *Lok Sabha* seats.

Table 7.1: States and UTs – BJP's likely performance in 2019

State/Union Territory	Total Seats	BJP in 2009	BJP in 2014	BJP in 2019 (likely scenario)
A and N Islands	1	1	1	Likely to remain largely similar
Andhra Pradesh	25	0	2	Likely to remain largely similar
Arunachal Pradesh	2	0	1	Likely to remain largely similar
Assam	14	4	7	Likely to remain largely similar
Bihar	40	12	22	High possibility of decline
Chandigarh	1	0	1	Likely to remain largely similar
Chhattisgarh	11	10	10	High possibility of decline
Dadra and Nagar Haveli	1	1	1	Likely to remain largely similar
Daman and Diu	1	1	1	Likely to remain largely similar
Goa	2	1	2	Likely to remain largely similar
Gujarat	26	15	26	High possibility of decline
Haryana	10	0	7	High possibility of decline
Himachal Pradesh	4	3	4	Likely to remain largely similar
Jammu and Kashmir	6	0	3	Likely to remain largely similar
Jharkhand	14	8	12	High possibility of decline
Karnataka	28	19	17	Increment possible
Kerala	20	0	0	Likely to remain largely similar
Lakshadweep	1	0	0	Likely to remain largely similar
Madhya Pradesh	29	16	27	High possibility of decline
Maharashtra	48	9	23	Increment possible
Manipur	2	0	0	Increment possible
Meghalaya	2	0	0	Likely to remain largely similar
Mizoram	1	0	0	Likely to remain largely similar
Nagaland	1	0	0	Likely to remain largely similar
Delhi	7	0	7	High possibility of decline
Odisha	21	0	1	Increment possible
Puducherry	1	0	0	Likely to remain largely similar
Punjab	13	1	2	Increment possible
Rajasthan	25	4	25	High possibility of decline
Sikkim	1	0	0	Likely to remain largely similar

State/Union Territory	Total Seats	BJP in 2009	BJP in 2014	BJP in 2019 (likely scenario)
Tamil Nadu	39	0	1	Likely to remain largely similar
Telangana	17	0	1	Likely to remain largely similar
Tripura	2	0	0	Likely to remain largely similar
Uttar Pradesh	80	10	71	High possibility of decline
Uttarakhand	5	0	5	High possibility of decline
West Bengal	42	1	2	Likely to remain largely similar
Total	543	116	282	

Note: BJP in 2019 (likely scenario) is based on our assessment and interpretation.

Source: Election Commission of India for number of *Lok Sabha* seats in a state and BJP's tally in 2009 and 2014.

For 2019, we think there is a chink in BJP's armour. Of the 247 seats where there is a possibility of decline in BJP's tally, BJP had won 212 in 2014 and this contributed 75 percent of the MPs the party have in 16th *Lok Sabha*. These are only 45 percent of total *Lok Sabha* seats where BJP had 85 percent plus success rate. This makes the party excessively dependant and vulnerable. Even if BJP falters in a few states which are large, the overall reduction in BJP's tally could be meaningful.

Of the 184 seats where there is a likelihood of no big change in BJP's tally of seats, BJP had won 27 seats in 2014 and this contributed less than 10 percent of the MPs the party have in the 16th *Lok Sabha*. These are 1/3rd of total *Lok Sabha* seats where BJP had 15 percent success rate. This number is susceptible to some change but that is unlikely to be very big and hence, this change may not really be material in altering the overall picture in 2019.

Of the remaining 112 seats where an increment is possible for BJP, the party had won 43 seats in 2014 and this contributed approximately 15 percent of the MPs the party have in the 16th *Lok Sabha*. These 112 seats represent approximately 20 percent of total *Lok Sabha* seats where BJP had 40 percent plus success rate. Even in the best case scenario, the overall tally for BJP in these seats is unlikely to cross 60-65 from the current number which is 43. Hence, this may not really be sufficient to compensate for the possible losses in those 247 *Lok Sabha* seats where BJP currently has 212 MPs today.

Table 7.2: The likely scenario for 2019 – Qualitative Assessment

	Total	BJP's seats in 2014	Percent of Total	Percent of BJP seats
High possibility of decline	247	212	45 percent	75 percent
Likely to remain largely similar	184	27	34 percent	10 percent
Increment possible	112	43	21 percent	15 percent
Total	543	**282**		

Note: 1) Percent of Total is calculated as number of seats divided by 543, 2) percent of BJP seats is calculated as number of seats divided by 282.

Source: Election Commission of India

We do agree that the following exercise is completely mathematical. But, let us try this out. What happens in a scenario where, a) High possibility of decline – BJP lose 1/3rd of its current tally, b) Likely to remain largely similar – BJP maintains its tally, and, c) Increment possible - BJP wins 1/3rd of the extra seats where the party doesn't have its MPs today. In this case, the BJP could lose approximately 50 seats from the number it has today and would have a tally of 234 in 17th *Lok Sabha*. This is good enough to form a coalition Government but the Government will be at the mercy of whimsical regional political outfits.

Table 7.3: The scenario ONE for 2019

	Total	BJP's seats in 2019	Percent of Total	Percent of BJP seats
From high possibility of decline	247	**141 (212 – 1/3rd of 212)**	45 Percent	60 Percent
From "Likely to remain largely similar"	184	**27 (same as 27)**	34 Percent	12 Percent
From "Increment possible"	112	**66(43 + 1/3rd of 69)**	21 Percent	28 Percent
Total	543	**234**		

Note: 1) percent of Total is calculated as number of seats divided by 543, 2) percent of BJP seats is calculated as number of seats divided by 234.

Source: Election Commission of India

In another similar mathematical scenario, let us see what happens in a situation where, a) High possibility of decline – BJP lose 50 percent of its tally, b) Likely to remain largely similar – BJP maintains its tally, and, c) Increment possible - BJP wins 50 percent of the extra seats where BJP doesn't have its MPs today. In this case, the BJP could lose approximately 70 seats from 282 and would have a tally of 211. Considering the aversion of several opposition parties towards BJP, this is most likely the scenario where a non-BJP coalition government looks more realistic. In this case even if BJP is able to form a Government, it would be hopelessly dependant on its allies and dysfunctional.

Table 7.4: The scenario TWO for 2019 in numbers

	Total	BJP's seats in 2019	Percent of Total	Percent of BJP seats
From high possibility of decline	247	**106 (212 – 1/2 of 212)**	45percent	50percent
From "Likely to remain largely similar"	184	**27 (same as 27)**	34percent	13percent
From "Increment possible"	112	**78 (43 + 1/2 of 69)**	21percent	37percent
Total	543	**211**		

Note: 1) percent of Total is calculated as number of seats divided by 543, 2) percent of BJP seats is calculated as number of seats divided by 211.

Source: Election Commission of India

In the next Chapter

We have seen in this chapter that though there are some states such as Maharashtra where BJP can improve its seats tally in 2019; this looks a very challenging task on an overall basis across the country. It is difficult to forecast what the exact number would look like but it is highly likely that BJP would end up somewhere between 220-230 seats. If things get a little bit more challenging for the party closer to the elections, the number could even fall further to somewhere close to 200. Please note that we are not making this assessment by making an assumption that Modi would experience a serious decline in his popularity. This means that in the most probable scenario for 2019, either we would see a non-BJP coalition Government or a BJP Government which is much more dependent on allies than today. In both these cases, this will be a qualitatively and materially different situation. In the next Chapter, we will take a look at what BJP can do to mitigate some of the challenges it has to face in 2019. In a real-time situation, the response of one player is determined by how the other is playing but under all situations, a better prepared side does better. If it wins, it wins with a better margin and even if it loses, it loses with a smaller margin.

8

THE KEY TAKEAWAYS FOR BJP FOR 2019

Be willing to lose a battle in order to win the war.

— H. Jackson Brown, Jr.[1]

What is important for BJP in 2019 elections?

On the basis of what we have discussed so far, we think a few important inferences can be drawn. And some of these inferences mean that the strategy and election campaign of BJP in 2019 may have to look very different vs. how the party had run this in 2014. This may also require accommodating allies a bit more. Another area is that the communication needs to get democratised and the local representatives need to get involved. Essentially, some of these things may also look very different as compared to how BJP is being seen today.

- Highlight the lack of alternatives to voters,
- Local Communication is the Key,
- Candidate selection has to be ruthless,
- Booth Management would be critical,
- Coalitions are important and need to be nurtured,
- Talk about the Unfinished Agenda.

Highlight the lack of alternatives to voters

For any Government which served a full term, it is natural to talk about its achievements. The case for NDA would not be different in 2019. The voters would be interested in seeing the NDA report card and evaluate them on the basis of performance vs. promise. Hence, it is likely that the BJP campaign would focus on the Government's performance in economy, job creation, inflation control, foreign policy, internal security and other vital areas. If BJP has a solid report card to display in front of the electorate, it will certainly help.

However, we think that it will be a faulty strategy because that alone is not going to be sufficient. We think more important focus area for BJP would need to be the comparison with its competitors. The party needs to emphasise that it is the best choice available for voters. BJP needs to tell the electorate that people don't have enough good choices available to reject BJP. This may sound like a message to the voters ***"OK, even when BJP may not be good enough compared to the expectations and NDA Government could have done better in five years from 2014 to 2019, the other choices are worse and voters still need to choose BJP".*** This is not an apology but an attempt to make the voters realise that irrespective of their view on BJP, the alternatives are far worse.

As discussed in the ***Chapter 2, 2014 Mandate: UPA – The Story of Self-Goals*** that it hardly matters if a candidate or a party is good or bad in absolute terms. The comparison is always relative and as long as a political party can convince the electorate that it is better than others, the job is done. This may require a shift in the campaign strategy from BJP. While it was seeking a positive vote on the issues of development and clean administration in 2014, BJP has to seek a negative vote against opposition in 2019 by convincing voters that other choices are far worse than BJP and they cannot trust the alternatives available.

Local Communication is the Key

The Central leadership of BJP is extremely particular about communicating to the electorate and does it very efficiently. Prime Minister is articulate and savvy in communication. The launches of programs like *"Mann ki Baat"*, Regular newsletters from the Prime Minister's Office (PMO) and other Ministries, use of new age communication mediums and effective use of social media indicate that BJP top leadership takes communication with voters very seriously. This may be in complete contrast with curtailed access to journalists and media at the Ministries and tight control on information dissemination by other constituents of the Government, but at least the general public can't really complain about not knowing what the Government and the Prime Minister are up to.

However, the same cannot be claimed about all the state leadership and elected representatives in their respective areas. One very pertinent and relatively recent example is of demonetisation. While the Prime Minister, Finance Minister and senior bureaucrats were speaking on this subject almost every day immediately after the notification to assuage the concerns of general public and highlight the rationale behind this move, many of the local representatives were either not too sure about the benefits of this step or didn't really feel that it was important for them to go to their respective areas and directly talk to people. The question is always not whether or not the voters would be convinced but in many instances the voters feel comforted that the elected representatives are listening to them and there is a two way communication.

This is also linked to the perception which has been created today that the Prime Minister is just too powerful in the NDA Government and the party affairs are in complete control of BJP President Amit Shah. It is not a bad thing *per se* because the party can always go to the voters asking for votes in the name of Narendra Modi. Similarly, Amit Shah is handling the party affairs with amazing dexterity and the results are there for everyone to see. In short, the Modi-Shah combination is successful. Ultimately, that is what matters and is the most important yardstick to determine a leader's political acumen in a democracy.

However, if there is a section of voters which believes that other leaders of BJP don't really matter, it may get disenchanted because the tight control of PMO on the Government could be seen as a reflection of authoritarian tendency by these voters. That may become really difficult to defend for party candidates in elections and could lead to loss of some popular support. That is a risk which we think is best avoided from BJP's perspective. There is also an argument that a typical Indian voter loves strong leaders and that means they don't mind a little bit of authoritarian trait in them. The success of Mrs. Indira Gandhi is considered a proof of that. However, it is a double edged sword and a more balanced mix can always work better.

Overall, it could be important for BJP that elected representatives and party functionaries are instructed to effectively communicate to the voters in their respective areas about how the Government is doing and the initiatives which are being taken for benefit of the people. In this age of social media and continuous flow of information, there is nothing called "over communication" and even if there is, it is unlikely to harm a party more than "under communication".

A case in point is the mistake committed by the previous UPA Government where all the prominent leaders including Congress President, Mrs. Sonia Gandhi, Congress Vice President, Mr. Rahul Gandhi and the Prime Minister, Dr. Manmohan Singh were seen hesitating in communicating to media and the public. This may have cost dearly to UPA and Congress. Of course, there is no such problem at the top with BJP but things are far from perfect when it comes to local BJP representatives.

Candidate selection has to be ruthless

If we look at Narendra Modi's tenure in Gujarat as the Chief Minister, it is possible that in 2002 Assembly Elections in the state, he may not have been allowed the complete freedom and final authority to choose all the BJP candidates who will contest. He was new at that time as Gujarat CM and had a lot many other battles to fight than worrying about putting his stamp of full authority in ticket distribution for Gujarat Assembly Elections in 2002.

However, this happened in 2007. In the Gujarat assembly polls in 2007, Modi had dropped as many as 47 members which eliminated anti-incumbency factor at grassroots level to a large extent. This was important to address the dissatisfaction of voters against some of the elected representatives.[2]

In 2012 Gujarat Assembly Elections, there was no need for Modi to do the same.

- By that time, Modi was already a big leader getting ready to move to the national stage and he was more self-assured than he would have been in 2007. He perhaps was also convinced that people will want to vote for Modi in those elections no matter who is contesting on a BJP ticket.
- There was also a minor threat from the outfit launched by ex-CM, Keshu Bhai Patel[3] that if Modi drops too many of his MLAs, they may create trouble for the official BJP candidates by joining the rival outfit.

However, Modi-Shah would need to be ruthless by dropping non-performing MPs in 2019 and that would be an important prerequisite for BJP to do well. There would be a serious need to get rid of deadwood both in terms of non-performing Chief Ministers and BJP's elected representatives across levels.

Booth Management would be critical

This is an interesting comparison between what had happened in 2014 and what could be the case in 2019. In 2014, the BJP and RSS cadre was very enthusiastic about Modi and as discussed in the ***Chapter 2, 2014 Mandate: UPA - The Story of Self Goals***, a large section of voters was so fed up and frustrated with UPA that they came to polling booths and voted for BJP. Now, this sentiment could become significantly weaker in 2019 both among party cadre and also among voters who formed the part of negative vote against UPA in 2014.

This may not really matter that much where BJP is just too strong or Opposition is just too weak, but if there is only a small gap, things might get more difficult for BJP in 2019. Please note that we are not making an assumption that party cadre would not be rooting for Modi and would not put in the hard work, but there could be some amount of complacency that might set in among the dedicated workers after seeing more successes than failures under PM's leadership in elections.

Whether we call them stray acts of indiscipline or a fundamental shift in behaviour, there were instances in last three to four years where even dedicated RSS workers have revolted against the entry of outsiders in BJP. These RSS volunteers have alleged that preferential treatment is being given to the outsiders and some of them also have the complaints that Central Goveernment and BJP's state Governments are not showing enough loyalty to the agenda of the organisation. Once a party is in power, it is natural that there would be difficulty in meeting the aspirations of each and every worker and some of the party leaders who have worked for decades, may feel ignored, sidelined and forgotten. That discontent could be a big source of potential risk for the party.

Similarly, the people who voted for BJP because they wanted to throw UPA out could become much less enthusiastic in voting for BJP in 2019. The negative emotions are more powerful than positive emotions when the stimulus remains equal and hence, these people felt very strongly about UPA's poor performance in 2014. They were very enthusiastically voting for BJP because any alternative to UPA would have worked and they also saw that Modi is a stronger alternative. They may not be unhappy with Modi's performance as the Prime Minister, but they would certainly not make a huge effort to go to the polling station on the day of the elections.

In this context, it would be extremely important for BJP to ensure that the cadre remains enthused and each and every BJP supporter casts his or her vote. For a very long time, this has been a key strength of cadre based parties. Their foot soldiers do a very good job in ensuring that no voter is left behind. BJP has been a huge beneficiary of having a efficient network on the ground which helps in converting supporters into BJP votes in a big way. This need to continue in 2019 and that is an absolute necessity for BJP to do well in the next General Elections.

Coalitions are important and need to be nurtured

No political party wants to be at the mercy of others. However, as the Congress became less powerful and BJP was yet to become a pan-India national party in the true sense despite making huge strides in last few years, coalition governments became a reality of Indian politics. Under these situations, running the Government gets even more complicated as the leading partner in a coalition has to invest a huge amount of time and effort in pacifying the allies.

If the allies are throwing tantrums continuously, why should not a party try to eliminate the need of a coalition at the first place? That is a great idea and BJP seems to be working very hard to achieve it. However, India is a large and diverse country and building a base at every nook and corner takes time. In fact, even if we look at the definition of a national party as per the guidelines of Election Commission (EC), we realise that it may not really come across as truly representative.

Today, we have a situation where even if we include some of the states with strong presence of regional parties such as Karnataka and Assam, there are only about 150 seats where the national parties in true sense (BJP and Congress) are in direct contest. These include Madhya Pradesh (29), Karnataka (28), Gujarat (26), Rajasthan (25), Assam (14), Chhattisgarh (11), Haryana (10), Uttarakhand (5), Himachal Pradesh (4), Goa and Arunachal Pradesh (2 each). In all other places there is a strong presence of either regional parties or the parties which cannot be called national parties in practical sense, such as Left parties. In this situation, it is more likely that mandates like 2014 would be few and far in between.

Another important factor is that for many parties in the country, BJP is still untouchable. For example, the Left parties are unlikely to ally themselves with BJP. Similarly, the core constituency of Samajwadi party is in direct conflict with BJP. Remember when Mulayam Singh Yadav had to backtrack almost instantly after declaring a tie up with ex-Chief Minister of Uttar Pradesh, Mr. Kalyan Singh[4]. Also, for many regional parties, the combination of Modi-Shah comes across as very aggressive and there is an impression that BJP is squeezing out the allies wherever possible. For example, the sentiment Shiv Sena expresses from time to time. This perception could be a challenge for BJP in case there happens to be a weaker performance by the party in 2019 as compared to 2014.

Hence, it is necessary that BJP should be prepared for an unclear verdict in 2019. That would require seeking support from regional parties and stitching an alliance which can reach the required number of 272+ in *Lok Sabha*. In case a party is not able to reach even 235-240 MPs, support from even more political parties than the required number of 272 is needed to govern effectively. Of course, BJP leadership would not want a repeat of 1999 when Atal Bihari Vajpayee led NDA Government lost the confidence of House by just one vote in the floor test. This strategy may work if some recalibration on BJP's part is carried out and the party leaves a little more space for allies. Tactical withdrawal and ceding a few inches in some battles are all part and parcel of the war strategy. BJP might have to adopt such a strategy in 2019.

Talk about the Unfinished Agenda

BJP can benefit by talking about two things simultaneously, a) the party has to convince the electorate that the situation in the country and for the economy was so bad in 2014 that it required a lot of effort to bring things back on track, and, b) BJP was not interested in adopting a short term approach based on quick fix, populist methods. If the BJP can convince the voters that in the 2014-19 phase, if the Government's performance is not up to their expectations, it is only because of the mess the country was in at the time of NDA taking over in 2014. BJP would benefit by highlighting that addressing policy paralysis and revival of sluggish economy requires considerable time and going for an overnight drastic change could have massively backfired.

One of the key themes for BJP could be the 'unfinished agenda' of the Government and it would help BJP to talk about the previous experiences. For example, BJP can tell voters that had Atal Bihari Vajpayee got another term in 2004, the country would have reached a different orbit of growth and development. The idea would be to tell people that if they make a wrong choice now, it will be impossible to rectify that mistake. Another approach could be to tell people about the dangers associated with a national party not getting a majority in *Lok Sabha*. At present it would require a herculean effort for Congress to compete well on its own in 2019 and the biggest danger for BJP may come from a coalition of regional parties led by Congress.

BJP would do well to highlight the previous experience of coalition Governments (1977, 1989, 1996 and 1998) which led to political instability and mid-term elections.

The message for the electorate is that they need to elect a strong and decisive Government and hence, the people's verdict needs to be unambiguous. Considering, it looks highly unlikely at this stage that there is a leader on the horizon who can offer himself or herself as a potentially good alternative to Modi and there is no non-BJP party which has magic figure of 272 in its reach, BJP will gain by rousing this sentiment in general public.

Facing a hostile opposition and belligerent media and yet winning three consecutive state elections and then remaining as popular and as loved even after three and a half years of running the Central Government is nothing short of a miracle and Narendra Modi has achieved this. He leads from the front and never shies away from taking the fight to the Opposition camp. Even after fifteen long years, Modi still has the image of a "clean and tough leader" and he is the best bet for BJP. In front of Modi-Shah combination, Opposition is struggling hard to get its moorings back. The Modi magic had worked so well in 2014 and it can work again in 2019 if BJP plays its cards well and Opposition continues to make the mistakes they made in 2014 and later. Make no mistake, Modi has delivered several firsts in his political career and his reelection in 2019, Opposition or for that matter, anyone else can discount at his or her own peril.

Table 8.1: SWOT of BJP as a Leading National Party

BHARATIYA JANATA PARTY			
S STRENGTHS	W WEAKNESSES	O OPPORTUNITIES	T THREATS
• Strong Cadre of BJP and RSS • The combination of PM Modi and Amit Shah as President of BJP is working well • No major Scams despite spending more than three years in the Government	• Economy is struggling in several areas and Job Creation is far from optimal • Excessive Dependence on Narendra Modi • Not All BJP led State Governments have performed well	• Weak and fragmented Opposition • Expansion of footprint in unchartered territories • Consolidation of Party's position as the leading and No. 1 national party in India	• True Impact of Demonetization and GST Implementation on the "Bottom of the Pyramid" Population is still unknown • Allies' Discomfort with BJP's Aggressive Approach • Consolidation of Opposition vote could lead to major electoral damage

In the next Chapter

We have seen in this chapter that BJP would need to adopt a strategy in 2019 which is different vs. what was successful for the party in 2014. Not just they would have to talk about their performance in this term, it would also help to highlight that the country lacks a credible alternative to BJP. In the next Chapter, we will take a look at what the opposition can do to challenge Modi effectively in 2019. The important characteristic of democracy is the fact that no matter how invincible a leader may appear, things can change rather quickly and history has enough examples to prove the same.

9

THE KEY TAKEAWAYS FOR OPPOSITION FOR 2019

> It's a long time until the next election, but it starts now. And if you truly want to see things change in the direction that our country is headed, you have to stay involved. You cannot quit now.
>
> — Deb Fischer[1]

In the previous chapter, we have looked at the strategies which may work for BJP in 2019 though some of them might even look counter intuitive. For example, less focus on NDA track record in this term and allowing the allies a little more breathing space. Naturally, there would also be a few things which Opposition may try to counter Modi in the next General Elections. In this chapter, we will look at some of them and if played well can help the Opposition. Despite the fact that Modi's effort so far has proved to be super-human in understanding the pulse of Indian voters and his electoral performance has been unprecedented, the vote share of BJP is a reasonable distance away from making him or his party, BJP invincible.

Though the national foot print of BJP is expanding, it is far from complete. There is least 1/4th of the country where the political presence of the party is at best on the fringes. As we have highlighted at several other places over the course of this book, this means that there is a chink in the armour of BJP and that could be the key for Opposition to do well in 2019 General Elections. The first thing which the combined Opposition can get solace from is that electoral politics is extremely fickle and even Mrs. Indira Gandhi had lost the elections in the Janata Party wave of 1977. Nothing is permanent in politics and each political battle is another chance of redemption for the vanquished.

Even big names have seen swift changes in political fortunes. Similarly, it might only be a very small scale experiment which needs to be replicated at the national level in *Lok Sabha* elections; AAP could sweep Delhi Assembly Elections by winning 67 out of 70 seats and relegating the national parties to become virtual non-entities (BJP with 3 seats and Congress 0) in a short span of time.

Before we get into the key inferences we can draw from the contrasting styles of Narendra Modi and other politicians and how that can be used by Opposition, it would be worthwhile to take a look at the political journey of Congress leader, Late Shri Madhav Rao Scindia who never lost an election and though we can only speculate, was a leader who could have been the Prime Minister in 2004, had he been alive. This story would be indicative that political fortunes could change very quickly for any leader irrespective of his or her popularity.

Late Shri Madhav Rao Scindia: Nine times winner in Lok Sabha elections

The Scindia royal family from Gwalior was one of the most powerful princely states during the times of British rule. The importance of Scindias can be understood from the fact that the ruler of Gwalior was only one of the five rulers across India, entitled to a 21 gun salute during British rule. After independence, the Late Smt. Vijaya Raje Scindia[2] (grandmother of Congress leader Shri Jyotiraditya Scindia and mother of Late Shri Madhav Rao Scindia and present Chief Minister of Rajasthan, Mrs. Vasundhara Raje) entered politics.

Smt. Vijaya Raje Scindia was one of the prominent faces of Jana Sangh (later BJP) not just in the Gwalior-Guna-Shivpuri region but also in the entire Madhya Pradesh and some adjoining areas. Following his mother and, as soon as he met the eligibility criteria to fight the elections, Madhav Rao Scindia entered *Lok Sabha* from Guna (in Madhya Pradesh) constituency and till the time he died in a tragic air crash in 2002, never lost an election.

There is a more interesting part. In 1984, Madhav Rao Scindia unexpectedly switched his constituency from Guna to Gwalior and defeated one of the tallest leaders of BJP and a future Prime Minister. When Madhav Rao had filed his nomination papers immediately before the close of the deadline, it was considered a politically suicidal move for Scindia. Gwalior was always a stronghold of BJP and there was no way someone like Mr. Atal Bihari Vajpayee could lose to a new entrant and novice like Madhav Rao.

However, the result was shocking as Vajpayee lost by a huge margin of more than 175,000 votes in 1984 *Lok Sabha* Elections from the Gwalior constituency. Though it came at the time of massive sympathy wave in favour of Congress and many stalwarts from Opposition lost in these elections (for example, Hemvati Nandan Bahuguna[3] to Amitabh Bachchan[4] in Allahabad), this huge defeat was so painful and humiliating for Atal Bihari Vajpayee that he never returned to Gwalior as a contestant after 1984.

Table 9.1: Madhav Rao Scindia's political journey seen through his election victories

Year	Constituency	Winner	Party	Votes	Nearest Rival	Party	Votes	Difference
1999	Guna	Madhav Rao Scindia	INC	443,965	Rao Deshraj Singh Yadav	BJP	229,537	214,428
1998	Gwalior	Madhav Rao Scindia	INC	284,365	Jaibhan Singh Pavaiya	BJP	258,086	26,279
1996	Gwalior	Madhav Rao Scindia	MPVC	337,539	Phool Singh Baraiya	BSP	113,545	223,994
1991	Gwalior	Madhav Rao Scindia	INC	195,212	Shejwalkar N.K.	BJP	96,156	99,056
1989	Gwalior	Madhav Rao Scindia	INC	279,799	Sheetla Sahai	BJP	130,374	149,425
1984	Gwalior	Madhav Rao Scindia	INC	307,735	Atal Bihari Vajpayee	BJP	132,141	175,594
1980	Guna	Madhav Rao Scindia	INC	203,176	Naresh Johri Balakram	JNP	87,050	116,126
1977	Guna	Madhav Rao Scindia	IND	184,513	Gurbakhsh Singh Thakur Singh	BLD	108,062	76,451
1971	Guna	Madhav Rao Scindia	BJS	209,950	Devrao Krishna Rao Jadhav	INC	68,860	141,090

Source: Election Commission of India, http://www.elections.in/madhya-pradesh/parliamentary-constituencies/gwalior.html, http://www.elections.in/madhya-pradesh/parliamentary-constituencies/guna.html

The story is not complete yet. As the Railway Minister in Rajiv Gandhi Government and later on, as a senior Minister in P V Narasimha Rao Government, Madhav Rao nurtured his constituency well and Gwalior became a very safe seat for Congress as a party and for Scindia as an MP. So much so that when he was expelled from Congress by Narasimha Rao and fought the *Lok Sabha* elections in 1996 as an independent candidate (under a newly floated, Madhya Pradesh Vikas Congress under the symbol of *The Rising Sun*), he recorded the best ever victory margin of his entire political career.

However, the story was entirely different a couple of years later. In 1998, BJP fielded a strong candidate, Jaibhan Singh Pavaiya and he ran a spirited campaign. Even after twenty years, we still remember watching "Madhav Rao Scindia – Gwalior – TRAILING" on a TV set near Vidyasagar Setu in Kolkata, this was something totally unbelievable. In the end, Madhav Rao scraped through with a very small margin of about 25,000 votes. This was the smallest victory margin of his career spanning nine *Lok Sabha* elections. Had Scindia lost, this could have been one of the biggest upsets of those elections.

The local grapevine suggests that in the 1998 elections, Scindia had inkling that he has a tough fight in hand and he had to make frantic calls to all his key supporters across the Gwalior constituency in the last 3-4 days just before the voting, asking them to mobilise voters in large numbers so that they cast their votes in favour of Scindia. The task was made even more difficult because after successive victories in 1984, 1989, 1991 and 1996 (with a massive and unprecedented margin even from the standards of Madhav Rao Scindia), his core support base had perhaps become complacent and was under the impression that Maharaj Scindia will eventually win, no matter what happens as his victory is a foregone conclusion.

It may only be a conjecture but many political analysts still believe that this was a difficult thing for even Scindia to digest and this dangerously thin victory margin in 1998 was one of the key reasons for him to shift his constituency back to Guna from Gwalior in the next elections of 1999. Madhav Rao Scindia remained (and he still is, even after almost 15 years of his untimely and tragic death) an extremely popular political figure in Gwalior, Guna, Shivpuri and many adjoining areas.

In Gwalior, a lot of old timers still fondly remember the privileges and development which come with being a VIP constituency (such as the extension of Taj Express to Gwalior, the compulsory stoppage of all the important trains at Gwalior despite being a short distance away and sandwiched between Jhansi and Agra, the India-West Indies cricket match in 1996 Cricket World Cup, Development of Malanpur as an Industrial area, the Railway Spring factory at Sithouli etc.).

Madhav Rao Scindia was a prominent leader of Congress for several years and he was also serving as the leader of Opposition in *Lok Sabha* at the time of his death, but he could not avert a near defeat experience in 1998. The message is simple: voters are fickle and the standard mutual fund investments disclaimer applies to politics as well: ***Past performance is not indicative of future returns.***

Coalition is the only way to effectively counter Modi

If they have to do well individually and collectively in 2019, it is necessary for the Opposition parties to set aside their differences and arrive at workable seat sharing arrangements among them. Despite Modi wave, BJP is still some distance away from being such a dominant force in Indian Politics that even a combined Opposition can't defeat it. It would be good for the anti-Modi forces if the Opposition realises that if they can't display unity in 2019, it may be too late for them to do so in 2024.

We have discussed the examples of Uttar Pradesh and Bihar in detail at various points in this book. Because these two states contributed 1/3rd of BJP's members in 16th *Lok Sabha*, they are extremely crucial for BJP to do well in 2019. More importantly, BJP would be vulnerable in UP if the Opposition parties are able to stitch a formidable coalition. In Bihar, it is likely to win less number of seats than the number it had in 2014 because after a tie-up with JDU, the seat sharing agreement will require that BJP allocates at least 18-20 seats to its allies in Bihar. If there is a united front of opposition parties across India, it would not be impossible to work out a solid plan to effectively counter and neutralise the Modi wave in 2019 General Elections.

There are several other states where its allies feel threatened due to BJP's aggressive approach and that sentiment can be exploited to forge a powerful coalition by opposition parties. For example, Maharashtra is a state where the relations between Shiv Sena and BJP are not at their best. Despite being allies in the state Government, BJP and Shiv Sena are continuously at loggerheads and that may provide an interesting opportunity for Opposition. While there are other states as well where BJP did not have enough vote share to win without a split in the opposition vote (such as Assam and Haryana), the prescription to Opposition remains generic that they need to avoid the split in the anti-BJP vote to be able to stop Modi in 2019 elections.

Frontal attack against Modi is a faulty strategy

Even in Gujarat, a frontal attack by Congress against Narendra Modi did not really work very well. The reasons may lie in the fact that Modi doesn't have the typical weaknesses which characterise politicians in India:

- it is difficult to argue that Modi is corrupt, the dirt simply doesn't stick to him and it is difficult to create an impression that he works for the benefit of a certain group of politicians or industrialists,
- the charges of nepotism doesn't work against him, he doesn't have a family of his own and his extended family continues to live under an ordinary or even sometimes less than ordinary existence,
- it is difficult to charge him with the allegation that he is working under the influence of a coterie, he is his own man and there is no proof to substantiate that allegation,
- it is difficult to argue that he ignores his responsibilities because he is extremely hard working and seems to be on the job 24x7,
- the opposition can't question his personal life and his lack of experience or lack of political acumen, he simply does not have those flaws (at least they are not common knowledge, if you insist) which Opposition can exploit.

To put it simply, Narendra Modi does not make many mistakes and as an Opposition, you don't get many chances against him. It is also difficult to accuse him of things which may strike a chord with general public, whether it is his personal or professional conduct. The continuous attack by Opposition on him in fact backfires because it creates an impression that;

- Opposition is trying to create issues when there are none and that makes the credibility of opposition parties questionable,
- People think that Modi is being targeted because he is trying to change the system and since he is an outsider, the Opposition is targeting him unfairly and unnecessarily.

This works towards Modi's advantage as voters sympathise with him for being an unfair target of opposition parties' attack. Once people see the attacks of Opposition on Modi as an attempt to target an innocent person who would be working with good intentions, they become immune to even genuine and fair criticism of Modi. They would see everything even things where Modi can be rightfully blamed as an unfair exercise and totally biased attempt.

It also makes some of the more neutral people pro-Modi because many of them think that the Opposition is not really allowing a fair chance to Modi and the opposition leaders are trying to impose their will on people by force. Many of those who were earlier indifferent may also become Modi supporters because in their view, not allowing democratically elected representatives of people to govern is also undemocratic and they think Opposition is guilty of doing that.

Targeting local representatives and State Governments is going to work better

Except for the hardened BJP supporters, though many people may not be too willing to listen anything against Narendra Modi, these same people may still be open to a discussion on the failure of various BJP state governments and the sub-par performance of BJP's elected representatives. This could provide Opposition parties a better opportunity to target Modi and his Government.

Instead of Opposition attempting and saying that Narendra Modi is inefficient, the general public may become more receptive when the Opposition highlights that the team of Modi, the BJP run state Governments and local MPs are really no better than others. The Opposition may be perhaps more successful in seeking and finding the usual weaknesses politicians are known for in Modi's colleagues. Hence, this may prove to be a smarter strategy.

An important point is recent influx of leaders from other parties to BJP. Keeping in view the immediate political compulsions and in an attempt to woo powerful leaders across parties and across constituencies, BJP has allowed many old faces from other parties to join the party and many of these political figures have also been awarded tickets in elections. Some of them have even become Ministers with important portfolios. This has not just antagonised the loyal cadre of the party but has also made the perception of people a little different about BJP.

Since it is expected that many of these new entrants would find it really hard to change their methods of working overnight, the Opposition theoretically should be getting enough opportunities to capitalise on them. This is not to claim that the BJP politicians and politicians belonging to other parties are qualitatively different or not, but only to highlight that there are enough people in BJP now who would not have risen through the ranks or who ideologically would be different vs. the core RSS and BJP cadre.

Not just BJP leaders, the sentiment against BJP run state Governments could also create an opportunity for Opposition. The state Governments always has a tough task at hand in meeting the expectations of people and fulfilling all the promises they may have made during previous elections. This is a different situation vs. the National Governments because the key factors which influence the elections at the state level are always more local. Hence, this is not really a big surprise that in many of the states, anti-incumbency remains an almost permanent theme and it is difficult to buck that trend.

It may work better for Opposition to make the 2019 elections a much more local affair because that is where the probability of success could be higher. **The idea is not to talk that much about why Modi Government is a failure but talk more about how the local state Governments in BJP ruled states and elected representatives belonging to BJP have not done a good job.**

Table 9.1: SWOT of Congress as Leading Opposition Party

INDIAN NATIONAL CONGRESS

S STRENGTHS	W WEAKNESSES	O OPPORTUNITIES	T THREATS
• Rich Legacy continues to attract votes • More Acceptable to smaller Allies and Left Parties • Principal Opposition Party "by Default"	• Rahul Gandhi is still seen as disinterested and not a natural leader • On Ground Presence is very weak in Key States of Uttar Pradesh and Bihar • The Party has not been able to gain political mileage from BJP's mistakes • Lack of Visionary Leaders at National Level and strong state leaders	• Little to Lose in 2019 and Everything to Gain and the party can become the Axis for Anti-BJP Vote • Can Target the Weak Economic Revival under BJP Led Government • Opportunity to groom strong and effective state level leaders and enhance local representation	• BJP has snatched the Primary National Party Status • Lack of effective communication strategy • Intra party factionalism could affect electoral prospects

Don't allow BJP to make 2019 General Elections like a US President elections

This is a real problem area for Opposition. Today, Narendra Modi is the tallest leader in BJP, and outside BJP. And it is clear that there is no credible alternative to Modi at this juncture. So, the Opposition is really struggling to find a leader who can match Modi in his or her oratory, political understanding and fan following.

BJP had sensed this opportunity early on and even before 2014 elections, one of the main points in Modi's campaign was that he will bring back the glory of Prime Minister's Office. It is very likely that even in 2019, BJP would prominently highlight that Narendra Modi would be the only choice for people when it comes to electing a strong, decisive and powerful Prime Minister for India.

Another challenge for Opposition is that the space for principal Opposition Party is virtually vacant. While Congress has been shrinking and the party is finding it really difficult to build the same kind of aura around Rahul Gandhi as it was existing at the time of Jawaharlal Nehru, Indira Gandhi, Rajiv Gandhi or even Sonia Gandhi, there is no other party that seems to be ready or capable enough to occupy that space.

The Left had already been on a decline and doesn't really look like reinventing itself to make its ideology relevant for today's voter. The rest of the most powerful parties in opposition are regional in nature and don't carry a national appeal. The new entrants like Aam Aadmi Party have already started to disappoint people in proving that they are really different vs. other political parties.

The most likely scenario for 2019 elections is that

Opposition may not be able to build a consensus on its common PM candidate before the elections. Or even if they do, the Opposition's PM candidate is not match enough to Modi. In such a scenario, it may really make sense to not let the parliamentary election become like Presidential elections of USA. The Opposition may offer the explanation that in a parliamentary democracy like India, PM is only first among equals and the head of the Government is only as good as his/her team.

The Opposition may benefit more if it says that people should focus on the team and not just on who would be leading that team. This is not the best of situations and lack of alternatives to Modi will surely hurt the Opposition but whether it is a war or it is an election, there will not be a side without any weakness. The challenge is the same; the trick is to ensure that the damage gets minimised.

Election analytics and the use of new age mediums is important

The times have changed and technology has become all pervasive. The way people source information and seek news has also changed. Moreover, the easy and instant availability of information has also impacted the attention span of the people. In an age when fame is for 15 seconds and people move on very quickly with so many different stimuli competing for their attention, it is very easy for people to get disengaged.

This means that brands and personalities have to evolve continuously to stay relevant to an audience which is extremely demanding and flooded with incessant bombardment of choices. The election campaigns have also evolved accordingly and the political parties are trying to maximise the impact through key influencing channels.

In addition, just like the marketing for consumer goods which has become more targeted today and profiling of customer has become extremely important, the elections are also working on the same principle. People do not want generic communication and that won't appeal to them. They want message that is personalised, specific and relevant to them and then only, it is possible to strike a chord with them.

The advent of web and social media based campaigning has increasingly started to play a critical role at least in urban areas and with the young voters (in the 18 to 25 years age bracket and especially among the first time voters). And as the urbanisation has been fast in India and the average population is getting younger, this is hardly an area which can be ignored by the political parties today.

Being responsive and changing with the times creates a positive aura around a party. The voters think that the organisation is not rooted in the past and can meet the aspirations of a young and modern India. For example, it would be pertinent to highlight that the use of unconventional mediums for campaigning and fund raising by Aam Aadmi Party played an important role in its formative years when the party lacked resources to compete with others, who were already well entrenched in the system. Another relevant point is that in some cases, the margins of victory is really small and even a small swing because of these factors could be the difference between a win and a loss.

On this count, BJP is already ahead and the party has been using the election analytics and new age mediums for a few years already. The Opposition has to play the catch-up game and they would have to play it fast. The too much "analysis paralysis" is not going to help but at the same time, completely ignoring the data is also not going to be beneficial for the Opposition parties.

The Opposition parties at their individual level need to devise the best possible method to reach out to the newer categories of voters and consolidate the existing supporters by remaining relevant to them. There is a fairly standard template on how they can use the internet, social media and data analytics more effectively and though this may require tweaks here and there, the task is not unmanageable.

Change is the only constant

There is a broader message in what we have discussed just now. As their audience undergoes a metamorphosis and the external environment in terms of technology and communication channels continues to evolve, the political parties in India certainly need to involve more professionals in the task of getting the right message across the targeted audience. The indiscriminate and old methods based campaigning had its utility in the past as there was no other alternative.

But, to continue with it on an exclusive basis in today's world without complementing with the latest trends and methodologies would not really have an excuse. Things don't always need to turn upside down but change is inevitable and irreversible. Many opposition parties need to learn new tricks and use them well in their campaigning. If they can do that and put aside their egos to forge a formidable alliance, 2019 may prove to be a difficult election for Modi and BJP, perhaps much more difficult than the elections in 2014.

It doesn't matter if a batsman (or batswoman, Yes we too enjoyed the performance of Indian women cricket team in the World Cup) is playing at zero or has already scored a triple century; it only takes just one delivery to get him out. Also, no matter how many runs a batsman scored in the previous innings, the scoreboard starts from zero in the next innings. The Opposition has to bowl well and wait for Modi to make a mistake. Democracy is a great leveler and every election is an equal opportunity, for Modi and for the Opposition.

EPILOGUE

> Election days come and go. But the struggle of the people to create a government which represents all of us and not just the one percent - a government based on the principles of economic, social, racial and environmental justice - that struggle continues.
>
> — Bernie Sanders[1]

The performance of BJP in 2014 General Elections was similar to a cricket team scoring 400+ runs in a One Day International. This is like a blue sky scenario[2]. It requires a good batting track, solid performance from the batting order, a relatively mediocre bowling from opposition team and some bit of luck like a few dropped catches or missed run outs or a few umpiring errors which went in favour of the batting side.

In other words, to put a 400+ score on the board, it has to be your day no matter how strong your team is or how weak the opposition is. That is exactly why it doesn't happen every day. 2014 performance for BJP was akin to 400+ score. While scoring 400+ is difficult, the law of probability suggests that scoring 400+ on two successive days, against two different opposition line ups is multiple times more difficult.

Theoretically speaking, there are three possible scenarios for 2019 verdict:

- BJP is not able to form a Government because it doesn't win enough seats on its own and the party is not able to win enough support from other parties.
- BJP doesn't win that well as it did in 2014 but the party still has a good enough number in *Lok Sabha* to hold on to power with support from allies.
- BJP is back with a thumping majority as good as it was in 2014 or even better.

We think the first two possibilities are more realistic and this has been the story throughout this book. The third one is unlikely in our view. But, as they say *"Never say Never";* nothing is impossible in politics and elections.

We have already discussed that a "Third Front Government" or "Weak BJP Government with excessive dependence on allies" is going to be bad for the country. A coalition government is never the most preferred outcome for the future of India. We have seen in 1977, 1989, 1996 and 1998 that coalition Governments are usually so caught up with their survival on a day-to-day basis that it is difficult for them to have a long term plan and the capability to execute it.

To be fair, these coalition governments also have a practical difficulty in deciding and implementing the core objectives for the Government because there are just too many stakeholders with each one having a different agenda. Many of them would also see this as a short term opportunity to influence policy at the highest level. So, decision making suffers in most cases due to a lack of political stability.

Similarly, the experience of Governments after the elections in 1999, 2004 and 2009 is that though it is possible to have more political stability when there is a dominant partner in a coalition, the push and pulls from coalition partners make it a tough battle for the senior partner in the Government. Who would have forgotten almost a permanent Vajpayee emissary in the court of Ms. Jayalalithaa[3] in Chennai and the famous remark of ex-PM, Dr. Manmohan Singh on the compulsions of coalition politics[4]?

So, while the Government may last a full five year term as it may have happened in 1999-2004 or 2009-14 but that alone is no consolation. Of course, it can be argued in case of UPA II (2009-14) that whether allies were responsible for a Policy Paralysis situation or the performance of Congress itself was so lackluster that it is unfair to blame the allies, but the net result was still the same. The Government was largely dysfunctional.

Table A: SWOT Analysis for NDA Government from Policy Perspective in 2019-24 term

NDA GOVERNMENT			
S STRENGTHS	W WEAKNESSES	O OPPORTUNITIES	T THREATS
• Strongly focused on Reforms • Will Push through difficult legislations • Strong Image of PMO without Any Serious Corruption Charges • New Vistas in Foreign Relations e.g. Modi is the First PM to visit Israel	• Less participative decision making e.g. Apparently Demonetization was not a consensus decision in the NDA Government • Excessive centralization of power with Prime Minister's Office (PMO) • At times Confrontational approach towards other political parties • Lack of Impactful initiatives for maintaining Forecasted Growth in Economy, Welfare Measures, Job creation and Spurring Innovation	• Continuity in Decision Making and less disruption is good for governance • Comfortable majority means more leeway to go for bold reforms • Utilizing the services of sector experts and proven administrators for better engagement and better execution • Strong Focus on Driving Ease of Doing Business	• Some of the recent decisions indicate a more populist approach and this may increase as we approach elections • Hawkish approach towards neighbors and sometimes the conflicts may escalate to unmanageable levels • Penchant for headline grabbing decisions and initiatives e.g. Bullet train project between Ahmedabad and Mumbai

Table B: SWOT Analysis for UPA Government from Policy Perspective in 2019-24 term

UPA GOVERNMENT

S STRENGTHS	W WEAKNESSES	O OPPORTUNITIES	T THREATS
• Consensus based decision making which is slow at times but lessens the probability of making mistakes • Grand vision for example, UIDAI (Aadhaar), Right to Information Act and MNREGA • Less ideological interferences as compared to RSS-BJP situation in NDA	• More populist in approach with less focus on governance • Serious charges of financial irregularities against functionaries in the Government • Less control over allies and party's state units • Demoralized since the losses in 2014 and lack of coherent Political Strategy at Grassroot Level	• Rahul Gandhi taking over as the Congress president will allow the party to reset the narrative • Consolidation of like minded parties and people who are against BJP by offering them a common minimum policy program • Focus on more harmonious atmosphere among different sections of the society	• Excessive political dependence on allies • Decision Making prone to pulls and pushes from various quarters • Lack of administrative experience with Rahul Gandhi and younger generation party leaders • Not being able to offer enough and credible alternatives to BJP in policy making

This means that it is difficult to choose between the two possibilities and decide which one is worse for the country, a) a rag-tag coalition with or without the support from Congress forms the Government in 2019, b) NDA is back in power but BJP is critically dependant on allies. The Central Government needs to be strong, decisive and stable to take the country forward. Also the working style of Narendra Modi is such that it requires him to be in complete control and that is not consistent with a BJP led coalition government which has no great chances of survival without allies.

Now, let us come to the third possibility which is that the charisma of Modi works again and BJP comes back to power in 2019 with a solid majority. As we have seen so far in this book that this scenario is difficult to foresee at this point but Narendra Modi has proved conventional political wisdom wrong, time and again and he may very well do the same once more in 2019. If it happens and BJP wins more than 250-260 seats at least, how would this play out for India?

Of course, history may not repeat itself but still it has important lessons. In India's 70 years of history, we have three full-fledged examples of second term Prime Ministers. They served a full term and then got reelected. Pandit Jawaharlal Nehru (he won in 1952 and after serving from 1952-57, got reelected in 1957. We are excluding 1962 because he didn't complete 1962-67 term), Mrs. Indira Gandhi (she served for some time before 1967 as well, but her first full term was effectively 1967-71 and then she got reelected in 1971, we are excluding Mrs. Gandhi's 1980-84 tenure because it was the first term after her return to power by defeating Janata Party) and Dr. Manmohan Singh (After UPA I from 2004 to 2009, he again led the UPA II from 2009 to 2014).

Pandit Nehru began very well. He was under 60 years old which is a relatively young age, when he became Prime Minister and he had a grand vision for India. He was focused on industrialisation, was a globally recognised leader and after the demise of Sardar Vallabh Bhai Patel[5] in 1950, was undisputed leader of Congress. Though the performance of Congress in the first General Elections under his leadership was not a surprise, he was never insecure and had great respect for public opinion and Parliament.

Nehru was reelected in 1957 but things had started to change for the Government, for the Congress party and for him. Leading the country for so long and in a turbulent phase took its toll and he was not in good health. There were a number of scandals in the Government with serious charges of financial misconduct against some of his cabinet colleagues. The country was not making enough progress and people had started to get frustrated and as an example, Congress lost power in Kerala. Finally, the debacle in war with China[6] happened in 1962 and Nehru was completely shattered. Pandit Nehru was never the same leader in his 1957-64 phases as he was in his earlier tenure.

Indira Gandhi was decisive in her first full term (1967-71) but she was never really unaware of ground realities. She used to understand pulse of the nation better than anyone else and was fully aware of what would work politically and what would not. Though she never shied away from taking big decisions (Nationalisation of Public Sector Banks[7] and Abolition of Privy Purses[8] are some examples), she was able to strike a fine balance between good governance and populist measures.

Mrs. Gandhi scaled the peak of her achievements in 1971 war, India comprehensively defeated Pakistan and a new nation of Bangladesh[9] was born. After this, she was well known for her iron will and strong persona across the world. For a leader of developing country, it was a huge achievement. Back home, the general public and even opposition parties were in awe and she had already won a much bigger mandate in 1971 as compared to 1967 elections.

But, it was all downhill after that. Interestingly, she is more remembered in history for her second term (1971-77) which culminated with imposition of an Emergency in 1975 and her defeat to Janta Party in 1977. Though she was reelected in 1980 General Elections and came back to power, she was never the same leader again. Even in 1980-84, she committed errors of judgment such as Operation Blue Star[10]. She had become emotionally insecure after the death of her younger son Sanjay in June 1980 and became much more susceptible to the maneuvers of people looking to take advantage of her. In short, she became a pale shadow of her earlier commanding and assured self.[11]

Pandit Nehru and Indira Gandhi were in a different category of leaders as compared to Dr. Manmohan Singh. While both Nehru and Indira were popular, democratically elected leaders, Dr. Singh owed his job to Mrs. Sonia Gandhi. While the primary reason for fall in standards in the case of Nehru was fatigue in his second term and in the case of Mrs. Indira Gandhi in her second term, was her inability to accept dissent, UPA II during 2009-14 phase suffered as a result of a strange and unexplainable meekness. Both Mrs. Sonia Gandhi and Dr. Manmohan Singh were a pale shadow of their UPA I avatar, we never saw Dr. Singh in the same confident manner while handling important issues as we did in UPA I tenure at the time of Indo-US Nuclear treaty[12].

In 2008, Dr. Singh had not only confronted the Communist Parties on the issue of nuclear deal between India and USA, he also ensured that Congress fully supported him when Communist Parties withdrew their support and had put the Government's survival under threat. Though Congress had won almost 50 percent more seats in 2009 as compared to 2004, the Congress party was always on a defensive and towards the end of UPA's second term, had almost resigned to its fate that it is not possible to salvage the situation and save the sinking ship.

Congress virtually surrendered in front of the aggressive campaign unleashed by BJP in 2014. Such an abject surrender from Congress in elections was unprecedented in the history of India and in the history of Congress over last 70 years. The Congress under the leadership of Mrs. Indira Gandhi had fought much better in 1977 and under Rajiv Gandhi in 1989. By no means, this made a small contribution to BJP's spectacular performance in 2014.

But more important than the victories and defeats of political parties and individual leaders was the fact that the 2009-14 phase was a wasted opportunity in the history of Republic of India. This might only be a coincidence but the curse of deficit in performance in their second term has been a powerful force for Indian Prime Ministers. Hopefully, this should not happen again in 2019-24 if Modi is back to power in next General Elections.

NOTES AND REFERENCES

Acknowledgments

1. William Arthur Ward was an American writer and his writings were published in many leading magazines and journals. He specialised in inspirational quotes and he is one of the most frequently quoted writers.
2. John Fitzgerald Kennedy, or JFK, was an American politician who served as the 35th President of the United States of America from January 1961 until his assassination in November 1963. JFK continues to rank very highly in historians' polls of US Presidents and with the general public.

The story behind this book – From Pankaj

1. Mitchell David "Mitch" Albom is an American journalist and bestselling author. *For One More Day* is a 2006 novel by Albom. He has also authored *Tuesdays with Morrie* and *The Five People You Meet in Heaven.*
2. Rakesh Jhunjhunwala is an Indian stock market investor and trader. He is also a qualified Chartered Accountant and manages his own portfolio as a partner in his asset management firm, RARE Enterprises. He is also one of the richest Indians.
3. Shri Narendra Modi is an Indian politician who is the 14th and current Prime Minister of India. He has been in office since May 26, 2014. Modi is a prominent leader of the Bharatiya Janata Party (BJP) and he was also the Chief Minister of Gujarat from 2001 to 2014. He is the Member of Parliament from Varanasi in Uttar Pradesh. Modi led the BJP in the 2014 General Elections, which gave the party a majority in the *Lok Sabha*, the first time a single party had achieved this distinction since 1984.
4. Donald John Trump is 45th and current President of the United States, in office since January 20, 2017. Before entering politics, he was a businessman and television personality. Throughout his campaign in 2016, Trump was trailing Hillary Clinton as per media reports and popular surveys. http://www.usnews.com/opinion/op-ed/

articles/2016-11-10/why-the-polls-got-donaldtrumps-2016-win-wrong, http://www.pewresearch.org/facttank/2016/11/09/why-2016-election-polls-missed-their-mark/ (Accessed in June 2017).

5. Theresa Mary May is a British politician who has served as Prime Minister of the United Kingdom and Leader of the Conservative Party since July 2016 after David Cameroon resigned subsequent to an unexpected "Brexit" result. The United Kingdom general election of 2017 took place in June. The election was not due until 2020, but a call by Prime Minister Theresa May for a snap election led to an early election. May had hoped to secure a larger majority for the Conservative Party in order to have more strength in Brexit negotiations, an expectation which didn't materialise.
6. The National Democratic Alliance (NDA) is a leading coalition of political parties in India. It is led by the Bharatiya Janata Party (BJP) and at the time of its formation in 1998, it had thirteen constituent parties. The coalition was in power from 1998 to 2004. The alliance returned to power in the 2014 *Lok Sabha* Elections and its leader, Narendra Modi is heading the central Government since May 2014.
7. The election to the 17th Uttar Pradesh Legislative Assembly was held from February 11 to March 8, 2017 in seven phases. Bharatiya Janata Party won this election by an overwhelming three-quarter majority. Subsequently, Yogi Adityanath was elected as the Chief Minister of Uttar Pradesh.

Introduction

1. George Orson Welles was a multi-dimensional theater and film personality. He was a successful actor, director, writer and producer.
2. Mahabharata is an Indian epic, which is primarily a story of Kauravas and Pandavas. The epic ends with a war at Kurukshetra between these cousins. It was written in Sanskrit and is considered to be one of the most complete and nuanced stories. Though the Mahabharata war was won by Pandavas, it led to total destruction and huge damage on both sides.
3. As the authors present in this book, the combinations of these two areas "Mathematics and Elections" are very nascent. However since the US Elections 2008, the area of Election Analytics has taken a completely different dimension. Even in India, there are studies and media reports that indicate how the core team of BJP was inspired from Barack Obama's victory during 2008 and 2012 elections in its preparation for 2014 *Lok Sabha* elections. This is an area that will continue to enhance its importance in elections in future.
4. It is pertinent to note that the usage of Social Media has never been as

well espoused and practiced as by the current government and Prime Minister's Office.

5. Barack Obama's election as the President of USA in 2008 saw him first getting the Democratic nomination and then the role of President by effectively using internet and media campaigns. Obama also used the Social Media to expand the outreach to voters.
6. Prashant Kishor is an Indian political strategist and campaign manager. He is known for his work on election campaigns that helped BJP in 2014 elections. Later on, he also played a key role in 2015 Bihar Assembly Elections by helping the Nitish Kumar-Lalu Prasad Yadav combination.
7. The Bharatiya Janata Party is one of the major political parties in India. The BJP's origins lie in the Bharatiya Jana Sangh, formed in 1951 by Shyama Prasad Mookerjee. After the *Emergency* in 1977, the Jana Sangh merged with several other parties to form the Janata Party. After three years in power, the Janata party lost in 1980, with the members of the erstwhile Jana Sangh reconvening to form the BJP. Although initially unsuccessful, winning only two seats in the 1984 General Elections, it grew in strength on the back of the Ram Janmabhoomi movement. In later years, it has been very successful in its electoral track record and has transformed itself into the dominant political force in India.
8. Amit Shah is an Indian politician and the President of BJP. He has been a member of Gujarat Legislative Assembly a number of times. He is also considered to be a close associate of Prime Minister Shri Narendra Modi. Amit Shah recently contested Rajya Sabha Elections from Gujarat and got elected to the Upper House of Indian Parliament.
9. Since the elections after Emergency in 1975-77, the role of national parties has diminished. At various points, the Political Parties have entered into pre-electoral and post-electoral alliances to gain the popular mandate in Indian Elections. In the seven successive elections between 1989 and 2009, the mandates resulted in hung Parliaments and coalition governments.
10. Dr. Manmohan Singh served as the Prime Minister of India from 2004 to 2014. Dr. Singh has held several key posts in the Government of India, such as the Chief Economic Advisor, Governor at Reserve Bank of India, Deputy Chairman of Planning Commission and Finance Minister in the Central Government.
11. United Progressive Alliance (UPA) was formed in 2004 soon after the 14th General Elections when none of the leading national parties emerged with majority. The Left Front, the Samajwadi Party and the Bahujan Samaj Party extended support to Congress to form the UPA government. Dr. Manmohan Singh served as the Prime Minister and the 2004 to 2009 term is known as UPA I.

12. The UPA was reelected in General Elections in 2009. Congress was even more successful than in 2004 in terms of number of seats won. Dr. Manmohan Singh again served as the Prime Minister and the 2009 to 2014 term of UPA and Dr. Manmohan Singh is known as UPA II.
13. The "Emergency" refers to a 21 months period (June 1975 to March 1977) in India. Then Prime Minister, Mrs. Indira Gandhi, declared a state of Internal Emergency under Article 352 on June 26, 1975. The 1977 General Elections in India took place in March and immediately after the elections, Emergency was lifted. The opposition to Mrs. Gandhi called for a restoration of democracy and the results of elections in 1977 were seen as voters' opposition to Emergency, https://en.wikipedia.org/wiki/Indian_general_election,_1977, http://indianexpress.com/article/opinion/columns/why-waves-dont-matter/ (Accessed in June 2017).
14. Mrs. Indira Gandhi was an Indian politician and one of the prominent leaders of the Indian National Congress party. She is also among the longest serving Prime Ministers of India (1966-1977 and 1980-1984) and was in office at the time of her death. She was assassinated on October 31, 1984 at her residence in New Delhi by her body guards. Subsequently in the December 1984 elections, Rajiv Gandhi led Congress and won an unprecedented majority in the *Lok Sabha* Elections. There was a strong sympathy wave especially in Northern and Western India in favour of Congress post Mrs. Gandhi's assassination. This had a meaningful impact on vote-and seat share margins and this positive impact helped Congress, https://en.wikipedia.org/wiki/Indian_general_election,_1984, http://indianexpress.com/article/opinion/columns/why-waves-dont-matter/, (Accessed in June 2017).

Chapter 1 – The Opposition will be better prepared for Modi

1. Sun Tzu was a Chinese General, military strategist, and philosopher who lived in ancient China around 2500 years back. Sun Tzu is traditionally credited as the author of *The Art of War*, a widely influential work of military strategy that has affected both Western and Eastern philosophy. Even after so many years, Sun Tzu remains a legendary historical figure in China.
2. Otto Eduard Leopold, Prince of Bismarck, Duke of Lauenburg known as Otto von Bismarck was a Prussian statesman who dominated German political scene in the second half of 19th century. In the 1860s, he engineered a series of wars that unified the German states under German Empire.
3. This is a form of governance where two major political parties are

dominant in government though not simultaneously. In this political system, the other political groups remain on fringes. The modern Political Party System in USA and United Kingdom (though it can be argued that this is not the case anymore) are examples of two party systems.

4. Ram Manohar Lohia was a freedom fighter and Indian Political Activist. He is well known for his role in the Quit India Movement and he was one of the top leaders of the Socialist movement of Congress. Later on, he quit Congress but remained an influential and respected political figure in India.
5. Samajwadi Party is a regional political party in India and its primary base is Uttər Pradesh (UP). The Samajwadi Party is led by Akhilesh Yadav. Akhilesh's father, Mulayam Singh Yadav was the founder of the party and it has been in power many times in UP over the last twenty-five years.
6. Nitish Kumar is an Indian politician of the Janata Dal (United) party. He has been Chief Minister of Bihar since February 2015. Previously, he served as the Chief Minister of Bihar from 2005 to 2014 and he has also been a Union Minister in India.
7. Lalu Prasad Yadav is an Indian politician from the state of Bihar. He was Chief Minister of Bihar from 1990 to 1997 and Minister of Railways from 2004 to 2009 with the United Progressive Alliance (UPA) government. He is the President of the Rashtriya Janata Dal.
8. Communist Party of India (Marxist) emerged from a split from the Communist Party of India in 1964. The CPI (M) was formed at the Seventh Congress of the Communist Party of India held in Calcutta in 1964. The party is strong in West Bengal, Kerala and Tripura.
9. *All India Trinamool Congress*, or commonly called the *Trinamool Congress* is a political party in India. The party is a dominant political force in Bengal. The founder and leader of Trinamool Congress is Ms. Mamata Banerjee, she had started her political career with Congress.
10. The Jammu and Kashmir Peoples Democratic Party (JKPDP or PDP) is a state level political party in Jammu and Kashmir. The PDP was founded by Mufti Mohammed Sayeed in 1998. His daughter, Mehbooba Mufti, succeeded him as party leader and as Chief Minister of Jammu and Kashmir following his death in 2016.
11. Rashtriya Swayamsevak Sangh (RSS), is a right-wing volunteer organisation, which is also the parent organisation of the Bharatiya Janata Party. It was founded in 1925 and the organisation grew into a prominent Hindu nationalist umbrella organisation.
12. Shiromani Akali Dal (or Akali Dal or SAD) was formed as a non-political organisation and as representative of the Sikh community. However, it is now the largest and most influential Sikh political party. The Akali Dal has run the state government in Punjab several times and at present SAD

is in partnership with its regional and national ally Bharatiya Janata Party in Punjab. SAD is also a part of NDA.

13. Vishwanath Pratap Singh (V P Singh) was an Indian politician and a prominent leader of the Congress. He was the Chief Minister of Uttar Pradesh and also Cabinet Minister at the centre. In mid 1980s, he quit Congress and became a key political figure of Janata Dal. He was the 7th Prime Minister of India from 1989 to 1990. He ran a coalition government and had to resign after BJP withdrew its support to the V P Singh run government.
14. Chaudhary Charan Singh served as the Prime Minister of India from July 1979 to January 1980. He is well recognised for his work as an able and popular administrator in the state of Uttar Pradesh. He had a strong following among peasant communities in the Northern India.
15. Chandra Shekhar was an Indian politician who served as the 8th Prime Minister of India from November 10, 1990 to June 21, 1991. He started his political career with Dr. Ram Manohar Lohia and became active in socialist politics. He had differences of opinion with Mrs. Indira Gandhi and when the *Emergency* was declared in 1975, he was arrested and sent to jail. He was fondly called a "Young Turk" for his unconventional and fearless political approach.
16. Chimanbhai Patel was an Indian politician and a former Chief Minister of Gujarat state in India. He was elected to the Gujarat Legislative Assembly in 1967 and served in cabinet under different Chief Ministers and later became CM himself. He was CM of Gujarat at the time of his death in 1994, https://en.wikipedia.org/wiki/Chimanbhai_Patel (Accessed in June 2017).
17. Bhajan Lal was a politician and three-time Chief Minister of Haryana. He first became the Chief Minister in 1979 and served till 1985. He again became CM in 1991 and served till 1996. He also served as Union Minister in the Central government. In this Jat-dominated state, he was the last non-Jat CM of Haryana before Manohar Lal Khattar (the current CM of Haryana). He passed away in 2011 after suffering from a heart ailment, https://en.wikipedia.org/wiki/Bhajan_Lal (Accessed in June 2017).
18. Ghanshyam Chhotalal Oza was the Chief Minister of Gujarat from March 17, 1972 to July 17, 1973. He was a member of the *Lok Sabha* from 1957 to 1967 and again from 1971 to 1972. Later, he was a member of the Rajya Sabha.
19. *Nav Nirman Andolan* (Re-construction movement) was a large socio-political movement in Gujarat by students and middle-class people against economic crisis and corruption in public life. It resulted in dissolution of state government.

20. Bhupinder Singh Hooda is an Indian National Congress politician who served as the Chief Minister of Haryana from 2005 to 2014.
21. In 2007, Bhajan Lal who was the ex-Chief Minister of Haryana announced that he would form a new party, called the Haryana Janhit Congress. This was after the suspension of his son, Kuldeep Bishnoi from the Indian National Congress, for criticising the party's central leaders. In April 2016, the party merged with Indian National Congress.
22. Kuldeep Bishnoi is son of ex-CM of Haryana, Bhajan Lal and is a prominent politician of the state. He was also a member of the *Lok Sabha* representing Hisar constituency in Haryana. He has also been an MLA in Haryana Legislative Assembly.
23. Pandit Jawaharlal Nehru was a prominent freedom fighter and the first Prime Minister of independent India. He was one of the tallest leaders Congress had and because of his role in the freedom struggle and after the death of Sardar Vallabh Bhai Patel in 1950, he was virtually unchallenged in Congress and the country. He served as the Prime Minister from India's independence in 1947 until his death in 1964.
24. Rahul Gandhi is an Indian politician and the Vice-President of the Indian National Congress. He represents Amethi as its Member of Parliament (MP). He is a member of the politically powerful Nehru–Gandhi family. He is the son of Rajiv Gandhi (the former Prime Minister of India) and grandson of Indira Gandhi (one of the longest serving Prime Ministers of India). His mother, Sonia Gandhi, is the President of Indian National Congress.
25. Bahujan Samaj Party is the third largest national political party in India, as per the votes polled in 2014 General Elections. In the beginning, the party's primary base was among the Scheduled Castes and Other Backward Castes. However, it has become more representative of the society over last decade. The party is led by Ms. Mayawati and its main base is in the state of Uttar Pradesh.
26. All India Anna Dravida Munnetra Kazhagam (AIADMK) is an Indian political party in the states of Tamil Nadu and Puducherry. It is currently in power in Tamil Nadu. It was founded by M. G. Ramachandran (popularly known as MGR) in 1972 as a breakaway faction of the Dravida Munnetra Kazhagam (DMK). From 1989 to 2016, AIADMK was led by J Jayalalithaa, who served as the Chief Minister of Tamil Nadu on several occasions. After Jayalalithaa's death, a bitter struggle for control over the party has started among different factions.
27. Telugu Desam Party or TDP is a regional political party in Andhra Pradesh. The party was founded by N. T. Rama Rao in 1982. Since 1995, the party is headed by Nara Chandrababu Naidu, the incumbent Chief Minister of Andhra Pradesh. Naidu has been the Chief Minister of Andhra Pradesh since 2014. Previously, he served as Chief Minister of

a United Andhra Pradesh from 1995 to 2004. He is well known for his reforms and development focused working style.

28. Shiv Sena is an Indian regional political party with its primary base in Maharashtra. It was founded in 1966. The party originally emerged from a movement in Mumbai demanding preferential treatment for Maharashtrians over migrants to the city. It is currently headed by Founder Bal Thackeray's son, Uddhav Thackeray.
29. The Biju Janata Dal (BJD) is a state level political party in Odisha led by Naveen Patnaik, the current Chief Minister of the state and the son of former Chief Minister Biju Patnaik, one of the tallest post-Independence era leaders from Odisha. Naveen Patnaik took over his father's *Lok Sabha* seat in 1996 as a member of the Janata Dal. In 1997, Patnaik split from Janata Dal and formed the BJD. Naveen Patnaik is known for his pro-poor, pro-development and clean image. He has been the Chief Minister of Odisha for more than fifteen years, with his popularity intact among masses.
30. The Janata Party was a large scale amalgamation of Indian political parties opposed to Emergency that was imposed from 1975 to 1977 by Mrs. Indira Gandhi. In the General Elections held after the end of the state of emergency in 1977, the Janata Party defeated Congress to form the first non-Congress government in the history of the Republic of India.
31. Rajiv Gandhi was the Prime Minister of India, serving from 1984 to 1989. He was the youngest Indian Prime Minister when he became PM at the age of 40. He was the grandson of first Prime Minister of India, Pandit Jawaharlal Nehru and son of Mrs. Indira Gandhi, one of the longest serving Prime Ministers of India. On May 21, 1991, at Sriperumbudur, Rajiv was assassinated in a human bomb explosion while on an election campaigning trail.
32. Election Commission of India (ECI) is an autonomous constitutional authority responsible for administering the electoral process in India. With Headquarters in New Delhi, the current Chief Election Commissioner (CEC) is Achal Kumar Jyoti. ECI conducts the general elections and Assembly Elections in India,http://eci.nic.in/eci_main1/statistical_reportge2014.aspx (Accessed in June 2017).
33. *Mahagathbandhan* literally means a grand alliance of major political parties. Here reference is to the political alliance in Bihar Assembly Elections, 2015 between Nitish Kumar of JDU and Lalu Prasad Yadav of RJD and Congress. The alliance was successful in defeating BJP in the Assembly Elections in 2015.
34. On December 6, 1992, Hindu volunteers demolished the disputed structure at Ayodhya in Uttar Pradesh. This structure was at the site of a sixteenth century Babri Mosque, which the Hindus believed was

constructed at the site of the birth place of Lord Rama, the revered Hindu God.

35. Mulayam Singh Yadav is a seasoned Indian Politician and he served as the Defence Minister of India under the United Front Government from 1996 to 1998 when he was elected to the *Lok Sabha* for the first time in 1996. He was also the Chief Minister of Uttar Pradesh three times and his last term was from 2003-2007. Akhilesh Yadav, his son took over as the Chief Minister of the State in 2012.
36. Akhilesh Yadav is the President of Samajwadi Party and served as the Chief Minister of the Indian state of Uttar Pradesh between 2012 and 2017. He has also been a member of the *Lok Sabha* earlier and represented Kannauj constituency in Uttar Pradesh.
37. Ms. Mayawati is an Indian politician and a prominent political leader from Uttar Pradesh. She has served four terms as the Chief Minister of Uttar Pradesh (UP). She is the national president of the Bahujan Samaj Party.
38. 2014 data for general elections by Election Commission of India,http://eci.nic.in/eci_main/archiveofge2014/17%20-%20State%20wise%20seat%20won%20and%20valid%20votes%20polled%20by%20political%20party.pdf (Accessed in June 2017).
39. 2017 data for State Assembly Elections by Election Commission of India. http://eciresults.nic.in/PartyWiseResultS24.htm?st=S24 (Accessed in June 2017).
40. Priyanka Gandhi is the daughter of Rajiv Gandhi and Sonia Gandhi. She is the granddaughter of Indira Gandhi. She is regularly tracked in the media due to her political influence on the Congress party in general and more specifically, in the constituencies of Amethi and Rai Bareily. Priyanka Gandhi is often seen as being the future leadership of Congress to revive its fortunes as a leading national party.
41. 2014 data for general elections by Election Commission of India, http://eci.nic.in/eci_main/archiveofge2014/17%20-%20State%20wise%20seat%20won%20and%20valid%20votes%20polled%20by%20political%20party.pdf (Accessed in June 2017).

Chapter 2 – 2014 Mandate: UPA – The Story of Self Goals

1. Anti-incumbency, not PM Narendra Modi's charisma behind poll results, says CPI. In these five state elections, it is anti-incumbency vote. In every state, the ruling party lost Reddy said,http://www.financialexpress.com/elections/anti-incumbency-not-pm-narendra-modis-charisma-behind-poll-results-cpi/587678/ (Accessed in June 2017).
2. Atal Bihari Vajpayee is an Indian politician who was the tenth Prime Minister of India, first for thirteen days in 1996, and then from 1998 to

2004. He was among the founding fathers and a prominent leader of the Jana Sangh first and then, the Bharatiya Janata Party (BJP).

3. National Rural Employment Guarantee Act 2005 (later renamed as the "Mahatma Gandhi National Rural Employment Guarantee Act" or MGNREGA) is an Indian social security measure that aims to guarantee the 'right to work'. It aims to enhance livelihood security in rural areas by providing at least 100 days of employment in a financial year to every household whose adult members volunteer for unskilled manual work, http://www.nrega.nic.in/netnrega/home.aspx, (Accessed in June 2017); https://en.wikipedia.org/wiki/National_Rural_Employment_Guarantee_Act,_2005 (Accessed in June 2017).
4. Lal Krishna Advani is an Indian politician and a senior leader of the Bharatiya Janata Party. Advani served as Minister of Home Affairs in the BJP-led National Democratic Alliance government from 1998 to 2004. He was the Leader of the Opposition in the 10th *Lok Sabha* and 14th *Lok Sabha*. In June 2005, he drew much criticism when he, while on a visit to the Jinnah Mausoleum at Karachi – his town of birth, praised and endorsed Mohammad Ali Jinnah and described him as a "secular" leader. This was not liked by the RSS and L K Advani was forced to relinquish his post as BJP President. However, he withdrew the resignation a few days later,https://www.telegraphindia.com/1050605/asp/nation/story_4828954.asp, (Accessed in June 2017); https://www.dawn.com/news/149722, (Accessed in June 2017); http://www.economist.com/node/4069498, (Accessed in June 2017);https://en.wikipedia.org/wiki/L._K._Advani (Accessed in June 2017).
5. Coal allocation scam (or Coalgate) is a major political scandal concerning the Indian government's allocation of the nation's coal deposits to private companies. In a report, the Comptroller and Auditor General of India (CAG) office accused the Government of India of allocating coal blocks in an inefficient manner which led to a loss of INR 1.86 trillion to the exchequer,http://indianexpress.com/article/what-is/manmohan-singh-cbi-coalgate-coal-block-allocation-cag-report-what-is-coal-scam-4668265/ (Accessed in June 2017); https://en.wikipedia.org/wiki/Indian_coal_allocation_scam (Accessed in June 2017).
6. The 2G spectrum scandal was an Indian telecommunications scam and political scandal in which politicians and government officials under the UPA coalition government charged less from mobile telephone companies for frequency allocation licenses. The Government chose NM Rothschild & Sons to design a first-of-its-kind e-auction mechanism in the world, a US$2.27 billion landmark deal. The difference between the money collected and that mandated to be collected was estimated by the Comptroller and Auditor General of India at Rs 1.76 trillion. The 2G

spectrum scandal was another major embarrassment for UPA coalition lead by Congress. This event turned out to be a major political scandal in which the supreme court of India ruled on Public Interest Litigation that the allotment of the 2G spectrum to the telecom companies was unconstitutional and arbitrary and cancelled the 122 licenses issued in 2008 under A. Raja (Minister of Communications and IT during 2007-09). https://en.wikipedia.org/wiki/2G_spectrum_scam (Accessed in June 2017).

7. In 2010, New Delhi witnessed the Commonwealth Games (CWG) scam, involving a pilferage of around Rs700 billion. All the accused, including Suresh Kalmadi, were charged of criminal conspiracy, cheating, forgery for purpose of cheating and under sections of Prevention of Corruption Act. https://en.wikipedia.org/wiki/Suresh_Kalmadi (Accessed in June 2017); http://timesofindia.indiatimes.com/miscellaneous/commonwealth-games-scam/articleshow/56032112.cms (Accessed in June 2017).
8. Anna Hazare is an anti-corruption activist and social leader in India. He is well known for leading the national anti-corruption movement in 2011. On April 5, 2011, he began a hunger strike at the Jantar Mantar in New Delhi with the aim of the movement to target corruption at senior political posts through introduction of the Jan Lokpal Bill,http://www.annahazare.org/, https://en.wikipedia.org/wiki/Anna_Hazare (Accessed in June 2017).
9. Jan Lokpal Bill also referred to as the Citizen's Ombudsman Bill, is an anti-corruption bill drawn up by civil society activists in India seeking the appointment of a Jan Lokpal, an independent body to investigate corruption cases. This bill also proposes improvements to the Lokpal and Lokayukta Bill 2011, https://en.wikipedia.org/wiki/Jan_Lokpal_Bill (Accessed in June 2017).
10. Arvind Kejriwal is an Indian politician who is the Chief Minister of Delhi since February 2015. He has previously served as the Chief Minister of Delhi from December 2013 to February 2014. He is one of the founder members of the Aam Aadmi Party and the most well-known face in his party. In 2006, Kejriwal was awarded the Ramon Magsaysay Award and has been closely associated with Anna Hazare's movement against corruption during UPA rule (the second term of UPA, 2009-2014).
11. Aam Aadmi Party is an Indian political party, formally launched on November 26, 2012, and is currently the ruling party in the state of Delhi. The party made its electoral debut in the 2013 Delhi Legislative Assembly election, where it emerged as the second-largest party, winning 28 of the 70 seats. In the 2015 Delhi Legislative Assembly election, AAP won 67 of

the 70 seats in the assembly,https://en.wikipedia.org/wiki/Aam_Aadmi_Party (Accessed in June 2017).

12. The Recession of 2008 was a period of general economic decline observed in world markets during the late 2000s and early 2010s. The scale and timing of the recession varied from country to country. In terms of overall impact, the International Monetary Fund concluded that it was the worst global recession since 1930s, https://en.wikipedia.org/wiki/Great_Recession#cite_note-New_IMF_Global_Recession_definition-3 (Accessed in June 2017).
13. Vibrant Gujarat is the name given to a biennial investors' summit held by the government of Gujarat state in India. The event is aimed at bringing together business leaders, investors, corporations, thought leaders and opinion makers. The summit is a platform to understand and explore business opportunities in Gujarat, https://en.wikipedia.org/wiki/Vibrant_Gujarat (Accessed in June 2017).
14. Gujarat has 5 percent of India's population and 6 percent of its land mass, but it accounts for 7.6 percent of India's GDP, almost a tenth of workforce, and 22 percent of country's exports. The state's annual GDP growth under Modi's regime from 2001 until 2012 averaged almost 10 percent, a faster rate than India as a whole. Other exporting states, such as Maharashtra and Tamil Nadu, also did well, https://www.economist.com/news/finance-and-economics/21638147-how-modi-nomics-was-forged-one-indias-most-business-friendly-states (Accessed in June 2017).
15. Sanjay Gandhi was the younger son of ex-Prime Minister of India, Late Mrs. Indira Gandhi and a member of the Congress party. After early 70s, Sanjay became an integral part of the prime ministerial office and influenced political decisions of Indira Gandhi. He died in a plane crash in June 1980.
16. Pranab Mukherjee was the 13th President of India and he was in office from July 2012 – July 2017. His term of office as President concluded recently. He was a senior leader of the Indian National Congress who occupied several Union ministerial portfolios in India. He was erstwhile Finance Minister in the UPA-II Government from 2009 to 2012. During the Congress Led UPA Government elected in 2004, he held key portfolios: Defence (2004-06), External Affairs (2006-09) and Finance (2009-12). He has withdrawn from public life after the completion of his term as President, he stays in Delhi.
17. P. Chidambaram is an Indian Politician and Member of Parliament. He served as the Finance Minister and Home Minister during the UPA Government. He held responsible positions earlier as well and he is widely known for his visionary Union budget for 1996–97. In this budget, Chidambaram brought discipline in government spending and

launched an ambitious tax reform programme to tackle an unwieldy fiscal deficit.

18. Sharad Pawar is the President of the National Congress Party which he founded in 1999 after separating from Indian National Congress. He previously served as the Chief Minister of Maharashtra thrice and also held the portfolio of Union Minister of Agriculture.
19. http://www.dailymail.co.uk/indiahome/indianews/article-2436031/It-torn-thrown-away-Rahul-Gandhi-turns-government-slams-law-saves-convicted-lawmakers-disqualificationhtml (Accessed in June 2017); http://timesofindia.indiatimes.com/india/Rahul-Gandhi-trashes-ordinance-shames-government/articleshow/23180950.cms (Accessed in June 2017).
20. The bottom of the pyramid, bottom of the wealth pyramid or the bottom of the income pyramid is the largest, but poorest socio-economic group. In global terms, this is the 2.7 billion people who live on less than $2.50 a day. Management scholar C K Prahalad popularised the idea of this demographic as a profitable consumer base in his 2004 book *The Fortune at the Bottom of the Pyramid.* Prahalad said that catering to the lowest economic category in population is also a profitable consumer base. Prahalad proposes that businesses, governments, and donor agencies stop thinking of the poor as victims and start seeing them as creative entrepreneurs and consumers, https://en.wikipedia.org/wiki/Bottom_of_the_pyramid (Accessed in June 2017).
21. The term pace battery in cricket was used for the fast bowlers of West Indies. These bowlers included Malcolm Marshall, Michael Holding, Andy Roberts and Joel Garner. West Indies Cricket team in 1970s and 1980s had top quality fast bowlers who were very successful even against the best batting line ups in those days.
22. In his public address on television on the evening of November 8, 2016, Prime Minister Shri Narendra Modi announced that Rs 500 and Rs 1000 banknotes would not be in circulation from the midnight of November 9. PM also announced that the new notes of Rs 2000 and Rs 500 have been launched. This banning of old notes is known as demonetisation. The RBI announced a window of fifty days until December 30, 2016 to deposit the demonetised banknotes.
23. Goods and Services Tax (GST) is an indirect tax applicable throughout India which replaced multiple cascading taxes levied by the central and state governments. The GST is governed by a GST Council and its Chairman is the Finance Minister of India. Under GST, goods and services are taxed at different slabs such as 0 percent, 5 percent, 12 percent, 18 percent and 28 percent, https://en.wikipedia.org/wiki/Goods_and_Services_Tax_(India) (Accessed in June 2017) .

Chapter 3 – The Role of Economy in Elections

1. "It's the economy, stupid" is a variation of the phrase "The economy, stupid", which James Carville had coined as a campaign strategist of Bill Clinton's successful 1992 presidential campaign against sitting President George H. W. Bush. Clinton's campaign had used the then-prevailing recession situation in the United States as one of the campaign's means to successfully unseat Bush, https://en.wikipedia.org/wiki/It%27s_the_economy,_stupid (Accessed in June 2017).
2. GDP (Gross Domestic Product) Growth Rate is a metric that is used to represent the economy's health. It is important for the readers to take a note of the changes in the formula in 2015. The estimates are released on a quarterly basis by the Government, http://statisticstimes.com/economy/gdp-growth-of-india.php (Accessed in June, 2017);http://mospi.nic.in/sites/default/files/press_release/PRESS_NOTE_PE_2016-17.pdf (Accessed in June 2017); http://www.livemint.com/Politics/Ig7hWnKkVbhVGXxovJOYGO/GDP-grows-at-61-in-fourth-quarter-below-estimate-of-71.html (Accessed in June 2017).
3. In economics, inflation is a sustained increase in the general price level of goods and services in an economy over a period of time. When the price level rises, each unit of currency buys fewer goods and services; consequently, inflation reflects a reduction in the purchasing power per unit of money – a loss of real value in the medium of exchange and unit of account within the economy. The measure of price inflation is inflation rate,https://en.wikipedia.org/wiki/Inflation (Accessed in June 2017).
4. Industrial Growth is an important measure of economic performance. The Index of Industrial Production (IIP) is an index for India which details out the growth of various sectors in an economy such as mineral mining, electricity and manufacturing. It is compiled and published monthly by the Central Statistical Organisation (CSO) six weeks after the reference month ends. The base year is 2011-2012, https://en.wikipedia.org/wiki/Index_of_industrial_production (Accessed in June 2017).
5. The exchange rate (also known as a foreign-exchange rate, forex rate, ER, FX rate) between two currencies is the rate at which one currency will be exchanged for another. It is also the value of one country's currency to another currency, https://en.wikipedia.org/wiki/Exchange_rate (Accessed in June 2017).
6. Dr. Raghuram Rajan is an Indian economist who is Professor of Finance at the Booth School of Business, University of Chicago. He was the 23rd Governor of the Reserve Bank of India between September 2013 and September 2016. Between 2003 and 2006, Rajan was the Chief

Economist at the International Monetary Fund, https://en.wikipedia.org/wiki/Raghuram_Rajan (Accessed in June 2017).

7. The growth in output of eight core industries — coal, crude oil, natural gas, refinery products, fertilisers, steel, cement and electricity,http://www.thehindu.com/business/Industry/eight-core-sectors-growth-slips-to-36-in-may/article19188416.ece (Accessed in June 2017).
8. Despite big announcements on rural infrastructure projects, irrigation projects have not taken off yet,http://www.livemint.com/Politics/SFo6B8rrvDy9s3QTClknhO/Has-the-Modi-governmentwalked-the-talk-on-reviving-public-investm.html (Accessed in June 2017).
9. Though no regular data is available in India at the moment, the Quarterly Employment Survey provide some estimates for the new jobs created, http://www.livemint.com/Opinion/B2gDpMIxRBQDNd2dGAYtzM/Government-limitations-in-job-creation.html (Accessed in June 2017).

Chapter 4 – 2014 Mandate: BJP's Statistical Peak?

1. Lawrence Peter "Yogi" Berra was an American professional baseball catcher, manager, and coach who played 19 seasons in Major League Baseball. He is widely regarded as one of the greatest catchers in baseball history, https://en.wikipedia.org/wiki/Yogi_Berra (Accessed in June 2017).
2. Sunil Gavaskar is one of the best opening batsmen in the history of Test Cricket. He represented India consistently in 1970s and 1980s and also captained the national team.
3. Gundappa Viswanath is a former Indian cricketer. He was one of India's finest batsmen throughout the 1970s. He is still considered one of the best in elegant stroke playing.
4. Sachin Tendulkar is a former Indian cricketer and captain. He is widely regarded as one of the greatest batsmen of all time. He is the only player to have scored one hundred international centuries and the first batsman to score a double century in a One Day International (ODI).

Chapter 5 – Modi's Pinnacle: Was it 2014 or Will it be 2019?

1. Mariel Margaret Hamm-Garciaparra (or Mia Hamm) is a retired professional soccer player, two-time Olympic Gold Medalist, and two-time FIFA Women's World Cup champion. She played as a forward for the United States women's national soccer team from 1987–2004 and was a founding member of the Women's United Soccer Association (WUSA), the first professional women's soccer league in US, https://en.wikipedia.org/wiki/Mia_Hamm (Accessed in June 2017).

2. Yuvraj Singh is an Indian International Cricketer, an All Rounder who bats in the middle order. He was the Man of the Tournament in the 2011 ICC Cricket World Cup, and one of the top performers at the 2007 ICC World Twenty20, both of which India won.
3. G.K. Moopanar was an Indian National Congress leader and parliamentarian. He was an All India Congress Committee General Secretary from 1980 to 1988. Tamil Maanila Congress was founded by Moopanar in March 1996,https://en.wikipedia.org/wiki/G._K._Moopanar (Accessed in June 2017).
4. Jagan Mohan Reddy is an Indian Politician of YSR Congress Party and Leader of Opposition in the Andhra Pradesh Legislative Assembly. He is the son of former Chief Minister of Andhra Pradesh, Y. S. Rajasekhara Reddy. YSR (Yuvajana Shramika Rythu) Congress is a regional political party in the state of Andhra Pradesh.
5. Janata Party had significant ideological and political divisions. The party consisted of veteran socialists, trade unionists and pro-business leaders, making major economic reforms difficult to achieve without triggering a public divide. Socialists and secular Janata politicians had an aversion to the agenda of the Rashtriya Swayamsevak Sangh, whose members belonged to Bharatiya Jana Sangh,https://en.wikipedia.org/wiki/Janata_Party (Accessed in June 2017).
6. Babu Jagjivan Ram (Babu ji) was an Indian independence activist and politician from Bihar. He was one of the tallest leaders of Dalit community post independence in India. He served as a Minister holding various portfolios in the Government. He was the Defence Minister of India during the Indo-Pak war of 1971.
7. Morarji Desai was an Indian independence activist and senior leader of Congress Party. He also served as the 4th Prime Minister of India for the government formed by the Janata Party during 1977-79.
8. The Mandal Commission was established in 1979 by the Janata Party government with an objective to identify backward classes other than Scheduled Castes and Schedule Tribes. A decade after the commission gave its report; then Prime Minister V P Singh tried to implement its recommendations in 1990.
9. P.V. Narasimha Rao served as the 9th Prime Minister of India from June 1991 to May 1996. He led an important economic transformation of India and he is often referred to as the father of India's economic reforms. With Rao's mandate, then Finance Minister Dr. Manmohan Singh launched economic reforms that implemented the International Monetary Fund (IMF) policies to rescue the almost bankrupt nation from economic collapse. Rao was known for his ability to steer tough legislation through the parliament when he headed a minority

government, https://en.wikipedia.org/wiki/P._V._Narasimha_Rao (Accessed in June 2017).

10. Naveen Patnaik is a politician and the leader of Biju Janta Dal. He is the current Chief Minister of Odisha and is known for his pro-poor, pro-development and clean image. He has been the Chief Minister of Odisha for more than fifteen years, with his popularity intact among masses.
11. Nara Chandrababu Naidu (or N Chandrababu Naidu) is an Indian politician who has been the Chief Minister of Andhra Pradesh since 2014. Previously he served as Chief Minister of a United Andhra Pradesh from 1995 to 2004. He is also the President of the Telugu Desam Party. He is known for his reforms and development focused working style.
12. Sheila Dikshit is an Indian politician who was the Chief Minister of Delhi from 1998 to 2013. She is a member of the Indian National Congress. Dikshit led the Congress to three consecutive electoral victories in Delhi. Subsequently, she was also the Governor of Kerala, https://en.wikipedia.org/wiki/Sheila_Dikshit (Accessed in June 2017).
13. Madan Lal Khurana is an Indian politician who was Chief Minister of Delhi from 1993 to 1996. He also served as Governor of Rajasthan in 2004. He is a member of RSS and Bharatiya Janata Party, https://en.wikipedia.org/wiki/Madan_Lal_Khurana (Accessed in June 2017).
14. Sahib Singh Verma was an Indian politician and the former senior vice-president of the Bharatiya Janata Party. He served as Chief Minister of Delhi (1996–1998) and was member of 13th *Lok Sabha* (1999–2004). He also served as the Union Labour Minister of India. He died on 30 June 2007 in a car accident, https://en.wikipedia.org/wiki/Sahib_Singh_Verma (Accessed in June 2017).

Chapter 6 – Anti-Incumbency Against State Governments

1. Marcus Buckingham is a British author, motivational speaker and business consultant. After extensive survey data from interviews with workers in countries around the world, he promotes the idea that people will get the best results by making the most of their strengths rather than by putting too much emphasis on weaknesses or perceived deficiencies, https://en.wikipedia.org/wiki/Marcus_Buckingham (Accessed in June 2017) .
2. Vasundhara Raje Scindia is an Indian politician who has been Chief Minister of Rajasthan since 2013. She served in the same post from 2003 to 2008. She has also been a Minister of State in the Union Ministry of External Affairs.
3. Chaudhary Devi Lal was an Indian politician who twice served as Chief Minister of Haryana, first in 1977–79 and then in 1987–89. He also served as 6th Deputy Prime Minister of India from 1989–91,https://en.wikipedia.org/wiki/Devi_Lal_(politician) (Accessed in June 2017).

4. Manohar Lal Khattar is a BJP politician and present Chief Minister of Haryana. He is a former RSS *pracharak* (campaigner or propagandist, depending on which side of the political discourse you are). In the assembly, he represents the Karnal constituency.
5. Jyotiraditya Scindia is an Indian politician. He is a titular Maharaja of Gwalior and is a Member of Parliament for Congress party. He was the 'Minister of State with independent charge' of Power in the cabinet of Prime Minister Dr. Manmohan Singh from October 2012 until May 2014,https://en.wikipedia.org/wiki/Jyotiraditya_Madhavrao_Scindia (Accessed in June 2017).
6. Madhav Rao Scindia was an Indian politician and Minister in Central Government from the Congress party. Earlier, in 1961, he had become the titular Maharaja of Gwalior being a descendant of the Scindia dynasty of the Marathas. He died in a plane crash on September 30, 2001,https://en.wikipedia.org/wiki/Madhavrao_Scindia#Death (Accessed in June 2017).
7. Kamal Nath is an Indian politician and the ex-Union Minister. He is a member of the current 16th *Lok Sabha* of India. He represents the Chhindwara constituency of Madhya Pradesh and is a member of Congress, https://en.wikipedia.org/wiki/Kamal_Nath (Accessed in June 2017).
8. Shivraj Singh Chouhan is a BJP leader and present Chief Minister of Madhya Pradesh. As of today, he has been one of the longest serving Chief Ministers in the country. He has also been a Member of Parliament, representing Vidisha seat in *Lok Sabha.*
9. Raman Singh is a BJP leader and present Chief Minister of Chhattisgarh. He has been a member of Madhya Pradesh Legislative Assembly consecutively and has also been elected for *Lok Sabha*. He has also served as a Union Minister.
10. Ajit Pramod Kumar Jogi was the first chief minister of the state of Chhattisgarh, India. He was earlier a member of the Congress party. He formed Chhattisgarh Janata Congress after Jogi and his son Amit Jogi were expelled from Congress because of anti-party activities, http://www.newindianexpress.com/nation/2016/dec/07/ajit-jogis-party-registered-as-janta-congress-chhattisgarh-j-1546593.html (Accessed in June 2017); https://en.wikipedia.org/wiki/Ajit_Jogi (Accessed in June 2017).

Chapter 7 – The implications for 2019

1. Simon O. Sinek is an author, motivational speaker and marketing consultant. He is the author of four books including the 2009 best seller *Start With Why: How Great Leaders Inspire Everyone to Take Action*,https://en.wikipedia.org/wiki/Simon_Sinek (Accessed in June 2017).

2. Devendra Fadnavis is the incumbent Chief Minister of Maharashtra holding the office from October 31, 2014. He is a member of Bharatiya Janata Party and the RSS. Fadnavis represents the Nagpur South West constituency in Maharashtra Legislative Assembly,https://en.wikipedia.org/wiki/Devendra_Fadnavis (Accessed in June 2017).
3. Captain Amarinder Singh is presently the Chief Minister of Punjab. He is Member of the Punjab Legislative Assembly from Patiala. He has also previously served as the Chief Minister of Punjab from 2002-2007. He has also been a Member of Parliament multiple times,https://en.wikipedia.org/wiki/Amarinder_Singh (Accessed in June 2017).
4. Yogi Adityanath is an Indian priest and Hindu nationalist politician who is the present Chief Minister of Uttar Pradesh, in office since March 26, 2017. He was chosen as the Chief Minister after the BJP won the 2017 State Assembly Elections. He has been the Member of Parliament from the Gorakhpur constituency, Uttar Pradesh for five consecutive terms since 1998,https://en.wikipedia.org/wiki/Yogi_Adityanath (Accessed in June 2017).

Chapter 8 – The key takeaways for BJP for 2019

1. H. Jackson Brown, Jr. is an American author best known for his inspirational book, *Life's Little Instruction Book*, which was a *New York Times* bestseller (1991–1994). Its sequel *Life's Little Instruction Book: Volume 2* also made it to the same best seller list in 1993,https://en.wikipedia.org/wiki/H._Jackson_Brown,_Jr (Accessed in June 2017).
2. http://www.hindustantimes.com/india/bjp-plays-it-safe-repeats-sitting-mlas-to-avoid-defection/story-,YzTPq9zgZVF4Epc1Xq4lFP.html (Accessed in June 2017);http://www.outlookindia.com/newswire/story/gujarat-poll-bjp-3rd-list-names-tainted-amit-shah/782061/?next (Accessed in June 2017).
3. Keshubhai Patel is an Indian politician who was the Chief Minister of Gujarat in 1995 and again from 1998 to 2001. He subsequently left the BJP in 2012, in opposition to Shri Narendra Modi and his policies. But this turned out to be an unsuccessful attempt.
4. Kalyan Singh is the Governor of Rajasthan since September 2014. He has served two terms as the Chief Minister of Uttar Pradesh. Kalyan Singh has been a member of RSS and BJP and he is also known for his role in the demolition of disputed structure at Ayodhya as he was Chief Minister of Uttar Pradesh at that time, https://en.wikipedia.org/wiki/Kalyan_Singh (Accessed in June 2017); http://www.ndtv.com/india-news/joining-hands-with-kalyan-singh-was-big-mistake-mulayam-singh-yadav-1451154 (Accessed in June 2017).

Chapter 9 – The Takeaways for Opposition for 2019

1. Debra Strobel Fischer (or Deb Fischer) is the senior United States Senator from the state of Nebraska. Previously, she was a two-term member of the Nebraska Legislature, representing the 43rd District. Fischer is a member of the Republican Party,https://en.wikipedia.org/wiki/Deb_Fischer (Accessed in June 2017).
2. Vijaya Raje Scindia was a prominent Indian political personality. She was the wife of last ruling Maharaja of Gwalior, Jivajirao Scindia. She became a politician of considerable influence and was elected repeatedly to both houses of the Indian Parliament. She was also an active member of Jana Sangh and later, Bharatiya Janata Party, https://en.wikipedia.org/wiki/Vijaya_Raje_Scindia (Accessed in June 2017).
3. Hemvati Nandan Bahuguna was a Congress Party leader. He served as the Chief Minister of Uttar Pradesh. He later joined Bharatiya Lok Dal and worked with Chaudhary Charan Singh,https://en.wikipedia.org/wiki/Hemvati_Nandan_Bahuguna (Accessed in June 2017).
4. Amitabh Bachchan is an Indian film actor. He first gained popularity in the early 1970s for movies like Zanjeer and Deewaar, and was dubbed India's first "angry young man" for his on-screen roles in Hindi Film Industry (Bollywood). In 1984 elections, Amitabh contesting on a Congress party ticket also defeated Hemvati Nandan Bahuguna from Allahabad *Lok Sabha* seat, https://en.wikipedia.org/wiki/Amitabh_Bachchan (Accessed in June 2017).

Epilogue

1. Bernard Sanders is an American politician who has been the junior United States Senator from Vermont since 2007. He is the longest serving independent in U.S. congressional history. He eventually lost but his campaign against Hillary Clinton for the party's 2016 U.S. presidential nomination raised many important issues. Sanders is considered pro-labour and emphasizes reversing economic inequality, https://en.wikipedia.org/wiki/Bernie_Sanders (Accessed in June 2017).
2. "Blue Sky" scenario means "best theoretically possible case scenario". In a "Blue Sky" scenario, the variable and unknown events are expected to turn positive and in your favour. All of it leads to the best possible result.
3. Ms. J Jayalalithaa was an Indian actor turned politician who served as the Chief Minister of Tamil Nadu, for over fourteen years between 1991 and 2016. He was the Chief Minister at the time of her death.
4. In 2012, then Prime Minister Dr. Manmohan Singh had referred to the challenges that a coalition government faces when making policy and other decisions. He had said difficult decisions were getting

"more difficult" because of coalition compulsions,http://timesofindia.indiatimes.com/india/Pained-by-Manmohan-Singhs-statement-on-UPA-allies-Sharad-Pawar/articleshow/12345682.cms (Accessed in June 2017).

5. Sardar Vallabhbhai Patel was the first Deputy Prime Minister of India. He was a leader of the Indian National Congress and played a key role in the integration of princely states with the Republic of India.
6. The China-India War also known as the Sino-Indian Border Conflict was a war between these two countries that occurred in 1962. A disputed Himalayan border was the main pretext for war, but other issues played a role. The war was a culmination of violent border incidents after 1959, when India had granted asylum to the Dalai Lama, spiritual head of Tibetan people, https://en.wikipedia.org/wiki/Sino-Indian_War (Accessed in June 2017).
7. The Central Government nationalised the Imperial Bank of India in 1955 and it was named as the State Bank of India. The seven other state banks became the subsidiaries of the new bank when nationalised on 19th July 1960. The next major nationalisation of banks took place in 1969 when the government under Prime Minister Indira Gandhi, nationalised 14 major banks, https://en.wikipedia.org/wiki/Public_sector_banks_in_India#Public-Sector_Banks (Accessed in June 2017).
8. In India, the Privy Purse was a payment made to the ruling families of erstwhile princely states as part of their agreements to first integrate with India in 1947. The Privy Purse was continued to the royal families until the 26th Amendment in 1971, by which all their privileges and allowances from the Central Government would cease to exist, was implemented, https://en.wikipedia.org/wiki/Privy_Purse_in_India (Accessed in June 2017).
9. The Bangladesh Liberation War was a revolution and armed conflict sparked by the rise of the Bengali nationalist and self-determination movement in what was then East Pakistan and the 1971 genocide. It resulted in the independence of the People's Republic of Bangladesh,https://en.wikipedia.org/wiki/Bangladesh_Liberation_War (Accessed in June 2017).
10. Operation Blue Star was an Indian military operation which occurred between 1st June and 8th June 1984, ordered by Prime Minister Indira Gandhi in order to establish control over the Harmandir Sahib Complex in Amritsar, Punjab, and remove militant religious leader Jarnail Singh Bhindranwale and his militant armed followers from the complex buildings. Jarnail Singh Bhindranwale had earlier occupied the Harmandir Sahib, fortified the complex and made it his headquarters in April 1983,https://en.wikipedia.org/wiki/Operation_Blue_Star (Accessed in June 2017).

11. *Indira: The Life of Indira Nehru Gandhi, a biography of Indira Gandhi* by Katherine Frank. Katherine Frank is a noted American author and biographer,https://en.wikipedia.org/wiki/Katherine_Frank (Accessed in June 2017);https://en.wikipedia.org/wiki/Indira_Gandhi (Accessed in June 2017).
12. The US–India Civil Nuclear Agreement was signed between USA and India. Under this agreement, India agreed to separate its civil and military nuclear facilities and to place all its civil nuclear facilities under International Atomic Energy Agency safeguards, and in exchange, the USA agreed to accord full civil nuclear cooperation with India.

ABOUT THE AUTHORS

PANKAJ SHARMA is an engineer (IIT Kharagpur, 1999) and MBA (FMS Delhi, 2003) with 15+ years of diverse work experience in various leadership roles with Global investment banks, Indian Equity brokerages, State Owned Enterprises and startups.

Most recently, he was heading Institutional Equities business for Equirus Securities. He was also leading the Equirus market strategy and macroeconomics team with an eye on political developments to make sense as to how the unfolding events would influence political line up in the country and their impact on equity markets. Before this, he was an Equity Analyst and used to track Power Utilities, Capital Goods and Coal for UBS India for more than seven years. In this role, he was ranked 'No. 1 Utilities Analyst' in Asia Money and 'Runner Up' in Institutional investor Polls. He had also received Thomson Reuters' Starmine Analyst Award for 'Best Earning Estimates' and 'Best Stock Picker'.

He also spent approximately one year with Citi and about three years with J P Morgan. Pankaj has also been involved with fund raising for start ups and has also been an entrepreneur. Pankaj has also been a regular contributor in print and electronic media.

SAURAV SANYAL has donned many hats successfully in an illustrious career so far. He has been a Scientific Research Officer, Business Leader, Sales and Marketing Professional and Organisation Builder. He is MBA from FMS Delhi (2003, Full Time Program) and M.Sc. from IIT Madras (1998) with a flair for keen observation and a sharp academic mind. He has over 17 Years of experience with Global Multinationals such as Unilever India, RB group and currently heads the business development for Elsevier Clinical Solutions in India. Elsevier is a RELX Group Company – a global provider of Information and analytics.

In his current role at RELX Group, Saurav has experience in developing and nurturing high performing teams. He works across Academic, Government and Healthcare organisations that are always at the cutting edge of research and new technology. His meritorious work has been recognised through Managing Director Awards at the APAC level (2010, 2011, 2014 and 2015) and Global Level (2012) within the Elsevier Organisation.

Earlier, Saurav worked at RB Group (earlier Reckitt Benckiser Plc). He championed Sales and Distribution projects, spearheaded the organisation's Key Account Management Practice and executed high value Trade marketing projects for the India organisation of Reckitt Benckiser (2003-2009). His achievements from this fruitful tenure include launch of Top global brands across the Modern Retail in India Market. At Unilever, Saurav worked in Chemical Engineering and Materials Science and was also awarded with Process Equipment and Technology Innovation Awards.

INDEX

A

Anti-incumbency against state governments
- Assembly Elections in 2014 *vs.* General Elections in 2014, results of
  - Haryana, 145
  - Jammu and Kashmir, 145
  - Jharkhand, 145
  - Maharashtra, 145
- Assembly Elections in 2016 *vs.* General Elections in 2014, results of
  - Assam, 143–144
  - Bengal, 142–143
  - Bihar, 144
  - Delhi, 144
  - Kerala, 143
  - Puducherry, 143
  - Tamil Nadu, 143
- Assembly Elections in 2017 *vs.* General Elections in 2014, result of
  - Goa, 142
  - Manipur, 142
  - Punjab, 142
  - Uttar Pradesh, 141
  - Uttarakhand, 141–142
- BJP, safe states for
  - Gujarat, 134
  - Madhya Pradesh
- changing election verdict, states
- Haryana, 129–131
  - Himachal Pradesh, 132–133
  - Karnataka, 126–128
  - Rajasthan, 128–129
  - Uttarakhand, 132
- employee's decision, 124
- 2014 general elections *vs.* subsequent Assembly Elections, 141
- local elected representatives
  - major issues, 147
  - proactive approach, 146
  - psychological pressure, 146
- local state governments, performance of, 125
- Lok Sabha and Vidhan Sabha elections, 125

B

Bharatiya Janata Party (BJP)
- anti-Modi forces, 189
- BJP's aggressive approach, 190
- BJP's MPs, 70 percent of
  - concentration risk, 100
  - performance, 99*t*
  - victory, 99–100
- booth management, 175–176
- candidate selection, 174–175
- coalitions, 177–178
- election analytics, 196–198
- 2019 elections
  - strategy and election campaign, 170
  - voters, lack of alternatives for, 170–171
- electoral politics, 184
- faulty strategy, 190–192

2019 implications. *see* 2019 implications
inevitable and irreversible change, 198–199
leaders, influx of, 193
local communication, 171–174
Lok Sabha constituencies, categories of
inconsequential player, 92
multi-polar contest, 94
one-on-one fight, 94
100 percent success rate in states, 96
80 percent success rate in states, 97
seat sharing with Shiv Sena, 93–94
smaller states and Union Territories, 94–95
vote percentage, 92–93
Lok Sabha elections
massive sympathy, 186
Scindia, Madhav Rao, 185, 186, 187*t*, 188
Scindia, Vijaya Raje, 186
victory margin, 188
new entrants, 193, 195
Opposition's PM candidate, 196
principal Opposition Party, space for, 195
seat sharing agreement, 190
state governments, 192, 193
struggling Opposition, 195
sub-par performance, 192
2009 to 2014, 100–101
unfinished agenda, 179–180
winners and candidates, 101–103
Bihar
Bihar Assembly Elections, 22
BJP performed, 32*t*
BJP's vote share, 31
critical states, 31
2019 general elections
coalition government, 24
JDU and BJP, 25
RJD-JDU alliance, 24
Uttar Pradesh and, 22–24
verdict, 16–18
Biju Janata Dal (BJD), 153
BJP. *See* Bharatiya Janata Party (BJP)

C

Centre for Monitoring Indian Economy (CMIE), 82
Communist Party of India (Marxist)/CPI (M), 3
Congress
anti-Congress ideology, 4
assassination of Mrs. Indira Gandhi, 1984, 107
Congress in 1977 and 1989, vote share of, 13
Congress's pathetic performance, 2014 election, 7–8
core vote banks loss, 107–108
1977 election verdict, 107
2014 – loss of power and face, 114
powerful regional satraps, 108
SP-BSP-Congress, 30
SP-Congress alliance, 27
SWOT of, 194*t*
UPA II
Congress party's allies, 48
Congress's loss, 42–43
Gandhi, Rahul, 49
Sonia Gandhi's image, 47
winning candidates, 54, 55*t*
Consumer food price index (CFPI), 70
Consumer Price Inflation, 62*t*

F
Farm loan waivers, 73
Food inflation, 70, 72

G
2019 general elections
Bihar
coalition government, 24
JDU and BJP, 25
RJD-JDU alliance, 24
implications, 35–36
Uttar Pradesh
2017 Assembly Elections results, 27
BJP and BSP, 29–30
BSP alliance issue, 28
BSP and SP, 28, 29
electoral battle, 30
King Maker, 28–29
2014 Lok Sabha elections results, 26*t*
Priyanka Gandhi, 30
SP-BSP-Congress, 30
SP-Congress alliance, 27

H
Haryana Assembly Elections and pre-poll alliance experiment, 130–131

I
Index of Industrial Production (IIP), 74, 75
2019 implications
BJP gain in 2019 *vs.* 2014
disappointing result, 154–155
Maharashtra, 152–153
concentration risk, 157
contributing factors, 157–158
decline, high possibility, 165, 166, 166*t*, 167*t*
Bihar, 161
Gujarat, 161
Lok Sabha seats, 164–165
Madhya Pradesh, 162
qualitative assessment, 165*t*
Rajasthan, 162
states and UTs, 162, 163*t*–164*t*
Uttar Pradesh, 161
increment possible, 165, 166, 166*t*, 167*t*
Karnataka, 158
Maharashtra, 158
Manipur, 159
Odisha, 159
Punjab, 159
OPS-EPS factions merger, 155–156
remain more/less similar result, 165, 166, 166*t*, 167*t*
Andhra Pradesh, 160
Assam, 160
Bengal, 159
Kerala, 160
Tamil Nadu, 159
Telangana, 160
Indian economy
economic factors, 87
Modi government
GDP growth, 66–70
2019 implications for BJP, 88
NDA government performing, 79–85
NDA *vs.* UPA, 86–87
struggling, UPA II rule
controllable factors, 60
core industries growth, 65–66
currency exchange rate, 63–64
electoral prospects, 60
GDP growth rate, 61, 61*t*
industrial growth, 63, 63*t*
inflation, 61–62, 62*t*
uncontrollable factors, 60
Indian Politics
1977 and 1989, feature of, 15–16

anti-Congress ideology, 4
anti-Modi coalition, 21
Bihar Assembly Elections, 22
Bihar verdict, 16–18
BJP, 4
BJP's spectacular victory in 2014, 14
BJP vulnerable, 32–33
Congress
  assassination of Mrs. Indira Gandhi, 1984, 107
  core vote banks loss, 107–108
  1977 election verdict, 107
  emergency, 107
  powerful regional satraps, 108
Congress in 1977 and 1989, vote share of, 13
2014 election
  BJP performance, 8–9
  Congress's pathetic performance, 7–8
  Prime Ministerial candidate, 6–7
  social media, 10
  third largest party, 9–10
2019 general elections
  Bihar, 24–26, 31–32
  implications, 35–36
  Uttar Pradesh, 26–32
Janata Party Experiment, failure of, 11
leader's popularity, massive decline in
  1984 after 1980, 108
  1998 after 1996, 108
  1999 after 1998, 109
  2009 after 2004, 109
  coalition experiment of 1989, 112
  1989 – Congress lost 10 percent vote, 110
  1996 election result, 113
  internal conflicts, 112
  1980 – Janata Party, 109
  2014 – loss of power and face, 114
  2004 – unexpected result, 113–114
  1991 – Vishwanath Pratap Singh, 111–112
Modi wave
  achievement of, 115
  important factors, 118
  Modi administration, performance of, 116
  Opposition leader, 116–118
  sustenance, 115–116
NDA Government, 120
non-BJP and non-Congress parties, 12, 21
onions and BJP's loss, 119–120
Opposition leaders, 13
parties
  BJP and Communist Parties, 3
  Chaudhary Charan Singh of Bharatiya Lok Dal and Chandra Shekhar` of Janata Dal, 3
  Rashtriya Swayamsevak Sangh11 (RSS) and Shiromani Akali Dal, 3
31 percent vote share, 11
political alliances, 5, 6
political careers
  Shri Chimanbhai Patel, 4
  Shri Bhajan Lal, 4–5
political events,
  2015 Assembly Elections in Bihar, 2
  Communist Party of India (Marxist)/CPI (M), 3
  Jammu and Kashmir Peoples Democratic Party (JKPDP/PDP), 3

reality, 14–15
results, 12*t*
seats won, BJP 2014
Assam, 34
Bihar, 34
Delhi, 35
Haryana, 34
Jharkhand, 34–35
Karnataka, 34
Maharashtra, 34
Uttar Pradesh, 33
Uttar Pradesh and Bihar, 22–24
Uttar Pradesh verdict, 18–20

J

Jammu and Kashmir Peoples Democratic Party (JKPDP/PDP), 3

L

Lok Sabha elections, 125, 136, 136*t*
BJP
massive sympathy, 186
Scindia, Madhav Rao, 185, 186, 187*t*, 188
Scindia, Vijaya Raje, 186
victory margin, 188
2014 elections results, 26*t*
2009 Lok Sabha Elections, UPA, 41–42

M

Modi government
Gross Domestic Product (GDP) growth
core industries growth, 77–78
demonetization, 68
economic survey, 69
financial year 2017 (FY 2017) and financial year 2018 (FY 18), 67, 67*t*
GST, 69
industrial growth, 74–77
inflation, 70–73
sub-sector data, 68
2019 implications for BJP, 88
NDA government performing
capacity utilization, 79, 80*t*
factory production, 82
investment cycle, 82
job creation, 83–85
new orders's flow, 80
OBICUS, 79, 81s
project execution, 81–82
Modi, Narendra
anti-Modi coalition, 21
anti-Modi forces, 189
BJP. *see* Bharatiya Janata Party (BJP)
government. *see* Modi Government
Modi's rule, 56–57
Modi wave
achievement of, 115
important factors, 118
Modi administration, performance of, 116
Opposition leader, 116–118
sustenance, 115–116

O

Order Books, Inventories and Capacity Utilisation Survey (OBICUS), 79

Q

Quarterly employment surveys (QES), 83

R

Rashtriya Janata Dal (RJD), 24

S

Safe states, BJP's
Gujarat, 134
Madhya Pradesh

Assembly Elections, results of, 135, 135*t*
Chhattisgarh, 140–142
farmer unrest and popular sentiment, 138–140
Guna and Chhindwara, 136–138
Lok Sabha Elections, 136, 136*t*
Samajwadi Party (SP), 19
Shiromani Akali Dal (SAD), 93
Struggling, UPA II rule
controllable factors, 60
core industries growth, 65–66
currency exchange rate, 63–64
electoral prospects, 60
GDP growth rate, 61, 61*t*
industrial growth, 63, 63*t*
inflation, 61–62, 62*t*
uncontrollable factors, 60

U

Unique Selling Proposition (USP), 138
United Progressive Alliance (UPA)
anti-incumbency, 52–54
BJP's winning candidates, 54, 54*t*
candidate's objective, 56
Congress's winning candidates, 54, 55*t*
2009 Lok Sabha Elections, 41–42
Modi's rule, 56–57
political tricks, 55
UPA I (2004-09), 41
UPA II
anti-corruption activist, 44
Congress party's allies, 48
Congress's loss, 42–43
corruption, issue of, 43
Gandhi, Rahul, 49
NDA, unexpected loss of, 51
policy paralysis and crumbling economy, 44–46
political model, 51, 52
public opinion, 48
Sonia Gandhi's image, 47
unruly allies, 50–51
Uttar Pradesh
and Bihar, 22–24
BJP performed, 32*t*
BJP's vote share, 31
critical states, 31
2019 general elections
2017 Assembly Elections results, 27
BJP and BSP, 29–30
BSP alliance issue, 28
BSP and SP, 28, 29
electoral battle, 30
King Maker, 28–29
2014 Lok Sabha elections results, 26*t*
Priyanka Gandhi, 30
SP-BSP-Congress, 30
SP-Congress alliance, 27
verdict, 18–20

WHAT HAS CHANGED FOR

BJP

IN LAST SIX MONTHS?

KW PUBLISHERS

20 YEARS OF PUBLISHING
1998-2018

Knowledge with Substance

www.kwpub.com

Copyright © 2018
Pankaj Sharma and Saurav Sanyal

All rights reserved. No part of this publication may be reproduced, stored in a retrieval system, or transmitted in any form or by any means, electronic, mechanical, photocopying, recording or otherwise, without the prior written permission of the copyright owner. The views expressed in this book are of authors and do not represent the viewpoint of the publisher.

ISBN 978-93-87324-17-6 Paperback
ISBN 978-93-87324-18-3 ebook

Published in India by Kalpana Shukla

KNOWLEDGE WORLD

KW Publishers Pvt Ltd
4676/21, First Floor, Ansari Road
Daryaganj, New Delhi 110002
Phone: +91 11 23263498/43528107
Marketing: kw@kwpub.com
Editorial: jose@kwpub.com
Website: www.kwpub.com

Printed and Bound in India.

We are extremely happy to receive strong encouragement which came in the form of our discerning readers' support to our book "2019: Will Modi Win?" and it gives us immense pleasure to share this latest update with our readers. The accompanied small text is a companion note to the main book and we believe that reading this will make the discussion for readers more relevant and current. The political developments are always continuous which means that there is a need to update the analysis and make modifications in the inferences we can draw on that basis. This is the objective we have in mind with this update as we have deliberately tried not to alter the flow of discussion in the main book by not opting for a complete revision of the book.

Notwithstanding the latest political developments some of which have been completely unexpected especially the bonhomie among opposition parties and continuous tantrums from BJP's allies, we believe that the main thesis which we had presented in "2019: Will Modi Win?" remains intact. As we have discussed and what was the underlying main theme in the November 2017 text, many Opposition leaders see BJP's defeat as "Priority No. 1" and their own victory as "Priority No. 2". This along with falling short on massive expectations of people will be the main obstacle for Prime Minister, Shri Narendra Modi to unfurl the national flag again from Red Fort in Delhi on 15th August 2019.

We hope that this update will receive the same or perhaps even bigger support from the readers. But before we close, we would like to express our sincere gratitude for Ms. Kalpana Shukla from KW Publishers to offer this suggestion for an update and to Jose Mathew for painstaking work on making the presentation of this update so much better than how it looked when we had submitted it initially. Thanks once again.

— Pankaj Sharma and Saurav Sanyal

PANKAJ SHARMA
SAURAV SANYAL
2019
WILL
MODI WIN
?

☆☆☆☆☆ **This book is not a light-hearted woolgathering at political predictions in India but well-assimilated political treatise**
By Monoj Chakraborty on 17 March 2018

Saurav and Pankaj have indeed done a daunting task. Not only have they tackled the complex and arcane subject of political predictions but have also done with , what else, 2019 and Narendra Modi in perspective....Doubting Modi's re-run in itself is a redoubtable task.
The fact that two seasoned professionals, highly educated (but in other sciences and not in political science or Psephology), would pick up a subject like this, in itself is laudable enough.
The Authors, with a very keen and objective mind, have used a lot of data to base their hypotheses, assumptions and predictions on.Their training in the corporate world would no doubt have come in handy in using various optics on the long history of electoral results in India.
It is their sharp analysis which tells us the huge dependence that BJP has on 4 large states - the results from which in 2014 may not be repeatable in 2019 and then which brings us to the possibilities of the tier-2 states and the pre/post alliances of the opposition therein.
They also touch upon, briefly though and completely contextual, on the evolutionary history of the the major parties - like Jan sangh; this will help the modern young reader in forming a historical perspective for the parties are they are today. The book also traces history , briefly again, on the how some earlier personalities shaped the political thought in our country (no discussion on Indian polity can be complete without at least touching upon Narsimha Rao, Deve Gowda, the brief yet eventful regimes of VP singh and Chandra Sekhar)
What I like about the approach that it eschews predictions (then it would become like exit polls) but build scenarios and ascribes probabilities - politics is the consummate art of possibility (Even Nate Sliver, [of "the noise and the signal" fame], who correctly predicted the Obama elections and the 2nd strike to WTC, got the trump elections wrong).
I particularly like the chapters on what should BJP do and what could the opposition do - these are choices to be made and only the satraps of the highest political acumen will know the right and optimum pay-offs.
Heartily enough they have sort of got a validation of their hypothesis in the UP by poll elections (but probably got Bihar wrong - which may have foxed many though); they are bang on in NESA and we will have to see how their hypotheses hold up in the upcoming state elections.
Overall a very entertaining book and even the uninitiated reader would find this a page-turner; I would not read this book with modi-non modi lens, but as a treatise on how the 2019 would look like basis 2014 and the previous electoral results.
I would urge Saurav and Pankaj to use some of their analyses here and go deeper into analysing the parties, their trajectories as a marketing/strategy theorists and probably even use game theoretic models to further their delightful journey so far....What next would be my question to them.

...more reviews at the end

WHAT HAS CHANGED FOR BJP IN LAST SIX MONTHS?

> *Political stability is an essential requirement for providing the right environment needed for peaceful communities and the vision of political leadership plays a key role in growth of a country. The NDA Govt has not done badly and BJP is certainly on a rise. With an expanding footprint across the country, it seems impossible to stop the Modi juggernaut in 2019. But, is the reality that simple and straight forward?*
>
> — From 2019: Will Modi win? by
> *Pankaj Sharma and Saurav Sanyal*

Where does BJP stand today?

We had finished writing "2019: Will Modi win?" in October 2017 and since then, there have been several important political developments. Despite BJP's win in Gujarat and North East, the previous six months have not been great for the ruling party. While the by-elections of Uttar Pradesh have provided the template on how to defeat BJP for the united Opposition, the party's failure to from the Govt in Karnataka despite emerging as the single largest party and the developments in between related with BJP's efforts to form the Government without a majority was also a big jolt. There are more signs of open dissent from BJP allies and some of the party's own leaders. On the other hand, the

Opposition is not letting go of any opportunities to even convert the non-political issues into rallying point against the BJP. ***The message is simple: the race for 2019 will be close. Winning is tough but winning again is even tougher and that will the predicament for the BJP.***

Fight for "Big Prize in 2019", Messages from By-Election Results

Till only three months ago, BJP was riding high on the success of party's victory in Gujarat followed by unprecedented success in the North East. However, after a series of successive electoral victories, the ruling Bharatiya Janata Party (BJP) suffered a big jolt in by-election results in Uttar Pradesh in March 2018. The loss at traditional BJP bastion Gorakhpur Lok Sabha seat (one which was vacated by Chief Minister of Uttar Pradesh, Yogi Adityanath and hence, necessitating a mid-term election) is much more humiliating for the Uttar Pradesh state government collectively and for Yogi Adityanath, personally.

It has been only little over twelve months since BJP had won a spectacular victory in assembly elections in Uttar Pradesh. The difference was that two major opposition parties (Samajwadi Party and Bahujan Samaj Party) were united in these recent elections. It is important to note that BJP had the biggest of its success in Uttar Pradesh in 2014 and that was primary reason for the party to have a comfortable majority in the 16th Lok Sabha. In the March 2017 Assembly Elections in Uttar Pradesh, BJP repeated the extraordinary feat. Hence, by-election results are much more disturbing for BJP.

In the by-elections of Rajasthan and West Bengal in January 2018 as well, the result was not good for BJP.

1. Ajmer Lok Sabha seat in Rajasthan - Congress defeated BJP.
2. Alwar Lok Sabha seat in Rajasthan - Congress defeated BJP.
3. Mandalgarh Assembly seat in Rajasthan - Congress defeated BJP.
4. Uluberia Lok Sabha seat in West Bengal - Trinamool Congress defeated BJP.
5. Noapara Assembly seat in West Bengal - Trinamool Congress defeated BJP.

Rajasthan result was more significant. Since 1993, the five Assembly Elections in Rajasthan have always seen a change in regime from BJP to Congress and then again from Congress to BJP. At present, BJP has a massive majority (more than 3/4th) in assembly and the next elections are due this year only. The change also reflects in the results of Lok Sabha elections. In 2014 Lok Sabha elections, BJP had achieved a clean sweep by winning 25/25 seats. The loss of both Lok Sabha seats is a sign that people are against BJP in the state and are not happy with its performance even if Modi is still popular with masses.

Even in a scenario which is more benign from BJP's perspective, it would be reasonable to expect that a reduction in BJP's tally is possible from 25/25 in Lok Sabha elections in 2019. There is serious anti-incumbency BJP will have to deal with in some of the sates where it is in power today and the party's performance was excellent in 2014 Lok Sabha elections. The important messages from these results are:

1. BJP has become stronger in last few years but it is still far from winning against a combined opposition in key states like Uttar Pradesh.

2. The Opposition parties are smart enough to understand that they can't take on BJP individually and will be ready to reconcile with each other.
3. The state level anti-incumbency remains a powerful force and when BJP is in power in more states, this will affect its prospects in 2019.

More 'Trial by Fire' Moments for BJP

After the loss in Phulpur and Gorakhpur in Uttar Pradesh against a united Opposition, loss for BJP is big political news and major encouragement for Opposition. It is very likely that BJP will have to face a united opposition in 2019 *Lok Sabha* polls. In Palghar and Bhandara-Gondiya in Maharashtra, there was an alliance between Congress and Nationalist Congress Party (NCP). Similarly, Samajwadi Party (SP) of Akhilesh Yadav and Mayawati led Bahujan Samaj Party (BSP) in Uttar Pradesh which didn't have an alliance in 2014, rectified their mistake and the loss of both Gorakhpur and Phulpur for BJP was attributed to support of BSP to SP candidates. In Kairana, BJP was again fighting the combined force of SP, BSP and Rashtriya Lok Dal (RLD). The result of Kairana was similar to the results in Phulpur and Gorakhpur and RLD defeated BJP.

BJP is in a predicament and frequent, well publicized by-elections have now started to reflect signs of fatigue and vulnerability in BJP's poll machinery which otherwise is far superior to any other political party in India. Regular elections are also leading to a more united opposition and the opportunities for other parties to learn from their mistakes on how to fight BJP better. Regular polls have important implications for 2019 General Elections. It is a well known fact that India is a noisy democracy but the "poll-mode" in which the nation finds itself almost on a continuous basis is testing the efficient machinery of BJP.

In 2018 itself, we have seen many elections after elections such as high profile by-elections in states like Uttar Pradesh and Rajasthan, State Assembly elections in North East and then in Karnataka and well covered local bodies' elections in West Bengal. The coverage then focused on by-elections scheduled for Lok Sabha seats in May-end at Palghar and Bhandara-Gondiya in Maharashtra and Kairana in Uttar Pradesh. The battle has become BJP vs. Rest as there is a heightened sense of insecurity among other parties from the BJP's rise and they have started to become more worried about their survival.

BJP has the best organizational structure among Indian political parties today and it also receives support from its parent organization (Rashtriya Swayamasevak Sangh or RSS). The dynamic, efficient and grounded in reality based leadership of Prime Minister Mr. Narendra Modi and party president, Mr. Amit Shah Shah has also been responsible for an expanding footprint of BJP across the country and the successful track record in elections. Starting with 2014 general elections, BJP has more "hits" than "misses" in its report card. This has started to change only in last few months but overall, the electoral performance of BJP is satisfactory when we see the results 2014 onwards.

However, regular elections make even BJP vulnerable because, a) there are more chances of mistakes e.g. the Karnataka misadventure, c) Regular elections provide more opportunities for Opposition to learn from its mistakes and also stitch the coalitions to defeat BJP, c) It is natural that elections require that a political party will have to make certain compromises and BJP is not an exception which attracts bad press, d) Even the non-political issues become political and there is an impact on governance, the incumbent suffers.

The continuous rise of BJP has led to disruption in equilibrium in Indian politics and naturally even the BJP allies don't like it. Regular elections provide an opportunity for them to throw tantrums. The regular elections also create problems of fatigue in the BJP cadre and overconfidence/ lethargy in state leaders. The bigger problem is that every time elections take place, BJP is expected to win and nothing short of a comfortable victory is seen as an achievement for the party.

Even BJP Members are showing discontent

If the other challenges are not bad enough, even some of the BJP members of parliament and party functionaries have questioned the intent of Modi Govt. The control of Modi-Shah on party affairs was considered absolute and hence, this was unthinkable. There were instances when BJP members have started openly questioning the party leadership. All of it will have implications for the future political environment in India and the 2019 elections.

The immediate was the Supreme Court ruling against the alleged misuse of an act which came into existence to stop the atrocities against the weaker sections of the society. Many BJP MPs have alleged that the Govt has not been doing enough to prevent the dilution of the Schedule Castes Atrocities Act.

1. BJP MP Savitri Bai Phule attacked her own government at the Centre over reservations. She is a Member of Parliament from Bahraich in Uttar Pradesh and she targeted the Govt over recent incidents of desecration of B R Ambedkar's statues and rise in crimes against the weaker sections of the society.
2. Yashwant Singh, MP from Nagina constituency in Uttar Pradesh, has targeted the Modi government alleging that even after four years of the party being in power at the Centre, nothing has been done for 300 million socially backward population of the country.
3. Ashok Dohre, Etawah MP from Uttar Pradesh alleged that police and BJP governments in different states are targeting members of SC and ST communities by lodging them in false cases in connection to the Bharat bandh called on Arpil 2 over the SC/ST Act.
4. Chhote Lal Kharwar, a BJP tribal MP has written to Prime Minister Modi about alleged shabby treatment he received at the office of Uttar Pradesh Chief Minister Yogi Adityanath. The Robertsganj MP has also accused the local administration officials of discrimination.
5. Dr. Udit Raj, who is a BJP MP from North West Delhi alleged that the members of scheduled castes arrested after protests on April 2 are being tortured in various BJP-rules states. He said that Dalits who participated in agitation are being tortured and demanded that it must be stopped.

A few months ago, Nana Patole who has been the BJP MP from Bhandara-Gondia Loksabha constituency in Maharashtra submitted his resignation from the party.

Patole raised the issue of the problems faced by farmers and BJP Govt's inability to address these issues. He expressed his frustration with the policies of the Govt pertaining to farmers.

It is possible that some of them could be unhappy with not getting enough importance in BJP and from the respective state Governments and in Centre. Some may be getting a sense that the party may not be nominating them as a representative in their seats in 2019 and they want to portray them as martyrs. Some of them may also be in touch with other parties and will be ready to switch loyalties at an opportune time. And they are making a case for the same. Nevertheless, the open rebellion has shattered the impression that the control of Modi-Shah over BJP is so tight that no dissent can be allowed.

What does this mean for 2019 elections? Modi's popularity with the BJP cadre doesn't ensure that even the state government heads remain popular with the BJP workers and leaders. The fair assessment of anti-incumbency against the local representatives means that BJP may not be able to re-nominate all its MPs in 2019 elections. These potential rebels will harm the party's prospects. Once the image of Modi-Shah as supreme leaders of BJP suffers, there could be many more such incidents and open expression of dissent will damage the image of party in front of voters.

Because of their perceived "ability to win", BJP has allowed the entry of several leaders from other parties in the past. If they realize that the party is on a shaky wicket, they will not hesitate to switch sides and join other political parties. These opportunistic elements could damage the party in 2019 elections. Though Modi remains the most popular leader in the country, Opposition is sensing an opportunity that he will be vulnerable in 2019 and this includes his party's allies and even his own party colleagues. Another key take away is that India is a complex country in terms of diverse social groups and managing aspirations of everyone is not an easy task.

BJP's Predicament – Allies have become more demanding

BJP allies have become more demanding and vocal in their criticism of BJP and its method of working. Not only did TDP quit NDA and Chandrababu Naidu decided to bring a no-confidence motion against the Govt, even Nitish Kumar of JDU and Ram Vilas Paswan of LJP also raised their concerns on how BJP functionaries are not behaving well and that is not in the interest of coalition. The most powerful ally in terms of members in Lok sabha, Shiv Sena already has a love-hate relationship with BJP.

Though BJP only has a wafer thin majority in Lok Sabha, these threats from allies do not pose any immediate danger for Govt's survival. The problem is in fact much larger. A weaker and vulnerable BJP means that allies will have more room for bargaining in seat sharing arrangements in 2019. The Govt may become less effective in pushing difficult but important policies which are in the long term interest of Indian economy. It is challenging for BJP that more than Opposition; it is the Allies which are causing trouble for BJP.

Many of the constituents of NDA see a chink in BJP's armor and will not let go of this chance. The TDP (Telugu Desam Party) which is in power in the coastal state of

Andhra Pradesh in South already exited NDA and it has also brought a no-confidence motion against the BJP Govt in the Parliament. The party's leader and Chief Minister of the state, N Chandrababu Naidu has also become extremely vocal in his criticism of BJP, Modi and Finance Minister, Arun Jaitley.

1. Chief Minister of Bihar and leader of Janata Dal United (JDU) had switched sides to enter NDA in July 2017. For the first time, he attacked the Union Ministers on the issue of spreading communalism. Giving voice to his growing discomfort with ally BJP, Nitish Kumar has made it clear that he would not compromise with "divisive forces". Kumar is extremely upset with BJP over recent incidents in the state.
2. Union Minister and Lok Janshakti Party (LJP) chief Ram Vilas Paswan is another important leader from Bihar and LJP is an important constituent of NDA. His party has six members in the Lok Sabha. In a direct attack, Paswan has said that BJP was in the need of adjusting its attitude towards Muslims and Dalits or else it could end up paying price at the ballot box.
3. Shiv Sena, partner of BJP in Maharashtra state Govt has said that the Telugu Desam Party's no-confidence motion has put an end to the "myth" that the BJP-led central Govt has an unshakable mandate. In a direct attack, Shiv Sena has alleged that there is an environment of mistrust in the country against the government. With its eighteen members in the Lok Sabha, Shiv Sena is the most important constituent of NDA after BJP.
4. Shiromani Akali Dal (SAD), an ally of BJP in Punjab has also voiced its concern over the treatment of alliance

partners within the NDA. SAD-BJP coalition was in power in Punjab for ten years before it lost to Congress last year. One of the important SAD leader has said, "The BJP leadership should be more accommodative of its alliance partners. This is precisely the reason why the TDP and Shiv Sena are unhappy."

5. The relationship between People's Democratic Party (PDP) and BJP in Jammu and Kashmir (J&K) has always been an uneasy one. Though the PDP-BJP coalition is in power in J&K, things have been far from cordial between these two parties. After the finance minister Haseeb Drabu, who was one of the architects of PDP-BJP alliance in the state, was removed from her council of ministers by J&K Chief Minister Mehbooba Mufti of PDP recently, things certainly don't look that bright.

Even the smaller parties are raising their voice against BJP. Om Prakash Rajbhar, chief of Suheldev Bhartiya Samaj Party, which is an ally of the Yogi Adityanath-led BJP Govt in Uttar Pradesh, has said that his outfit might not support the ruling party during the Rajya Sabha polls in the state. Also, former Chief Minister of Bihar and Hindustani Awam Morcha (Secular) leader Jitan Ram Manjhi quit the NDA and joined the RJD-led grand alliance. Mr. Manjhi hit out at the Nitish Kumar-led NDA government in Bihar as "anti-poor" and said that they are not getting due respect in NDA.

BJP has been making each and every attempt to grow its strength and eliminate its dependence on smaller parties, which is perfectly fair. However, this has not gone down well with its allies. For example, the allies have not been consulted with on ministry expansion and portfolio distribution. The allies may not quit NDA in a hurry, but many of them find BJP on the defensive and they want to bargain hard in seat sharing arrangements before the next year elections.

There is a perception that Modi-Shah combination (Prime Minister, Narendra Modi and BJP President, Amit Shah) has been much less accommodative towards BJP's allies. This approach may have to change and BJP may be required to make more proactive effort to pacify its allies. As in the case of UPA (United Progressive Alliance, which was in power from 2004-2014), more power in the hands of allies could mean poor outcome for Govt's efficiency and effectiveness.

More Bad News for BJP, from the States across India

There was a huge political controversy over recommendations of "Finance Commission", the constitutional body which recommends revenue sharing between Centre and the States. The Southern states are against 15th Finance Commission which they allege is considering population from 2011 census instead of 1971 as basis for calculating allocation of tax revenue among states. This issue has worked as a strong reason for the Opposition parties to get united against the BJP and Prime Minister Narendra Modi.

15th Finance Commission considering 2011 census implies that the Southern states which implemented population control measures more efficiently will be penalized for their good work. The issue is similar to representation in Lok Sabha. The number of Lok Sabha and Rajya Sabha seats from various states in India's Parliament is based on an almost fifty years old data point i.e. the population of 1971 in the Indian states. The number of

MPs per state is based on 1971 census and the states that had lower birth rates afterwards don't want to change the status quo because if the seats are reallocated on the basis of population today, they will lose out.

In previous NDA rule under Atal Bihari Vajpayee (1998-2004), the idea to reallocate the number of seats was put forward by the Govt but the southern states were vehemently against it and the idea had to be dropped. There are vast differences in population and development achieved between the Northern and Southern states. The North-South divide is real and is a sensitive issue no doubt. In case of Finance Commission, the southern states are opposing terms of reference (ToR) of the 15th Finance Commission on using the 2011 census to calculate population for allocation of union tax revenue among states.

These states which include Tamil Nadu, Kerala, Karnataka, Andhra Pradesh and Puducherry (as of now in raising this issue) are saying that it is unfair because this would greatly impact them because they have efficiently implemented the population control measures. These state governments from the states in South are seeking amendment of these terms. This week, finance ministers of many of these states met and unanimously decided that ToR were in contradiction to the principles of federalism and would also result in revenue loss to performing states.

It is turning out to be a BJP vs. Opposition issue. The Finance Commission deliberations rarely capture the media headlines but unfortunately for BJP, the party is not in power in any of these states. While Southern states technically have a solid ground to argue their case, the worst part is that the issue has taken a political turn. Kerala is especially more aggressive on this issue as it has the state government run by the Left parties, staunch rivals of BJP. The Chief Ministers of Andhra Pradesh and Karnataka have also criticized the Modi government on this issue.

In the recent past, there have been incidents in several states which have created political environment difficult for BJP. The Central Government and aggressive agenda of some of the BJP's associate organizations have come under intense scrutiny from media and Opposition like. In this regard, the silence and inability of PM Modi to rein in these elements have also been questioned.

1. Jammu & Kashmir - Ever since the PDP-BJP alliance came to power in Jammu & Kashmir (J&K) in 2014 after assembly elections in the state, the coalition of PDP and BJP has been marred by numerous controversies. After the incidents over some BJP members' active support to anti-state government protests after the rape and murder of an eight year old girl in Kathua, things have become worse between these two partners.
2. Uttar Pradesh - The image of BJP Government has taken a serious beating in the state after recent incident involving one of his legislators. BJP Member of Legislative Assembly (MLA) Kuldeep Singh Sengar in Uttar Pradesh is accused of raping a minor girl in Unnao and the premier investigation agency in India, Central Bureau of Investigation (CBI) is conducting enquiries in the case. After intense media pressure and protests from Opposition parties, Yogi Adityanath government handed over the probe to CBI. The MLA is also an accused of hatching conspiracy to kill the rape survivor's father in police custody.

The political narrative in the country has become more challenging for BJP because of these incidents and unless controlled in time, this may escalate further. BJP which is now in power at Centre and across several states in India is possibly going to be struggling with anti-incumbency in future elections as the image of the party has suffered because of these developments. This will be bad for the return of Narendra Modi to power in 2019.

Is BJP Trading 'Small Gains' today for 'Big Losses' tomorrow?
In the recent past, BJP has been guilty of taking perceived missteps over entry of some of the corrupt, infamous and criminal elements into the party. The latest in this series is the nomination of Bellary's mining barons (the Reddy brothers and their associates) for Karnataka Assembly elections on BJP ticket. This created a huge media backlash and this is a warning sign. In 2014 elections, BJP's PM candidate Narendra Modi's clean image was a big asset and he had won strong support from educated, middle class and youth voters. If these inductions into BJP end up damaging that image of Modi, it could become a serious issue for the party in upcoming assembly election and also in 2019 general elections.

In democracy, winning elections is the only thing that matters for a political party, but the calculations go haywire at times. No matter what a political party says and irrespective of the moral high ground it takes, the fact is that it is 'the ability to win' which is the most important parameter when deciding on allocations of party tickets in Indian democracy. The entry of criminals and moneybags in electoral fray is politically beneficial and it is encouraged by almost all the political parties. While that is not a new thing as such, the entry of 'outsiders', 'criminals' and 'unwanted' elements is often resented by old timers and loyal party workers.

However from the top leadership's point of view, there is a trade off. No matter what the media says and what a section of ordinary and common people think, many of these candidates score very highly on 'the ability to win' quotient. In most of these cases, these elements are 'assets' and not 'liabilities'. However, there are also situations when the outrage is so massive that the parties backtrack and withdraw their decisions. This happens mostly when these people become an 'electoral liability'. Some of the more infamous examples from last few decades are:

1. One of the root cause behind escalation of an internal feud in Samajwadi Party in Uttar Pradesh between founder Mulayam Singh Yadav's brother, Shivpal Singh Yadav and Mulayam's son, Akhilesh Yadav was over the entry of some of the local powerful politicians to the party who didn't have a clean image. Finally, these people were expelled from the Samajwadi Party.
2. In the demolition of disputed structure at Ayodhya, then Chief Minister of Uttar Pradesh, Kalyan Singh had allegedly played an active role. After a few years, he joined Samajwadi Party and was inducted by Mulayam Singh Yadav himself. However, this created a severe backlash and fearing a massive political damage from some of his core voters including Muslims, Mulayam immediately withdrew Kalyan's induction.
3. More than a decade ago, Bharatiya Janata Party had to withdraw membership for D.P. Yadav, a powerful Don

and influential politician in Western Uttar Pradesh. Yadav was welcomed to the party by the big guns but his entry led to severe backlash.

The examples are not limited to any particular political group. But the rule is simple: background doesn't matter as long as the political leader is useful but if the "potential losses' could be higher than 'potential gains', the risk-reward becomes adverse and these leaders needs to be dropped. When the situation was desperate for BJP in Karnataka Assembly elections, in a last minute attempt to boost party's chances of winning in some of the key constituencies, BJP brought back the 'Reddy brothers' from Bellary as candidates in assembly elections.

Is BJP making tactical errors?

While it is difficult to forecast how good or bad this decision will ultimately be but the initial reaction does not look good. Many of these decisions which are beneficial in the short term have often come back to haunt the party in the past. Some of the recent examples are:

1. The recent controversy over arrest of BJP's MLA from Unnao in Uttar Pradesh has once again led to questions over the party's strategy to allow leaders from other parties and ticket allocation to them.
2. The entry of a regular party hopper, Naresh Agrawal in Uttar Pradesh and his controversial comments on Ms. Jaya Bachchan led to strong protests even from BJP MPs and also from media. Incidentally, Mr. Agrawal had joined BJP after he was denied a Rajya Sabha ticket by Samajwadi Party.

3. The BJP leadership was seen hobnobbing with some of the independent MLAs who are notorious for their criminal background in order to win an extra seat in recent Rajya Sabha elections in Uttar Pradesh, This led to severe criticism. For example, Raghuraj Pratap Singh alias Raja Bhaiya and Amanmani Tripathi.
4. Some of the BJP MPs who have been very vocal against party leadership recently have not risen through the ranks and joined BJP from other parties. Now, they are causing serious heartburn for the party..

In 2014, BJP and Modi had won strong support from educated, middle class and youth voters and if these incidents damage this "clean" image of Modi, it could become a serious issue for the party.

Conclusion

The combined opposition, unhappy allies, anti-incumbency against state government, disgruntled party functionaries and some mistakes which BJP could make in desperation will be critical to determine the outcome for 2019 and as we have seen in last few months, the road to get re-elected for BJP will be far from smooth. An interesting battle is on the cards and the observers will have to wear their seat belts tight.

☆☆☆☆☆ **The book is an easy and simple read**

By Sandip on 2 March 2018

A must read for all interested in politics...read it for its analysis, its detailing and its objectivity. Have not come across a book on this topic that combines all these aspects and that too so finely. The facts & figures presented and the associated narrations/comparisons/arguments provide the reader the wherewithal to draw his/her own conclusions. The book is an easy and simple read, but is data/numbers heavy..so go ahead if the subject fascinates you.

☆☆☆☆☆ **Interesting Topic as the Nation stands on the Crossroad**

By Subrato on 10 May 2018

An interesting topic specially considering the changing dynamics of politics.... The book is concise and the statistical data helps to analyse which side the tables might turn.

The best take away is the SWOT analysis for the ruling party and the opposition.

The research done by both the authors is commendable....

☆☆☆☆☆ **It's great read for all political analysts in the Country**

By Pavitra on 4 March 2018

It's great read for all political analysts in the Country. Tonnes of well Researched Data for Think Tank & Media Cells Of Top Regional and National Parties in India before 2019 Dawns

Pankaj Sharma is an engineer (IIT Kharagpur, 1999) and MBA (FMS Delhi, 2003) with 15+ years of diverse work experience in various leadership roles with global investment banks, Indian equity brokerages, State Owned Enterprises and startups. Pankaj has also been a regular contributor in print and electronic media.

Saurav Sanyal has donned many hats in an illustrious career so far. He has been a Researcher, Sales and Marketing Professional and Organisation Builder. He is a seasoned professional (MBA from FMS Delhi, 2003) and researcher (M Sc at IIT Madras 1998) with a flair for keen observation and an academic bent of mind.

₹ 599.00

KNOWLEDGE WORLD

KW PUBLISHERS PVT LTD

www.kwpub.com

ISBN 978-93-87324-17-6

9 789387 324176